Audiovisual Alterity

The Oxford Music / Media Series

Daniel Goldmark, Series Editor

Tuning In: American Narrative Television Music
Ron Rodman

Special Sound: The Creation and Legacy of the BBC Radiophonic Workshop
Louis Niebur

Seeing Through Music: Gender and Modernism in Classic Hollywood Film Scores
Peter Franklin

An Eye for Music: Popular Music and the Audiovisual Surreal
John Richardson

Playing Along: Digital Games, YouTube, and Virtual Performance
Kiri Miller

Sounding the Gallery: Video and the Rise of Art-Music
Holly Rogers

Composing for the Red Screen: Prokofiev and Soviet Film
Kevin Bartig

Saying It With Songs: Popular Music and the Coming of Sound to Hollywood Cinema
Katherine Spring

We'll Meet Again: Musical Design in the Films of Stanley Kubrick
Kate McQuiston

Occult Aesthetics: Synchronization in Sound Film
K.J. Donnelly

Sound Play: Video Games and the Musical Imagination
William Cheng

Sounding American: Hollywood, Opera, and Jazz
Jennifer Fleeger

Mismatched Women: The Siren's Song Through the Machine
Jennifer Fleeger

Robert Altman's Soundtracks: Film, Music and Sound from M*A*S*H *to* A Prairie Home Companion
Gayle Sherwood Magee

Back to the Fifties: Nostalgia, Hollywood Film, and Popular Music of the Seventies and Eighties
Michael D. Dwyer

The Early Film Music of Dmitry Shostakovich
Joan Titus

Making Music in Selznick's Hollywood
Nathan Platte

Hearing Haneke: The Sound Tracks of a Radical Auteur
Elsie Walker

Unlimited Replays: Video Games and Classical Music
William Gibbons

Hollywood Harmony: Musical Wonder and the Sound of Cinema
Frank Lehman

French Musical Culture and the Coming of Sound Cinema
Hannah Lewis

Theories of the Soundtrack
James Buhler

Through The Looking Glass: John Cage and Avant-Garde Film
Richard H. Brown

Cinesonidos: Film Music and National Identity During Mexico's Época de Oro
Jacqueline Avila

Sound Design is the New Score: Theory, Aesthetics, and Erotics of the Integrated Soundtrack
Danijela Kulezic-Wilson

Rock Star/Movie Star: Power and Performance in Cinematic Rock Stardom
Landon Palmer

The Presence of the Past
Temporal Experience and the New Hollywood Soundtrack
Daniel Bishop

Metafilm Music in Jean-Luc Godard's Cinema
Michael Baumgartner

Acoustic Profiles
A Sound Ecology of the Cinema
Randolph Jordan

Four Ways of Hearing Video Game Music
Michiel Kamp

Defining Cinema
Rouben Mamoulian and Hollywood Film Style, 1929–1957
Michael Slowik

Mobilizing Music in British Wartime Film
Heather Wiebe

Audiovisual Alterity: Representing Ourselves and Others in Music Videos
Michael L. Austin

Audiovisual Alterity

Representing Ourselves and Others in Music Videos

MICHAEL L. AUSTIN

OXFORD
UNIVERSITY PRESS

Oxford University Press is a department of the University of Oxford. It furthers the University's objective of excellence in research, scholarship, and education by publishing worldwide. Oxford is a registered trade mark of Oxford University Press in the UK and certain other countries.

Published in the United States of America by Oxford University Press
198 Madison Avenue, New York, NY 10016, United States of America.

CIP data is on file at the Library of Congress

ISBN 978–0–19–027779–6 (pbk.)
ISBN 978–0–19–027778–9 (hbk.)

DOI: 10.1093/oso/9780190277789.001.0001

Paperback printed by Marquis Book Printing, Canada
Hardback printed by Bridgeport National Bindery, Inc., United States of America

For my mother, Kelly Austin

Contents

Figures

Acknowledgments

Thanking everyone who deserves gratitude for making this book a possibility in the space of only a few pages is nearly impossible, but I would like to express sincere appreciation to several people who gave of their time, talent, and trust for this project.

I first want to thank everyone at Oxford University Press for making this book a reality. I cannot express a sufficient amount of appreciation to Norm Hirschy, Senior Editor, with whom I began this journey a somewhat embarrassing number of years ago. Not only has your insight and thoughtfulness made this project much better than it would have otherwise been, your grace and patience with me as I struggled through the agonizingly long process of working through such difficult material and controversial topics, especially the ones that affect me directly, is sincerely appreciated. Thanks also to Daniel Goldmark, Series Editor, for including this book in such a remarkable series, to Laura Santo, Project Manager, for your guidance and assistance through the production process, and to Tim Rutherford-Johnson for his thoughtful and thorough copyediting.

For their timely and sound advice, encouragement, and/or inspiration, I would like to thank a number of friends and professional colleagues: James Buhler, William Cheng, Amy Coddington, Dean Disher, Kevin Donnelly, Jarek Ervin, Luis Manuel Garcia-Mispireta, William Gibbons, Claudia Gorbman, Sumanth Gopinath, Robin James, Phil Jackson, Matthew J. Jones, Loren Kajikawa, Jesse Kinne, Victor Merriman, James Millea, Claire Parkinson, Matthew Pateman, Rebekah Pritchard-Adair, Victor Szabo, Amy Skjerseth, Robynn J. Stilwell, Indira Somani, Timothy Summers, Carol Vernallis, and Jennifer Woodward.

Further, thank you to my colleagues at Howard University, especially Carolyn Byerly, Judi Moore-Latta, and Sonja Williams for their mentorship and support. I would also like to thank my department heads during my time there, Bishetta Merritt and Yanick Rice Lamb, for their kind words and encouragement. Likewise, I am very grateful for the support of my colleagues in the College of Liberal Arts at Louisiana Tech University, especially Benjamin Bergholtz, Nicole de Fee, Erin Singer, and John Worsencroft, and the faculty and staff of the School of Music, and my colleagues at Edge Hill University.

Thanks also to my friends Chance Browning and Jessie Garcia for sharing their music video expertise with me, and Mark Carter Hash for his invaluable help in matching obscure scenes in viral videos to their sources, and to the Revs. Amber Henry Neuroth and Jeffrey B. MacKnight for their encouragement and understanding when I needed weekends off from my various church jobs to attend conferences to present early versions of, and to receive critical feedback about, some of the work included here.

Of course, I am grateful for the support of my family. Most of all, I would like to thank my mother, Kelly Austin, for instilling in me a love for music videos from a very early age, and my husband, Paul Tran Austin, for his unwavering support and encouragement.

Introduction

"I Want My Hegemony!"

MTV and I have grown up together. On August 1, 1981, at 12:01 a.m. Eastern Standard Time, the pioneer audience of MTV saw footage of the Columbia space shuttle launch and the Apollo 11 moon landing; however, instead of hearing Neil Armstrong's famous "one small step for man" quote, they heard John Lack say, "Ladies and gentlemen: rock and roll." Just after the rockets blasted off, a single electric guitar and drum kit blasted the original MTV theme music and viewers watched the "moon man" plant MTV's flag on the moon. The "moon man" was actually Buzz Aldrin, with the image of MTV's blocky "M" in place of the American flag, but the constant shifting of that animated logo appropriately foreshadowed MTV's remarkable ability to adapt and change throughout the coming years. After introducing the first class of "video jockeys," or VJs, MTV wasted no time in symbolically staking its claim on music by playing its first video: The Buggles' VIDEO KILLED THE RADIO STAR (1979).

I was born at 8:01 a.m. on December 17th of that same year to considerably less pomp, circumstance, media acclaim, or cultural capital. Some of my first and fondest memories involved jumping on the furniture with my mom and brother as the music video for Van Halen's JUMP (1983) played on MTV in the background. I recall being terrified to take a bath, but not for the same reasons most kids hate to bathe; when I saw Ric Ocasec, lead singer of The Cars, become a periscope and rise out of the bathtub drain to watch model Susan Gallagher bathe in YOU MIGHT THINK (1984), I was sure it could happen to me, too. I also had a sneaking suspicion that comic books and the Lincoln Memorial could come to life someday, as in a-ha's TAKE ON ME (1984) and Starship's WE BUILT THIS CITY (1985), respectively. I really wanted a red leather jacket like Michael Jackson's and some M.C. Hammer parachute pants with lots of zippers, but I didn't know I wanted either sartorial relic until I saw each of them on MTV. As a teenager, I watched in envy as Alanis Morissette chauffeured herself around the snowy countryside in IRONIC and as the Danish-Norwegian pop group, Aqua, rode together in a toy convertible in BARBIE GIRL (1997) as I waited impatiently for my early morning ride to driver's education class. Instead of spending my spring breaks at home in the arid High Plains of West Texas watching daytime TV shows, such as *People's Court* and *The Young and the Restless*, I was young and

Audiovisual Alterity. Michael L. Austin, Oxford University Press. © Oxford University Press 2024.
DOI: 10.1093/oso/9780190277789.003.0001

restless and desperately wanted to be at the beach with the party animals I saw on *MTV Spring Break*. And just as I came of age and was forced to face the reality of being an adult in the real world, MTV focused more and more on what became known as "reality shows"—the first of which was aptly titled *The Real World*—despite the fact that the situations and characters in these shows were often only tangentially based in *actual* reality. We young people (or more accurately, those of us who were young at the time) were MTV's prime audience. We were not as interested in reality as much as we craved the cultural cachet that MTV seemed to afford its viewers, even if we could not afford to live the aspirational lifestyles seen within its music videos. Nevertheless, many of us saw ourselves in those videos, or we at least saw ourselves as we hoped to be seen.

Throughout this book, readers will find that, for better or worse, music videos are one of the major lenses through which many of us see both ourselves and others. And recently, through the democratizing power of social media and easier access to film equipment and software used to create and edit video and audio, music videos have also become a reinvigorated medium through which "others" represent themselves. This book focuses on a number of the various (and often controversial) ways in which alterity, or otherness, is represented and misrepresented in music videos by dominant forces in the music industry, and it highlights the various ways in which "others" use this same medium as a tool for self-representation; share narratives about life from their own perspective; appropriate, counter-appropriate, and redeem harmful tropes in music videos; and take control of conversations about the ways in which they are represented by others.

Perhaps the most well-known and most often cited "other" misrepresented in music videos is women. Plenty of cultural commentary, journalistic think-pieces, and academic research on women in music videos point to the problematic ways in which women are often depicted as sexualized subjects in the service of the male gaze. Whether the sexy school teacher-turned-beauty pageant winner in Van Halen's HOT FOR TEACHER (1984), the high-heeled strippers of Mötley Crüe's GIRLS, GIRLS, GIRLS (1987), or the silent, mannequin-esque models pretending to be Robert Palmer's band in ADDICTED TO LOVE (1986), these women played the role of objects of desire. Their objectified presence within the video often did not even need to be especially germane to the plot of the song, or even the video for that matter, such as Tawny Kitaen's appearance in Whitesnake's IN THE STILL OF THE NIGHT (1987) or, to a certain extent, Courteney Cox's artificially impromptu appearance in Bruce Springsteen's DANCING IN THE DARK (1984). And although MTV's three staple genres—pop, rock, and rap music—seem to be the most scrutinized for the sexualization of women in music videos, one could easily see that country music also features its fair share, especially in examples of "Bro Country," such as Luke Bryan's army of video vixens in COUNTRY GIRL

(SHAKE IT FOR ME) (2011), the bathing beauty in Florida Georgia Line's CRUISE (2012), and the *literal* parade of sexualized music video tropes in Big & Rich's SAVE A HORSE (RIDE A COWBOY) (2004).[1]

If they were not "video vixens," women would sometimes be portrayed as domineering disciplinarians. They could be scolding mothers who set out to ruin a young man's life, as in DJ Jazzy Jeff & The Fresh Prince's PARENTS JUST DON'T UNDERSTAND (1988), or against whom young men needed to fight in order to preserve their inalienable right to have a good time, as in the Beastie Boys' (YOU GOTTA) FIGHT FOR YOUR RIGHT (TO PARTY) (1986). A confluence of these two tropes is represented by Stacy's mom in STACY'S MOM (2003) by Fountains of Wayne and the model who plays Trace Adkins' wife in HOT MAMA (2003). Another version of this trope is the nagging (ex-)wife/(ex-)girlfriend, as seen in Luke Combs' WHEN IT RAINS IT POURS (2017) and in country music supergroup, The Notorious Cherry Bombs' IT'S HARD TO KISS THE LIPS AT NIGHT THAT CHEW YOUR ASS OUT ALL DAY LONG (2004), a video in which several members dress in drag to play each other's nagging wives.

The misrepresentation and objectification of subjects within music videos is obviously worthy of scrutiny and has heretofore been discussed in great detail by critics and scholars. But the under-representation, misrepresentation, or non-representation of many marginalized groups within commercial music videos has ironically been overlooked and/or understudied within music video scholarship. Although I share with many other Americans from my generation nostalgic feelings about MTV and the music videos featured on that channel, I was shielded from many of the ills that accompanied the representation of "others" in many videos by my white privilege. While I am able to identify with characters and artists seen in most music videos, members of marginalized communities may never have had the chance to do the same. In the rare instances when they have seen themselves in a music video, they may have viewed a damaging misrepresentation or misappropriation of their race, gender, sexuality, religion, or culture.

For example, at the time of MTV's launch, with the exception of J.J. Jackson (the sole Black person on MTV's original roster of VJs) seldom were audiences able to see other Black faces on the channel. Early on, the station battled claims of racism for not playing enough music videos that featured Black artists. And although they did actually play videos that included Black musicians, even on their first broadcast day,[2] MTV initially claimed that the reason they played few videos that featured Black artists was because there really weren't any to play. In a 2006 interview for *Jet Magazine*, MTV co-founder Les Garland said:

> There was a shortage of Black videos by urban artists . . . the success of this AOR (album-oriented rock) format in radio certainly had its influence on MTV. But,

> there were no music videos. They weren't being made. We had nothing to pick from. Fifty percent of my time was spent in the early days of MTV convincing artists to make music videos and convincing record labels to put up money to make those videos because this was a whole new area of expense that they never had before. MTV put music on television and it began to work. It began breaking artists.[3]

But the claim that there were no music videos from Black artists was not entirely true. Rick James accused MTV of "blatant racism" when the channel refused to broadcast his video for SUPER FREAK (1981) or those of other Black artists, claiming, "There are no Blacks on MTV's program list except for Tina Turner, and she stopped being Black about 10 years ago. MTV puts on little white punk groups who don't even have record deals. Blacks are missing exposure and sales."[4] And it was true that "little white punk groups" were getting more exposure on MTV at the time. Music videos were already popular in Britain at the beginning of the 1980s, so a majority of MTV's broadcast schedule was drawn from punk and New Wave videos from the UK, ushering in a second "British Invasion." And although the androgyny and gender-bent performances featured in many of the videos of this type gave queer audiences a very rare, small glimpse of themselves in popular music videos (albeit extraordinarily over-the-top and camp), they famously did not feature many Black performers, especially not as frontmen or frontwomen. In fact, one of the main reasons MTV did not play videos featuring Black artists was more deleterious, having more to do with respectability politics and message control than a dearth of videos by these artists, and MTV's original head of Talent and Acquisition, Carolyn B. Baker said as much, admitting in an interview, "It wasn't MTV that turned down 'Super Freak.' It was me. I turned it down. You know why? Because there were half-naked women in it, and it was a piece of crap. As a black woman, I did not want that representing my people as the first black video on MTV."[5] Market research and audience preference were often cited by MTV as the reason to shy away from R&B and other genres that more prominently featured Black artists, but MTV's early audience was primarily comprised of white, suburban Americans.[6] Further, channel executives argued that MTV was fundamentally designed to be a rock music channel, and that "it was difficult for MTV to find African-American artists whose music fit the channel's format that leaned toward rock at the outset."[7] Realizing that this research was likely flawed and potentially tainted by systemic racism, Baker did argue that *some* Black artists should be broadcast:

> I said, "We've got to play James Brown." And Bob [Robert Pittman] said, "The research says our audience thinks rock n' roll started with the Beatles." I came through the civil rights movement. I was a member of SNCC. I believe in

> opening doors. The party line at MTV was that we weren't playing black music because of the "research." But the research was based on ignorance. I told Bob that to his face. We were young, we were cutting edge. We didn't have to be on the cutting edge of racism.

It took several years for MTV to concede and to begin to consistently put videos by Black artists into heavy rotation. After ratings began to increase once MTV played videos by Michael Jackson, such as BILLIE JEAN (1983) and BEAT IT (1983), executives could see the commercial viability of Black music and Black performers. Ironically, even though he did not fit MTV's original rock 'n roll-only format, Michael Jackson's videos saved MTV from financial ruin. In an interview with *The Root*, music journalist Rob Tannenbaum contends:

> It's not enough to say the *Thriller* videos forced MTV to integrate. Michael Jackson helped save the network from being shut down. MTV executives had expected to lose $10 million before they showed a profit. The network quickly lost $50 million, and its parent company was prepared to shut down MTV and call it quits. Jackson's three *Thriller* videos came out in 1983. In the first three months of 1984, MTV had their first quarterly profit.[8]

But even commercial viability did not always help to bring the music of minority communities to MTV's airwaves. Despite hip-hop's growing popularity throughout the 1980s, it took until 1987 for MTV to launch an entire program dedicated to the genre. *Yo! MTV Raps* was a hip-hop program initially broadcast on MTV Europe that was not available to US audiences until August 1988. Despite being initially released in an inhospitably late Saturday nighttime slot, the show was a breakthrough hit that launched the careers of many hip-hop artists during the 1990s. Due to its astonishing success, MTV created a daily version of the show called *Yo! MTV Raps Today* in March 1989. Still, hip-hop was ghettoized and relegated to special, and separate, programs. But rather than becoming a space for accurate representations of hip-hop artists and their culture, African and African American Studies scholar Mark Anthony Neal argues that—even despite MTV's "apartheid-like programming" during the early 1980s—hip-hop was sufficiently sanitized and mainstreamed to the point that the "Hip-Hop music video would open the form to an audience of mid-American youths, who relished the subversive 'otherness' that the music and its purveyors represented. By the time 'Gangsta Rap' . . . became one of the most popular genres of Hip-Hop, a significant portion of the music was largely supported by young white Americans."[9]

Four decades have now passed since our birth, and MTV has ruled as the chief arbiter of youth culture for most of those forty-something years. As such, the music videos it broadcast around the globe represented the leading edge of popular music, fashion, style, and culture of the world, and in doing so, shaped global culture through those representations. And as readers will see throughout this book, the politics of representation in music videos is a perennial topic of utmost importance that is as old as the medium itself.

Hegemony

The myriad issues related to representing ourselves and other people can all be traced to a single root source: power. The ability to represent oneself or others within popular media is a form of power not afforded to everyone, especially not in mainstream media, and this power is less attainable for members of many minority groups, classes, and cultures. Most of this power is consolidated by the privileged among us through hegemony, or "the power of the ruling class to convince other classes that their interests are the interests of all."[10] This power is not usually forced upon those of us who are not part of distinctive minority communities through noticeable, active persuasion, but instead, we are subtly taught to accept the interest of the ruling class (i.e., the rich, the racial or religious majority, etc.). For example, Christian hegemony has been established in the United States to the point that Christmas pervades almost every facet of life in December for Christians and non-Christians alike. Rare is the grocery store, coffee shop, or shopping mall that does not play Christmas music from at least the end of November through December 25 each year. And many insist that people who work at these places say "Merry Christmas" to all patrons without regard to the religious adherence of either party; many more people offer and accept this greeting uncritically during the holiday season as it has become so tightly woven into the fabric of Western culture. Further, although many religions celebrate holidays throughout the month of December, almost every public school, government office, and business across the country is closed on Christmas Day (and usually a few days before and/or after).

We can see the exertion of hegemonic power within music videos in a number of ways. Record companies, MTV, and other media outlets exert hegemonic control over Western culture, dictating to us what music is cool, who our celebrities should be, what clothes are fashionable, and which items and activities are worth our time and money. As described previously, the inherent power of media hegemony is given freely. Even in its heyday, MTV did not have a monopoly on programming for youth, and no one was forced to watch MTV, but it became a dominant cultural force and the voice of several generations who shouted "I want my MTV," and MTV gave them what they wanted. However, the increasingly interdependent relationship that record labels had with MTV gave the channel (and others like it, such as VH-1) more control over what words songwriters could use in their songs and which images music video directors could include in their videos by exerting pressure through standards policies. Producers began to insist that songs, and the music videos that featured them, conform to MTV's standards to such an extent that "bland conformity in videos that are loaded with hackneyed visual clichés" became preferred over ground- and rule-breaking content that MTV may refuse to broadcast.[11] We will see throughout this book that clichés can quickly become harmful tropes when the dominant power continues to rely on them to represent "others."

"Others," their cultures, their communities, and their cultural artifacts also appear in music videos through the hegemonic tool of cultural appropriation. Through the process of *enculturation*, we learn and internalize elements of our own culture. When we come into contact with another culture, *acculturation* can occur. Acculturation is a form of cultural exchange in which individuals come into sustained contact with another culture and willingly take on the customs, beliefs, values, and so on of the other culture (such as learning the local language when moving to a foreign country, for example). However, this seemingly mutually beneficial exchange can become one-sided. The process of enculturation, or the process of learning to become part of another culture, can become forced on "others" by the dominant culture with an expectation to assimilate and discard one's original heritage culture or to separate oneself from one's original culture in order to fit into the dominant culture. In many cases, the dominant culture altogether rejects another culture, leading to the marginalization of those from that culture, never accepting them as part of the dominant culture; however, that often does not prevent them from taking elements of the "other" culture through the act of *cultural appropriation* and using them inappropriately and/or making them part of their own culture without benefiting the culture from which they came.

Richard A. Rogers identifies four categories of cultural appropriation that vary in degrees of hegemonic power relations, subjugation, and exploitation:

1. Cultural exchange: the reciprocal exchange of symbols, artifacts, rituals, genres, and/or technologies between cultures with roughly equal levels of power.
2. Cultural dominance: the use of elements of a dominant culture by members of a subordinated culture in a context in which the dominant culture has been imposed onto the subordinated culture, including appropriations that enact resistance.
3. Cultural exploitation: the appropriation of elements of a subordinated culture by a dominant culture without substantive reciprocity, permission, and/or compensation.

4. Transculturalization: cultural elements created from and/or by multiple cultures, such that the identification of a single originating culture is problematic, for example, multiple cultural appropriations structured in the dynamics of globalization and transnational capitalism creating hybrid forms.[12]

Here, we see that cultural appropriation is always a matter of power (hegemony), but it isn't always necessarily a bad thing. It certainly is fine to appreciate another culture, especially when a cultural outsider is invited to participate in that culture by cultural insiders. It is also perfectly acceptable to exchange cultural values, ideas, and artifacts when there is a mutually beneficial exchange between cultures, as long as it is done with respect and proper credit is given to the originating culture. Cultural appropriation becomes unethical when the power dynamic and benefit from using a cultural artifact becomes unequal; when the dominant culture claims elements of another culture as their own without giving the originating culture credit; or when the dominant culture recontextualizes a cultural artifact to such an extent that its original cultural significance is ignored, reduced, lost, or forgotten.

We will see throughout this book that appropriative acts can be used as rhetorical tools within music videos for the benefit of marginalized communities to enact resistance. Because of the cultural hegemony they often face, marginalized "others" are incentivized or forced to assimilate into a dominant culture in order to have access to rights and opportunities and to avoid various forms of discrimination. In order to do so, they are often expected to appropriate elements of the dominant culture. Here, "others" also engage in cultural appropriation, but the act is not unethical as it is necessary to participate in the dominant culture—and at times, it is necessary for survival. For example, Katy Perry's decision to wear cornrows in her video, THIS IS HOW WE DO (2013) is an example of cultural appropriation because she is adopting an African American hairstyle for fashion without providing any credit or mutual benefit to African American culture by doing so; in fact, African American women are fired from jobs and are not allowed to wear natural or ethnic hairstyles to work as they are still often deemed to be "unprofessional" in contemporary American culture. Conversely, no one can reasonably suggest that Beyoncé is guilty of unethical cultural appropriation for wearing a long, straight honey blonde wig in PRETTY HURTS (2013) since American culture still values white beauty standards and its markers, where light skin, blue eyes, and blonde hair are highly valued and generally considered to be more attractive, and people who identify as women who are not white still find themselves unfairly expected to meet these same standards.

In this form of appropriation—what I call "redemptive appropriation"—members of subaltern groups appropriate rhetoric or artifacts from the dominant culture and use them, ascribe redeeming qualities to them, or otherwise "rescue" them, in order to construct and express their own narratives and ideology. In her essay, "Counterhegemonic Acts: Appropriation as a Feminist Rhetorical Strategy," Helene A. Shugart describes ways in which

> members of various disenfranchised social groups . . . claim and utilize labels conventionally applied by their oppressors in a derogatory manner as a way of challenging their original meaning. Some lesbians and gay men, for example, refer to themselves as *dykes* and *faggots*, respectively; some African Americans defiantly refer to themselves as *niggers*; and some women celebrate their identities as *whores* and *bitches*.[13]

Another example of this type of counterhegemonic appropriation is the myriad uses of the anthem "God Save the King." Dating back to the eighteenth century, the tune serves as the National Anthem of Great Britain and the Royal Anthem of many of the other countries of the British Commonwealth. In colonial America, the anthem was a touchstone for British loyalists who came to New England on royal charters, but parody tunes were composed as symbols of American anti-monarchism. In 1831, "My Country 'Tis of Thee" (or "America"), written by Samuel Smith, was premiered in Boston and began its life as an American anthem in its own right, used as a tool for music educators and other social reformers. During the Civil War, abolitionists used parodied versions of the "America" text in their fight against the institution of slavery in America. Other appropriations of the text and tune were used in the nineteenth and early twentieth centuries in the temperance and suffrage movements.[14]

We can find many similar examples of redemptive appropriation in music videos. In the Eurythmics' video, SWEET DREAMS ARE MADE OF THESE (1983), Annie Lennox redemptively appropriates a tailored men's suit, white dress shirt, gray tie, black gloves, and a crew-style haircut. She claims that these sartorial choices helped her to express the point that "appearance is just temporary, and I want to be as strong as a man . . . I'm as good as a man, I'm as strong as a man."[15] In his video, THIS IS AMERICA (2018), Childish Gambino (Donald Glover) redemptively appropriates poses, facial expressions, and other physical characteristics of Jim Crow, a racist caricature of African-Americans from nineteenth- and twentieth-century blackface minstrel shows, to represent the prevalence of Jim Crow laws and other forms of extreme racial injustice that continue to plague the United States. Throughout this book, I will discuss many other examples in which "others" use redemptive cultural appropriation to adopt and/or adapt elements from the dominant cultural milieu in order to critique their representation and treatment within the dominant culture or to better represent themselves.

When discussing cultural appropriation, the power dynamic between dominant and non-dominant cultures or communities is key. There are, however, as we will see in this book, instances wherein members of a marginalized group will take and use elements from the culture of another marginalized group. Sometimes, this adoption or borrowing of the elements of another culture is done out of solidarity, "fictive kinship," or as a way to assimilate into another minority culture into which they feel more accepted.[16] At other times, the use of these elements is more unethical and exploitative and done without mutual benefit or sufficient attribution. In order to address this phenomenon within the nuanced relationship between two non-dominant cultures, fashion and media studies scholar Minh-Ha T. Pham coined the term "racial plagiarism" to highlight

> the racial relationships and inequalities that are obscured by terms like cultural appropriation, cultural appreciation, and piracy. In the fashion context, racial plagiarism occurs when a designer copies racial and indigenous styles, forms, practices, and knowledges without permission and without giving adequate (or any) attribution to the source model and community. As with other plagiarisms, racial plagiarism covers verbatim copying (or in fashion terms, the line-by-line copying of a racially marked garment) and unacknowledged paraphrasing (a reworked but still recognizable derivative model).[17]

Even though this use of elements from another culture may be questionable, controversial, exploitative, or otherwise unethical, the term racial plagiarism helps us recognize the fact that, indeed, there are perceptible power dynamics at play in the relationships among marginalized racial groups, with some group having more influence with and among the dominant culture in a particular place at a particular time, while recognizing that true cultural appropriation involves the hegemonic power and privilege that lies with the dominant culture alone. As with most forms of cultural appropriation, racial plagiarism (and by extension, *cultural plagiarism*, when discussing this type of interaction between marginalized groups in which other elements of their identity beyond race is the key factor) is a form of erasure in which the originator of a cultural artifact is ignored, forgotten, and ultimately replaced.[18]

Conservative cultural critics are quick to argue that culture is not property that can be owned and is therefore free for the taking because no one can be expected to educate themselves or do enough due diligence to keep track of the various meaning(s) of the culture we continually exchange in our globalized society. Willfully ignoring the force that cultural and economic hegemonic power exerts on marginalized communities, they claim that cultural "cross-fertilization" is always a good thing and presume the fact that they have access to a culture and its artifacts gives them permission to use any element from that culture as they please.[19] Some go to great lengths to find and point to a few members who belong to particular marginalized communities who personally do not have a problem with the cultural appropriation of their own culture's artifacts, as if anecdotes and a few individual opinions reflect the views of an entire community.[20] Throughout this book, we will also see these ham-fisted, unscrupulous arguments resurface when members of a dominant culture are questioned about their use of elements of another culture in their music videos, even when done out of what they argue is sincere appreciation for the culture in question, as they gain cultural (and often literal) capital through their cultural appropriation while simultaneously pushing the "others" who created them even further toward the margins of our society. No matter how much of our dominant culture is built upon elements unethically appropriated from other marginalized cultures or how unavoidable cultural appropriation seems to be in our creative process and practices, we still have an ethical responsibility to handle the culture of others with care and respect.

Others and Ourselves

But what do we mean when we talk about "others?" Edward Said was among the first theorists to describe the centuries-old practice in which colonial powers from the West asserted dominance and cultural superiority by setting themselves up against "others" they wished to colonize, conquer, and/or otherwise exploit for capital. In his treatise *Orientalism*, Said explains that the West defines itself by constructing an image of what it is *not*—exotic, sensual, emotional, feminine, and despotic. In this way, the Orient (i.e., the Middle East and Far East) became the "other," a stark contrast and false dichotomy used by the West to further bolster its self-aggrandizement as characteristically reasonable, rational, virtuous, objective, masculine, stoic, and so on, essentially crafting its own identity, that is, what it is, by describing what it is not:

> The development and maintenance of every culture require the existence of another, different competing alter ego. The construction of identity . . . involves the construction of opposites and "others" whose actuality is always subject to the continuous interpretation and reinterpretation of their differences from "us."[21]

Further, this dichotomy helped secure the belief that the Orient—considered to be homogenous—was incapable of defining itself and required the assistance of Western intellectuals in order to make sense of itself and to help institute the superior Western values of justice, democracy, and capitalism.[22] And it was this false dichotomy that provided the philosophical justification and framework for conquering the East symbolically, ideologically, and literally. Said argues, "Orientalism can be discussed and analyzed as the corporate institution for dealing with the Orient—dealing with it by making statements about it, authorizing views of it, describing it, by teaching it, settling it, ruling over it: in short, Orientalism as a Western style for dominating, restructuring, and having authority over the Orient." This "othering" also helped the West make ethical and value judgements about the people of the "Orient," and by extension, established the representation and validation of the Orient as an overtly Occidental undertaking. In fact, Said explains how the logic of Orientalism renders self-representation by Eastern peoples impossible:

> The Orient and Islam have a kind of extrareal, phenomenologically reduced status that puts them out of reach of everyone except the Western expert. From the beginning of Western speculation about the Orient, the one thing the Orient could not do was to represent itself. Evidence of the Orient was credible only after it had passed through and been made firm by the refining fire of the Orientalist's work.[23]

These representations of "the other" rely heavily on clichés, stereotypes, myths, and fetishes about Eastern people and their cultures in order to make them seem exotic, inferior, less threatening, and altogether more palatable for Western consumers and domineers. In fact, the theorist and cultural critic bell hooks refers to these types of misrepresentations as the "eating the Other," wherein difference is exploited by the dominant culture as a conscious aesthetic choice, writing "within commodity culture, ethnicity becomes spice, seasoning that can liven up the dull dish that is mainstream white culture."[24]

The Orientalist project is not a relic of Imperial Britain or France relegated to the nineteenth century but lives on in representations of the Middle East, Asia, and Africa (as we will see in subsequent chapters). There are countless instances of orientalism and exoticism in canonic classical music, many examples of which are among the most famous works of well-known composers: *Les Indes Galantes* (1735) by Jean-Philippe Rameau, the rondo movement of Mozart's Piano Sonata No. 11 in A major, K. 331 (nicknamed "Rondo alla Turca") (1783/4), Rossini's *The Barber of Seville* (1816), Franz Liszt's *Hungarian Rhapsodies for Piano*, S. 244, R.106 (1846–1853), Giuseppe Verdi's *Aïda* (1871), Georges Bizet's *Carmen* (1875) and *The Pearl Fishers* (1863), Saint-Saëns' *Samson et Dalila*, Op. 77 (1877), Maurice Ravel's *Bolero* (1928), Puccini's *Madama Butterfly* (1904), Gilbert and Sullivan's *The Mikado* (1885), much of the work of Impressionist composers such as Claude Debussy, and Philip Glass's operas

Satyagraha (1980) and *Akhenaten* (1984), to name just a handful of a great many examples.

The Italian neo-Marxist philosopher and politician Antonio Gramsci developed his notion of the "subaltern" over several years, writing in notebooks while he was imprisoned by the Italian Fascist regime from 1929–1935. He first uses the term in his first notebook (1929–1930) in its literal and more prevalent usage as a term for second lieutenant (or any officer below the rank of captain) in the British army. He later adapts the term to describe someone who is of lower status or subordinate to authority, or someone who has lost status. Later he expands the use of the term even more to describe differences in class, writing, "Subaltern classes are subject to the initiatives of the dominant class, even when they rebel; they are in a state of anxious defense."[25] Later still, Gramsci expands the term yet again to include "slaves, peasants, religious groups, women, different races, and the proletariat as subaltern social groups."[26]

Adopting the term from Gramsci, a group of historians and literary theorists known as the Subaltern Studies Group (SSG) defined the term "subaltern" as "the general attribute of subordination in South Asian society, whether this is expressed in terms of class, caste, age, gender and office or in any other way."[27] Gayatri Chakravorty Spivak, a leading Indian literary theorist, cultural critic, translator, pioneer in postcolonial theory, and member of the SSG, describes why she prefers to use the term "subaltern" to other alternatives:

> I like the word subaltern for one reason. It is totally situational. Subaltern began as a description of a certain rank in the military. The word was under censorship by Gramsci: he called Marxism "monism," and was obliged to call the proletarian "subaltern." That word, used under duress, has been transformed into the description of everything that doesn't fall under strict class analysis. I like that, because it has no theoretical rigor.[28]

Like Gramsci, Spivak has also changed her definition of "subaltern" over time. But rather than broaden the concept to include more people, she has narrowed her definition to essentially only include the colonized people of India:

> [E]verybody thinks the subaltern is just a classy word for oppressed, for Other, for somebody who's not getting a piece of the pie . . . The subalternist historians take it from Gramsci and change it. They define it as the people, the foreign elite, the indigenous elite, the upwardly mobile indigenes, in various kinds of situations: everything that has limited or no access to the cultural imperialism is subaltern—a space of difference. Now, who would say that's just the oppressed? The working class is oppressed. It's not subaltern. It's in capital logic, you know what I mean?[29]

Generally, the broader and less exclusionary concept of subalterity (sometimes subalternity) as a way of recounting "history told from below" remains most prevalent and refers to any marginalized group that is seen as "inferior" or that is denied a voice in society because of its race, class, sexual orientation, gender, religion, and so on. According to critical theorist Robert Young, "subaltern" can describe a single "person rendered without human agency, by his or her social status" or entire "social groups who are excluded from a society's established structures for political representation, the means by which people have a voice in their society"[30]

In her groundbreaking essay, "Can the Subaltern Speak?," Spivak focuses on this voice (or lack thereof). She examines the ways in which those of us in privileged positions write and talk about the subaltern. Skillfully confronting several giants of modern Western thought, such as Michel Foucault, Gilles Deleuze, Karl Marx, and Walter Benjamin (among others), Spivak argues against the universal application of Western theories to subaltern cultures (and emphasizes that "the subaltern" is rarely one homogenous group, but represents multiple groups, and the various social, political, and economic strata with those groups), as they tend to essentialize the non-Western subject as a monolithic whole and serves as a form of epistemic violence (i.e., to inflict harm through discourse).[31] Further, she argues that the representation of the third-world subject within Western discourse and intellectual production also tends to conflate representation, "as in 'speaking for,' as in politics, and representation as 're-presentation,' as in art or philosophy."[32] As a result, Spivak argues, the subaltern (in this case, female Indian women) have no space within hegemonic discourse from which to speak, and since their message is not heard, it is almost as if they are not able to speak at all. The apparent irony here is not lost on me. Spivak is arguing that most forms of academic interpretation, however well-intentioned, can easily be seen by subaltern groups as an act of epistemic violence. marginalization, and systematic oppression, wherein the Western interpreter assigns the subaltern a voice or grants them agency, rather than letting them speak for themselves. The goal of my book is not to speak for "others," to give them metaphorical voices, or even to amplify their voices. People who would generally be classified by the academy as "others" or "the subaltern" do not need my assistance and continually speak for themselves. Discussing the large body of text about "the Orient" from which he drew his analysis for *Orientalism*, Edward Said writes, "Orientalism is after all a system for citing works and authors."[33] It is my intention to disrupt this recursive and self-referential cycle by taking care to make room for "the subaltern to speak" as it were, and when possible, intentionally citing authors and thinkers from subaltern communities who may or may not have access to the traditional academic publishing avenues made available to me, but instead, disseminate their work through cultural journalism, blogs, YouTube videos, and other public venues that often lack the academic cachet one would expect to cite in an academic monograph. I understand that because I am not a member of most of the subaltern groups represented in the music videos discussed in the chapters of this book, many people may believe that I do not even deserve a seat at the proverbial table where discussions about race, gender, class, and so on are discussed, and to a certain extent, I agree. My personal opinions about these topics, even when informed by rigorous study, careful listening, or personal experience, are not necessarily welcomed or appreciated. I am certainly not *entitled* to express them. For example, my experience as a white professor who taught for over five years and earned tenure at a prestigious Historically Black College or University (HBCU) has not earned me the right to express my opinions about the lived experience of African Americans or members of the African Diaspora in America, and it certainly does not make me an expert on the lived experiences of members of those communities. And it is especially important for me to recognize the fact that the expression of my opinions *ipso facto*, even when they are positive, does nothing to assuage any of the epistemic, economic, political, or even physical violence committed against these communities through colonialism, racism and systematic oppression, homophobia, misogyny, and so on. Therefore, this book is not designed to serve as a compendium of my opinions on identity politics and the representations of various "others" in music videos. Instead, it is a sort of reckoning with my personal complicity with systems of oppression within the media—not as a result of my misrepresentation of "others" in media objects that I have created, per se, but the complicity that results from my silence in the face of misrepresentation, appropriation, and the commodification of the subaltern identities. It is not the job of the subaltern to end their own symbolic (or literal) oppression, or even to resist it. Writing about a blog post in which she shared her decision to no longer discuss race with white people, journalist and author Reni Eddo-Lodge explains the emotional labor involved in taking on a task that should be the duty of those of us who hold any sort of privilege (white, cis-, male, Christian, etc.) and retain various degrees of hegemonic power, writing:

> I cannot continue to emotionally exhaust myself trying to get this message across, while also toeing the very precarious line that tries not to implicate any one white person in their role of perpetuating structural racism, lest they character assassinate me.[34]

Racial minorities should not be forced to teach us to be less racist; it is our job to teach ourselves and each other. Likewise, members of the LGBTQIA+ community are not responsible for our sex education or for ridding us of our transphobia. Members of religious minorities should not have to teach us the grace and tolerance that we claim Christianity teaches us. And the incarcerated should not have to teach us that their lives have value on both sides of a prison wall.

Additionally, this book is also not meant to serve as an indictment on music video directors, performers, or the entertainment industry writ large, nor is it a condemnation of American popular culture, capitalism, or people who do not fall within the category of "others" described herein, per se. But even though I argue that this book is not necessarily a forum for my personal opinions, it is my duty as a musicologist and media studies scholar with a certain degree of privilege and power to assess the various representations of subalterity within music videos—both positive and negative—and offer criticism where criticism is due. In this way, using my privilege to speak truth to power is altogether different from offering my uninformed and/or uninvited opinions on the experience of subaltern communities.

I should note that what I am attempting to do here is much different from what many might label as my participation in "cancel culture" (or even the more innocuous-sounding "call out culture"). Increased video recording and dissemination capabilities have made smartphones and other mobile video recording devices essential tools in fighting for social justice in today's world. Perhaps the best example of their use is the Black Lives Matter movement, which gained momentum in the mid-2010s as supporters demanded justice for victims of brutality and murder at the hands of police which had been recorded on smartphones by bystanders or police officers' own bodycams. Likewise, social media plays an increasingly important role in the ways in which abusers are held accountable. The #MeToo movement has successfully held many sexual abusers to account by publicly pointing out their behavior on social media, both as a way to seek justice for themselves and to protect others who may have been or who may become victims at the hands of an abuser. Social media is also now riddled with videos of "Karens" behaving poorly in public, belittling service industry workers and demanding to speak to a store's manager, refusing to follow clearly posted rules from which they feel exempted, or weaponizing the police by calling them when BIPOC people happen to share a public space with them, all of which is recorded and posted online to hold accountable people who have historically gotten away with this type of atrocious behavior.[35]

Critics of this mode of ensuring accountability have labeled it "cancel culture," lamenting the fact that they miss out on professional opportunities or are altogether shunned or "blacklisted" when the traditional institutions that have usually shielded them from accountability are less effective in the court of public opinion. However, ham-fisted attempts at "holding others accountable" by simply recording and attempting to publicly shame someone for behavior with which one does not agree can sometimes strengthen the argument of naysayers who dismiss all attempts at holding abusers accountable as bullying. It is also easy to see how many attempts at "calling out" bad behavior can quickly slip into performative activism, where policing the tone or behavior of others becomes much more important than seeking justice for those who have been harmed. Rather than the self-indulgence and drama of unnecessary public call-outs, academic and activist Loretta J. Ross argues instead for "calling-in" which "engages in debates with words and actions of healing and restoration."[36] Ross argues that call-outs are justifiable when "challenging provocateurs who deliberately hurt others, or for powerful people beyond our reach," but she also points out that most contemporary public shaming is horizontal and is motivated more by respectability politics than seeking justice. Further, while some call-ins arguably need to be made in public, they can still be done with respect and without the "weaponization of suffering that prevents constructive healing."[37]

Throughout this book, I analyze, and at times harshly critique, some extremely harmful representations of subaltern communities that appear in music videos. However, I do so not in an attempt to destroy careers or reputations or publicly shame those involved, but rather seek to call-in those who profit from discrimination and white fragility (or Christian fragility, or other types of fragility experienced by dominant cultures when their position is challenged). I am just as interested in centering inclusive, healthy representation and positive change in the representational politics of music videos as I am in pointing out harmful stereotypes and unjust power dynamics. It is my hope that this book contributes to the work of activists and academics advocating for broader and healthier representations of subaltern communities in contemporary media. In doing so, I also employ my various forms of privilege, taking responsibility for my own community and culture by doing emotional labor that those who have been misrepresented should not be asked to do and who are not responsible for the personal and professional growth of those who have unknowingly or intentionally misrepresented them (but who have tirelessly done it out of necessity—and with astounding grace—nonetheless). Likewise, I have no unrealistic expectation that artists or music video directors will even read this academic monograph.[38] Nor do I naïvely think that this is the best way to change the hearts and minds of an entire industry or presume that any creator of questionable representations seen or heard in a music video or their supporters and defenders in academia and cultural criticism would even make a good faith effort to engage with the material in this book. But that does not mean that this effort is not worthwhile. Further, I do not believe we should completely dismiss decades-old (or hours-old) music videos because of the harmful representations they contain, as it is exceedingly difficult to learn from the historical artifacts we hide out of shame; much like Confederate statues and Nazi memorabilia, these harmful parts of our culture absolutely do not deserve to be given pride of place to be celebrated, but they should be analyzed, contextualized, and presented appropriately to serve as a reminder of what *not* to do.

Scholars who use their privilege as a means of "calling-in through analysis" may feel uneasy about doing this vital work, but it is one of our primary duties as public figures, especially for those of us with sufficient institutional support and even more so for those of us who enjoy the protection of tenure. I have struggled with this duty for many years, concerned that I am speaking for others or essentializing communities for whom I have no business speaking. Reni Eddo-Lodge explains that "[d]iscussing racism is not the same thing as discussing 'black identity.' Discussing racism is about discussing white identity. It's about white anxiety. It's about asking why whiteness has this reflexive need to define itself against immigrant bogey monsters in order to feel comfortable, safe and secure."[39] Thus, by discussing and critiquing the cultural appropriation of Native American culture by wearing a war bonnet in a music video, for example, I am not offering my opinion about Native American identities nor am I attempting to validate their cultural identity in some way (as if that were possible). Rather, I am using my privilege to call the appropriative act into question and engage others in positions of hegemonic power in discussions about the pitfalls of this type of cultural appropriation.

In her essay "Marginality as a Site of Resistance," bell hooks describes the margin of society not as a site of domination and colonization, but rather as a site of "radical possibility, a space of resistance."[40] Here in the margin, hooks argues that the oppressed have the freedom to resist the oppressor and colonizer. But in a soliloquy of sorts, hooks presents the thoughts of the academic—of me, and perhaps you, the reader—as one who inhabits this marginal space in search of difference, colonizing, annihilating, and erasing as we go:

> No need to hear your voice when I can talk about you better than you can speak about yourself. No need to hear your voice. Only tell me about your pain. I want to know your story. And then I will tell it back to you in a new way. Tell it back to you in such a way that it has become mine, my own. Re-writing you as I write myself anew. I am still author, authority. I am still colonizer, the speaking subject and you are now at the center of my talk.[41]

I fully acknowledge that no matter how benevolent my intentions, a certain amount of "epistemic violence" and erasure is done to subaltern communities when they are not allowed to speak for themselves and, instead, I do most of the speaking. In an effort to mitigate this tendency, discussions of the various ways in which subaltern communities speak for themselves in (and through) music videos will be a prominent feature of this book. Mythologist and postcolonialist Marc Colavincenzo reminds those of us who write about groups to which we do not belong that doing this kind of engaged scholarship comes with responsibility:

> [I]t is all too easy to be postcolonially clever and theoretical about issues of race and ethnicity if one is not affected by this personally . . . I am not arguing for a sort of "nativism": i.e. that only indigenous scholars can discuss these issues. But I do think we need to be acutely aware of the privileged position from which we make our pronouncements.[42]

Similarly, white privilege can function as a hermeneutic lens through which white audiences and spectators interpret the cultural contribution of others. As hooks reminds us, "[i]t is a sign of white privilege to be able to 'see' blackness and black culture from a standpoint where only the rich culture of opposition black people have created in resistance marks and defines us. Such a perspective enables one to ignore white supremacist domination and the harm it inflicts via oppression, exploitation, and everyday wounds and pains."[43]

Wholeheartedly accepting this responsibility for this kind of reflexivity, I endeavor to use my position of privilege to amplify and augment the voices of "others" to the best of my ability, without usurping the inherent power of their message, voice, and personal agency. It is also for this reason that all of the chapters in this book include case studies that focus on music videos that are created and controlled by subaltern community members themselves. When possible, my analysis will be informed by interviews and other writings (both formal and informal) that connect more directly with video makers, performers, and their associated fan communities.

Chapter Outlines

On May 7, 2013, Aisha Harris, a columnist for *Slate Magazine*'s culture blog "Brow Beat," published an article titled "The Troubling Viral Trend of the 'Hilarious' Black Neighbor," wherein she discusses sound bites from news interviews that become viral videos on the Internet. She argues that because the interviewee is almost always Black, candid, and often perceived as flamboyant, the act of heroism or bravery for which they are being interviewed is overshadowed by their portrayal as being poor, undereducated, and working class. In addition to their "viral" status as news clips alone, these videos have found even more popularity in being "auto-tuned" or "Songified," that is, the audio from the interview is processed through a phase vocoder and transformed into pop music.

In my first chapter, I examine several of these auto-tuned viral videos, the sound bites from which they are created, the songs created from them, and some of the ethical, sociopolitical, and racial issues surrounding this type of aesthetic labor, as well as issues surrounding representations of ethnicity and mental disability in the original online videos and their subsequent remixes.

Chapter 2 discusses music videos that depict East Asian and Pacific Islander communities and cultures. Asian culture and aesthetics have long influenced Western pop music, and recently, Asian aesthetics have again struck a chord with young performers. This chapter traces the long history of sexualization, demonization, and exclusion of East Asians in American history and the roots of many stereotypes and tropes about this community we see and hear in contemporary media, even music videos. This section also covers music videos that include Pacific Islander communities; while some mainstream films and music videos, such as Elvis Presley's *Blue Hawaii* and Nicki Minaj's STARSHIPS (2012) only feature Islanders as exoticized backup singers and/or dancers, there are other views, shared mainly via the internet that showcase Pacific Islander cultures prominently.

Chapter 3 discusses the issues surrounding "redface" in music videos, that is, instances in which non-Native people adopt Indigenous dress and customs, and reinforce racist stereotypes with the inclusion of "Indian princesses," "noble savages," or "sexy squaws" in music videos. This chapter also addresses *aegyo* (애교), a term used to describe a South Korean "cute" aesthetic (similar to Japan's *kawaii*) and is often used to describe the childlike and submissive attitudes and behavior of K-Pop stars. Ironically, several K-Pop music videos employ a "Native American chic" aesthetic, awash with teepees, headdresses, and war paint, as an expression of *aegyo*. While this genre of K-Pop music videos shares many similarities to other videos discussed in this chapter, I will argue that these videos demonstrate a unique type of misappropriation as K-Pop music video directors adopt these elements from the already-debased and exploitative representations of Native Americans in Western pop culture. I also discuss ways in which Native communities represent themselves in music videos—especially younger community members who live in poverty on reservations—feel a kinship with hip-hop artists who grow up in poverty in the inner city; in solidarity, some artists create hip-hop music videos that share similar aesthetic elements with hip hop music videos but also include native instruments, dance, costumes, and so on. Other videos demonstrate artists' dual affiliation with their native roots and their integration into the dominant culture.

Chapter 4 explores how the slow turn toward acceptance in country music of the LGBTQIA+ community and drag performers can be viewed in these and other country music videos by investigating the representations of these groups and their relationships within country music videos. It also examines the reception history of these videos and discusses the success many of them enjoy, despite appearing only online or in niche markets rather than on mainstream outlets such as Country Music Television (CMT). Further, it sheds light on the delicate aesthetic and career choices country music stars make when creating country music videos with queer themes.

Chapter 5 traces the development of religious music videos and scrutinizes many of the ways religious minorities, especially those who ascribe to the beliefs of "New Religious Movements," namely in Scientology and the Church of Jesus Christ of Latter-day Saints, are represented through the use of sacred images, symbols, icons, and the performance of religious rites and traditions in music videos.

The prison population is one of the most often overlooked groups of "others" in the United States and other Western countries, but it is regularly featured in music videos. There is a wide range of contested and contradicting narratives regarding incarceration and life behind bars; those who have been to prison seldom *want* to go back to such a horrifying place; others who only know of prison from media representations find jail to be an intriguing—and sometimes even sexy—place about which they fantasize. The final chapter deals with the fetishization of prison life and representations of the incarcerated in music videos.

Readers may notice that, at times, quite an extensive overview of beliefs, customs, or the historical treatment of a particular marginalized group is provided within these chapters. This background information has not only often escaped the attention of the general public, either purposefully or unintentionally, but is also vital to understanding the root causes of many stereotypes and tropes used to represent these groups in Western media, including in music videos.

Representing Music Videos in Print

There is currently no academic standard for citing music videos, and confusion arises because music videos almost always share their name with the songs they were produced to promote. Following the lead of Diane Railston and Paul Watson, the emerging convention is to cite songs, albums, films, and so on conventionally, and to display the titles of music videos in small capital letters. In their book, *Music Video and the Politics of Representation*, Railston and Watson use the following example:

> The music video AMERICAN IDIOT promoted Green Day's song "American Idiot" which featured on their 2004 album *American Idiot*.[44]

Some of the discussion around YouTube and TikTok videos throughout this book involves citing viewership statistics as a measure of popularity and a mark that a particular video has or has not gone "viral." In their book, *Going Viral*, Karine Nahon and Jeff Hemsley define virality as:

> a social information flow process where many people simultaneously forward a specific information item, over a short period of time, within their social networks, and where the message spreads beyond their own [social] networks to different, often distant networks, resulting in a sharp acceleration in the number of people who are exposed to the message.[45]

In other words, the virality of an online music video is determined by four things: the willingness of audiences to share the video among their own social networks, the speed at which the video spreads, the number of people reached and exposed to the content, and the distance the video travels as it spreads beyond one network to others. So while an online music video may be viral at the time I am writing this book, it is likely that it is much less "contagious" even just a short time after publication. Likewise, some videos that currently are not so viral may find incredible popularity many years after they are first produced, perhaps in an altogether different medium and cultural context. For example, Rick Astley's NEVER GONNA GIVE YOU UP (1987) was a chart-topper when it was first released, but like almost all pop songs, its popularity faded with time. Unlike most pop songs, NEVER GONNA GIVE YOU UP enjoyed a spectacular second life beginning in May 2007 when members of 4chan and other online forums engaged in a relatively harmless prank called "Rickrolling," which involves tricking other people into watching Astley's video by mislabeling a hyperlink or other deceptive means.

So, while the virality of music videos waxes and wanes over time, the figures published herein represent a snapshot of a video's virality and popularity at the time of writing. The issues surrounding the representation of subaltern communities in music videos, however, seem to be perennial, so while viewership statistics quickly become obsolete, the obsolescence of harmful misrepresentations and misappropriation cannot come soon enough. Further, it is my hope that this book and the ideas and theories presented within it prove to be useful in the analysis of not only music videos but also other audiovisual media—television, film, online videos, art installations, and so on—since concerns and controversy surrounding the representation of subaltern communities in the media is not confined solely to music videos.

1

"Dead Giveaway"

Blaxploitation Aesthetics and Viral Music Videos

Viral videos are everywhere. Thanks to many of the technological innovations that have made the Internet more social, more collaborative, more conversational, and especially more user-generated, viral music videos are becoming ever more ubiquitous. If you don't happen to catch a viral video online, either by receiving an especially popular video in an e-mail from a colleague, or if you haven't yet seen it posted by a friend on social media or on your favorite blog, or if you haven't stumbled upon it as you've browsed through videos on YouTube, there's still a good chance you will see it played on the local news or featured by your favorite late night television host; in fact, an entire format of television program has been designed around playing viral videos from the Internet, such as Comedy Central's *Tosh.0* (2009–2020) and MTV's *Ridiculousness* (2011–), *Deliciousness* (2020–), *Messyness* (2021–), and *Adorableness* (2021–). If you do not see it on TV, you might yet hear the video's audio content on a morning radio show during your commute. In fact, viral videos can proliferate both in popularity and cultural significance so quickly and so furiously that they often make the jump from the Internet to radio and television, each transmediation a sort of viral media zoonosis.[1]

In late 2008, Brooklyn musician Michael Gregory released on YouTube his first viral music video, titled "Debate Highlights—in song and dance," using footage of the first presidential debate of the 2008 US election cycle. At the encouragement of his brother, Evan, Michael used footage of that year's US Vice-Presidential debate between Sarah Palin and Joe Biden to create a video using Auto-Tune, an audio processor that alters the pitch of vocal and instrumental music, often to correct mistakes. Soon after this first video's release, "The Gregory Brothers," a band that includes Michael, Evan, their other brother Andrew Rose Gregory, and Sarah Fullen Gregory (who is married to Evan), began to create their "Auto-Tune the News" series of YouTube videos (later rebranded as "Songify the News"), sharing them on their website and their YouTube channel called "Schmoyoho."

In addition to music videos created from videos of politicians and news anchors, the Gregory Brothers have found what they call "unintentional singers" in historic figures, stars from film and TV, and Internet stars from already-viral

Audiovisual Alterity. Michael L. Austin, Oxford University Press. © Oxford University Press 2024.
DOI: 10.1093/oso/9780190277789.003.0002

videos. It is from this last source, particularly news footage documenting interviews with people whom *Slate* columnist Aisha Harris calls the "hilarious black neighbor,"[2] that the Gregory Brothers have drawn material that has both led to their most successful videos and also elicited the most consternation from critics. In some cases, it seems the subjects in these videos are lauded and made more famous for being featured by the Gregory Brothers than they were for performing the heroic acts for which they were initially interviewed.

In this chapter, I examine several of these auto-tuned viral videos, paying particular attention to relatively popular videos created by the Gregory Brothers and others, namely:

BED INTRUDER SONG!!! (2010): A music video featuring Antoine Dodson, a young man who chased a suspected rapist out of his sister's bedroom. He was subsequently interviewed by Elizabeth Gentle, a reporter for WAFF-48 News, and after his animated interview, the video went viral, prompting the Gregory Brothers to "songify" it.

MOMMY & DADDY SONG (2010): This song/music video is based on material from the viral video "Make Sure the Kiddies Are Sleeping Before . . ." posted to YouTube by user "Freshalina." In it, a toddler recounts having heard her parents having sex.

AIN'T NOBODY GOT TIME FOR THAT (2012): In this video, Kimberly "Sweet Brown" Wilkins speaks to KFOR-4 in Oklahoma City, OK about a fire in her apartment building. She discusses how she was getting ready to leave her apartment to get a soda, smelled indications of a fire, and left without putting on her shoes. She also talks about the effect of the smoke on her voice. In the Gregory Brothers' version, the spoken account of her ordeal is played, alternating with a "songified" phrase, created from her exclamation "Ain't nobody got time for that."

DEAD GIVEAWAY (2013): This music video is created from an interview given by Charles Ramsey, a Cleveland, OH resident who rescued three women and a baby who were being held as prisoners by captor Ariel Castro for over a decade. In his televised interview, Ramsey discussed his involvement with the rescue and his thoughts surrounding the ordeal.

Further, this chapter will also investigate the sound bites from which these music videos are created, the derivative songs and videos created from them, and some of the ethical and sociopolitical issues surrounding this type of aesthetic labor, especially those regarding representations of race, ethnicity, the discomfort of some white people with various expressions of Blackness, and mental disability in the original news footage, in the resulting "songified" video versions, and in subsequent remixes.

To understand the political dynamics and social ramifications of these music videos, it is important for us first to understand how they are made. Take the Gregory Brothers' video DEAD GIVEAWAY (2013), for example. It is composed mostly of clips from an interview with John Kosich from Cleveland's ABC affiliate, WEWS NewsNet5, and includes brief clips from a different interview with Kevin Freeman, a reporter with the local Fox affiliate in which Ramsey also repeats the words "dead giveaway." In his interview with Kosich, Ramsey explains how the situation surrounding his heroic rescue of three young women and a baby unfolded after he first heard screaming coming from the house next door:

KOSICH: And when did you see Gina?

RAMSEY: About . . . About five minutes after the police got here. See that girl Amanda, told the police "I ain't the only one. There's some more girls up in that house." So they go up in there, 30, 40, deep. And when they came out, it was just astonishing. 'Cause I thought they would come up with nothing. Like I said my neighbor, you got to have some pretty big testicles to pull this off, bro. Because we see this dude every day. I mean every day.

KOSICH: How long have you lived here?

RAMSEY: I've been here a year. You see where I'm coming from? I barbeque with this dude. We eat ribs and whatnot and listen to salsa music. You see where I'm coming from?

KOSICH: And you had no indications?

RAMSEY: Bro, not a clue that that girl was in that house. Or anybody else was in there against their will. Because of how he is. He just comes out to his backyard, plays with the dogs, tinkering with his cars and motorcycles, go back in the house. So he's somebody you look, then look away. He's not doing anything, but the average stuff. You see what I'm saying? There's nothing exciting about him. Well, until today.

KOSICH: What were the reactions on the girls' faces? I can't imagine to see the sunlight . . .

RAMSEY: Bro, I knew something was wrong when a little, pretty white girl ran into a black man's arms. Something is wrong here. Dead giveaway. Dead giveaway.[3]

For the creation of DEAD GIVEAWAY, the Gregory Brothers cut selected sections from the original news clip, re-arranged the text of the interview in an order that established a rhyming scheme for the stanzas of the song, and often repeated parts of the original video several times within the context of the new musical work to form the song's hooks, a chorus, and other recognizable pop song elements. As you can see, once the edits have been made, the song lyrics are recognizable derivatives of the initial interview, but depending upon the part of the song they comprise, particular phrases become repeated, and therefore emphasized, within the new context of the song. Further, rearranging the order in which Ramsey's story is told and which words are used (or not) to tell that story can drastically change or even create an altogether new account of the events that occurred that day. This is a marked subversion of conventional journalistic ethics where editing to re-contextualizing content and distorting interview material for emphasis is normally eschewed. After editing, the interview was transformed into these song lyrics:

Spoken:
(Kosich) "I'm talkin' with Charles Ramsey; he's a neighbor. Uh, t—, walk me through again what happened this afternoon."
Pre-chorus:
I knew somethin' was wrong when a little pretty white girl ran into a black man's arms
Chorus:
Dead giveaway, dead giveaway
My neighbor got big testicles 'cause we see this dude ev'ry day
We eat ribs with this dude
but we didn't have a clue
That that girl was in that house; she said, "Please help me get out!"

Dead giveaway [*repeated 7 times (with echoes)*]

Chorus repeated

Verse:
So I opened the door, we can't get in that way
A body can't fit through the door, only your hand
So we kick, kick, kicked the bottom
And she comes out, and she says
"It's some more girls up in that house
Call 911," and they caught him at McDonald's

Pre-chorus
Chorus
Dead giveaway[4]

Reading these song lyrics, several things are apparent. As with other viral videos, the Gregory Brothers capitalized on the most outrageous parts of Ramsey's interview, placing these statements—namely, "I knew somethin' was wrong when a little pretty white girl ran into a black man's arms," "My neighbor got big testicles 'cause we see this dude every day," and of course "Dead giveaway"—in the most prominent places within the song, that is, the pre-chorus and first lines of the chorus. Also, although Ramsey and Kosich said Amanda Berry's name several times throughout the course of the original interview, and her name is inextricably linked to the case, it is conspicuously missing from the song's lyrics. By removing Berry, the song has the potential to reach well beyond the specificity of Ramsey's rescue of Amanda Berry, Michelle Knight, Georgina "Gina" DeJesus, and Berry's six-year-old daughter born in captivity after they were held as sex slaves in Ariel Castro's house for over a decade. Without the visual representation of Ramsey from the news footage and the aural representation of Amanda Berry through the speaking of her name, one can imagine this song could be interpreted in a number of different ways; for example, it could be about rescuing a white woman from an abusive inter-racial relationship; or, rather than being about Amanda Berry and her situation specifically, it could be about almost any attractive white woman running into the arms of any Black man. By describing the actual breakout from the house and Castro's eventual arrest at a local McDonald's, the verse is the only part of the song that alludes to Ramsey's rescue specifically, but the details therein still do not explicitly point to Ramsey, Berry, or the other women who were rescued, essentially erasing them from the narrative.

Although the rearrangement and recontextualization of several chunks of news footage has resulted in creative new song lyrics, another essential element of the music video is missing: the music. Having selected parts of Ramsey's interview for its content (narrative flow, rhyme, etc.), his speech pattern is still irregular in rhythm and indiscrete in pitch. In order to be usable as musical material, the Gregory Brothers needed to lengthen or shorten Ramsey's spoken phrases to convert his speech pattern into the usable, musical rhythm necessary for a pop song. Also, although Ramsey's speech already had pitch, it was not necessarily musical; many words could have been spoken on an exact pitch (such as an A or an F#), but many others could just as easily have fallen between two notes. The Gregory Brothers therefore used the software Auto-Tune to assign each of Ramsey's spoken syllables to the nearest discrete pitch. Now they could adjust them to be any pitch they desired within the contour of the melody they were writing, finally transforming Ramsey into an "unintentional singer."

In the pre-chorus, notated in Figure 1.1, notice how Ramsey's speech was transformed from regular speech, spoken as dialog within the context of a news interview into a rhythmic phrase of regular eighth and sixteenth notes, the discrete pitches of which outline a D# minor 7 chord, accompanied by a synthesized tom-tom.

Figure 1.1 Notation of auto-tuned speech and tom-tom in the pre-chorus of the Gregory Brothers' "Dead Giveaway."

Figure 1.2 Vocal part and chords from the chorus of the Gregory Brothers' "Dead Giveaway."

In the chorus that follows, as seen in Figure 1.2, Ramsey continues to "sing" his responses to Kosich's questions, but instead of hearing the response he gave in the order he gave them, we hear a lilting, rhapsodic melody with a relatively high tessitura and difficult passages, especially the second-inversion B major triad outlined on the word "ev'ry day" and the treacherous descending leap of more than an octave between the F# of "ribs" and the E of "with" from the phrase "we eat ribs with this dude . . . ." Ramsey seems to handle these potential pitfalls effortlessly, singing his part of the interview to a steady rock beat and chords played on synth pads.

Many of the Gregory Brothers' videos end with advertisements, and DEAD GIVEAWAY is no exception. Backed by the accompaniment from the song, Michael Gregory appears at 1:30 of the video, dressed in a black blazer, white shirt with no tie, purple sunglasses and a white baseball cap;[5] he raps:

> Tell us what to do next and we'll Songify that
> Do it to yourself on the Songify App
> Just like this (just like this, just like this, just like this)

Here, Gregory demonstrates the app on a smartphone, points the phone toward the viewer, and makes a cheeky face with his finger pointed to his puckered lips like a pin-up girl. In the top left corner of the screen are clickable links to viewer-created covers (a drum cover, a ukulele cover, and a cover in the style of Johnny Cash) and an admonition for viewers to download the karaoke track they created for this song, further commodifying Ramsey's voice. The upper right corner is filled with a link that allows viewers to subscribe to the "Schmoyoho" YouTube channel. Gregory finishes: "Schmoyoho—accent on the 'yo.'"

At this point in the video, Sarah Gregory appears in a zip-up hoodie and orange toboggan singing a cover of "Dead Giveaway" into a retro-styled ribbon microphone. The video fades out as she sings the chorus.

Here Sarah Gregory assumes the voice of Ramsey, whose voice was already appropriated to create the song, further reinterpreting and recontextualizing Ramsey's harrowing experience and perhaps even further disconnecting the victims from the story.

As you can see, an enormous amount of aesthetic labor is invested in the creation of these music videos. Not only does the creator need to be competent in using a wide variety of video and audio editing software, including digital audio workstations and synthesis software, but he or she must also spend hours poring over footage to select and extract the desired text, and must possess the musical talent required to auto-tune the speech into a catchy hook and to compose a suitable and equally memorable instrumental accompaniment.[6] However, no amount of talent or impressive output can be used to justify insensitivity to the representation of subaltern groups and the ways in which their images and voices are manipulated for aesthetic purposes.

"I Got Bronchitis": How the Subaltern Lose Their Voices in Musical Appropriation

Of course, the central element of these viral music videos is the human voice. In the context of these videos, the voice serves to identify the subject of the video and supply the creator of remixed music videos with melodic material. The voice is perhaps the only sonic indicator of who we are; no other parts of our body make a sound that is as recognizable, distinctive, and understandable as human speech. Few things in this world can signify a person sonically like his or her own voice. A speaker's tone, timbre, accent, rate of speech, and choice of words can provide a wealth of information to a listener; based on what they hear, this listener then makes inferences about the speaker's sex, race, class, emotional state, whether or not the speaker was telling the truth or lying, and a host of other distinguishing features of a speaker's personal and collective identity.[7] The political philosopher Adriana Cavarero extols the virtue in listening to the voice for its power in communicating individuality:

> What [the voice] communicates is precisely the true vital and perceptible uniqueness of the one who emits it. At stake here is not a closed-circuit communication between one's own voice and one's own ears, but rather a communication of one's own uniqueness that is, at the same time, a relation with another unique existent. It takes at least a duet, a calling and a responding—or, better, a reciprocal intention to listen, one that is already active in the vocal emission and that reveals and communicates everyone to the other.[8]

Within this duet, the communicative power of the voice gives expressive control to the speaker and interpretive control to the listener. The voice affords sonic opportunities for speakers to express a sense of belonging, for example, by sharing regional accents and using standard language, slang, and idioms common within a culture or subculture. However, when this position of power is usurped and the voice and its embodied performance of identity are used for aesthetic purposes, what epistemic damage is done to personal agency and identity expression of subaltern voices, especially in instances in which those in positions of privilege appropriate the voice of the subaltern? In other words, what is the harm in borrowing—or even stealing—someone's voice for artistic purposes, especially when the voice belongs to a member of a minority group?

Appropriation is a perennial issue within the history of music, and over time, opinions regarding its legitimacy as an artistic practice vacillate widely between acceptance of appropriated material as musical quotation to protestations and allegations of theft. On the one hand, appropriation is expected, or at least understood to be part of the creative process; after all, Igor Stravinsky (along with T.S. Eliot, Pablo Picasso, and others) is often quoted as allegedly having said, "A good composer does not imitate; he steals" (or something to that effect depending upon the attributed speaker's artistic medium of choice). Some celebrate composers who appropriate and incorporate the music of other cultures into their own framework of Western art music for undertaking such a valiant endeavor and for accepting musical "others" as valid alternatives to Euro-centric material, seemingly calling into question the hegemonic power of Western culture on their own artistic output. Others, however, view this aesthetic labor as an example of cultural imperialism. Wim Mertens writes, of the use by Steve Reich,

Philip Glass, and other minimalist composers of elements of Indian, Indonesian and West African musics, "This use of non-European techniques should not be regarded as the foundation of their work, but rather as a symptom of the ability of the modern culture industry to annex a foreign culture, strip it of its specific social-ideological context and incorporate it into its own culture products."[9]

Using a sample in commercial popular music requires artists to obtain sample clearance, often involving diplomatic negotiations in securing permissions from copyright owners (usually the record company or publishing company), negotiation of royalties to which the original artist is entitled, and paying a fee for the clearance license.[10] A major part of these negotiations is also ensuring that the original artist gets proper credit for having created the initial musical work from which the sample is derived. But as time passes, and especially as the derivative work becomes more successful and popular than the work from which it borrows material, the original artist is rarely known to the general public. This information can usually be found in the liner notes of physical, published copies of the music, but now that more consumers download music online instead of purchasing physical media, the originator of a sample is often long forgotten. This credit they are denied is not only important to the originator in financial or economic terms but also ensures that their individual identity as an artist is attached to the work. As discussed in the previous chapter, sampled music can be seen as colonized music when new artists seem to stake a claim on something belonging to someone else; even the rhetoric surrounding the way an artist "discovered" a sample (as if it were the first time the music was ever heard) is reminiscent of imperial powers colonizing the land they "discovered" in the New World. The damage of cultural imperialism ensues when the identity of the sample's original creator is removed, detached, or forgotten to the benefit of the appropriator and the originator's creation is re-contextualized and voided of its original intent, meaning, or social signification.

A well-known example of such a case from the avant-garde electroacoustic art music tradition is Steve Reich's *Come Out* (1966), a piece in which Reich used the voice of Daniel Hamm, a young Black man who was beaten in Harlem's 28th precinct station during the Harlem race riots of 1964. Hamm was recorded as he recounted the fact that he would not receive any medical care unless he was visibly bleeding, so he "had to like open the bruise up and let some of the bruise blood come out to show them." Through tape looping processes, Reich takes the final segment of that sentence—"come out to show them"—and repeats it, chops it up, and plays bits and pieces simultaneously, in the process of which Hamm's speech loses its syntax and context, becoming simply speech (or musical) sounds, devoid of its original intent and meaning, and on a superficial level, drained of its emotional content as well. However, Reich reassures listeners this is not the case, arguing:

By using recorded speech as a source of electronic or tape music, speech-melody and meaning are presented as they naturally occur. By not altering its pitch or timbre, one keeps the original emotional power that speech has while intensifying its melody *and* its meaning through repetition and rhythm. (Emphasis in original).[11]

In a critical assessment of Reich's use of Hamm's voice in *Come Out*, and also the voice of a Black street preacher in *It's Gonna Rain* (a similar work also composed in 1966 by applying the same analog tape-looping technique), Lloyd Whitesell writes:

> Each piece's frame is filled with black vocal presence. Whiteness is thematically absent; yet a white author has set up the frame. The authorial "voice" occupies a comparatively mute position, vaguely apprehended as a set of background assumptions and an unfolding structural matrix. To begin with, the black voices are melodious and expressive, occupying the position of dramatic subjects. The composing persona attempts to disappear within an attitude of rigorous objectivity. But as the musical process is set in motion, the snippets of speech are treated as manipulable voice-objects, to be reiterated and knocked out of phase. Gradually, through the phase distortion, semantic articulation and expressivity are utterly drained from the voice-objects. They slowly alter from foreground performers to background noise. It becomes clear that the true "subject" of the music is the man behind the curtain; though the subject position he occupies is as reduced as possible.[12]

Pointedly, Whitesell contends that this aesthetic labor separates the whiteness of Reich from the Black subjects, cementing the alterity of Hamm, and serves as a means to afford Reich "a powerful conceptual position of exemption from troubling particulars."[13]

While one could argue that Reich had no ill intent when creating this piece, Mitchell Morris points out that the Reich's aesthetic labor can lead to several exegetical possibilities:

1. "The disappearance of speech can be taken as a metaphor for the crushing of individuality under one or another Ideological State Apparatus."
2. "The disappearance of speech signals Reich's triumphant ability to absorb the materials of someone else's voice and someone else's pain into his own serene compositional processes . . . [that is possibly] unaccountable and ultimately inconsequential."
3. "The disappearance of speech comes as a result of Reich's articulating something quite profound about violence, time, and repetition," representing

trauma cycles and the experience of lost time during particularly violent incidents.

4. "The disappearance of speech signifies an act of mourning."[14]

Morris's first three interpretations, in particular, are especially applicable to the viral music videos examined in this chapter. In having their speech chopped up and looped, and their voices auto-tuned, do the music videos' subjects lose their individuality? Are their voices, their identities, and their cultures somehow being colonized?

Auto-Tune itself is a technology that has become infamously associated with inauthenticity, fraud, the undermining of (art) work, and the destruction of self—or others—through the manipulation of the voice. Patented in 1998 by creator Andy Hildebrand, Auto-Tune was an artistic application of principles Hildebrand used as a geophysicist, called autocorrelation, in which oil companies used soundwaves to search underground for petroleum deposits. Distributed by his company Antares as a software plugin for digital audio workstations, it was designed as a way to imperceptibly correct a singer's pitch or tuning mistakes, but Auto-Tune's sonic effect and artistic potential were first noticed by the general public in Cher's "Believe" (1998) when the album's producers, Mark Taylor and Brian Rawling, "misused" the software, aggressively adjusting the settings much more than would be required to address an errant pitch, and distorting Cher's voice into a mechanized, robotic chimera. Although Cher was praised for the creative audible use of this technology, others who used it afterward—especially T-Pain, who used the technique extensively in the early 2000s—were excoriated for applying the same technique to hip-hop. T-Pain faced serious scrutiny by other hip-hop artists, even to the point that it had profoundly negative effects on his mental health. Discussing an interaction he had with Usher on an airplane en route to the 2013 BET Awards for the Netflix docuseries *This Is Pop* (2021), Faheem Najm (T-Pain's real name) recounts:

> Usher was my friend. I really respect Usher. And he said, "I'm gonna tell you something, man. You kinda fucked up music." . . And then he was like, "Nah, man, you really fucked up music for real singers." I was like, "Oh, you're serious," and he was like, "Yeah man, look what you did. Look what you're doing." I was like, "What did I do? I came out and I used Auto-Tune." He was like, "Yeah, you fucked it up." I'm like, "But I used it, I didn't tell everybody else to start using it." That is the very moment, and I don't even think I realized this for a long time, but that's the very moment that started a four-year depression for me.

It wasn't until T-Pain performed for an NPR Tiny Desk Concert in late 2014 that he was able to legitimize his musical ability and regain the respect of audiences by singing without the use of Auto-Tune software. It is no wonder, then, that if Auto-Tune had such a bad reputation among the American public generally, and among hip-hop artists in particular to the point of ostracizing a prolific artist and blaming them for having ruined music, that the artificial manipulation of Black voices may cause some to be wary of both the technology and its associated techniques.

The various ways in which these videos are shared also play an important role in the politics of representation, cultural appropriation, and agency; this discussion begins with a video's rise to viral status. I began this chapter with a biological image, describing the recent spread of viral videos as an epidemic. We have all heard the terms "meme" and "viral" used as biological metaphors to describe the ways in which media is spread from one person to another on the Internet; these terms have become conflated as their use becomes ever more ubiquitous. Before I proceed, I feel as though a brief explanation of these terms is in order, especially as they apply to Internet music videos. When Richard Dawkins coined the term "meme" in his 1976 bestseller *The Selfish Gene*, he used it to describe the way in which ideas, behaviors or styles spread from person to person in "unit[s] of cultural transmission, or . . . unit[s] of imitation;"[15] therefore, I want to emphasize the fact that the ideas, the behaviors, the styles, the prejudice, the value judgments, and the cultural baggage ensconced within these videos is the essence of "a meme," not the videos (or image macros, or chain letters, or LOLcats) themselves.

In her book, *Memes in Digital Culture*, communications scholar Limor Shifman succinctly delineates the main difference between Internet memes and viral media in one word: *variability*, writing, "Whereas the viral comprises a single cultural unit (such as a video, photo, or joke) that propagates in many copies, an Internet meme is always a collection of texts."[16] In other words, a viral video exists as a singular media entity in and of itself that is spreadable by virtue of its original content. Memetic videos, on the other hand, fall into two categories: those that are created in many versions using most of the same original footage or content (defined by Shifman as "founder-based memes"), and "egalitarian memes" through which people relate to a particular formula rather than a specific video, and create many videos based on that formula. Shifman concedes, though, that these terms are not mutually exclusive, and argues that many videos are often associated with both categories, "by first spreading virally and then spawning numerous derivatives."[17] The videos described in this chapter are videos of this type: found video footage + a phase vocoder (the technology used to auto-tune their voice) + music. Each is "viral" in its own right; many of them have received millions of views on the Internet and on network and cable TV, and they are collectively part memes based on a specific formula.

These viral videos can also be meta-memetic; together, some videos within this collection constitute yet another level of memetic material. In part due to their viral status and popularity, often because they are created by rather talented musicians, and many times because they are encouraged by the videos' makers, viewers will sometimes create their own videos based on the original videos—these usually take the form of remixes, mash-ups, or covers of the original songs. These videos are third-order Baudrillardian simulacra par excellence—Giving up all pretense of being faithful reflections of reality, they are so far removed from the original news footage that they neither imitate the voice captured in the original video nor do they retain the same set of values and meaning (good or bad) from the auto-tuned videos they more directly seek to imitate.

Blackface, Blaxploitation, and "Hilarious Black Neighbors"

If the meme is really comprising cultural values, and not necessarily the music videos, what cultural values are these videos spreading? What is gained by plugging the "hilarious black neighbor" into this formula? On a very superficial level, the similarities between these viral music videos and earlier forms of exploitative entertainment. In several critical readings of BED INTRUDER SONG!!!, many were concerned that not only did the video reflect poorly on the Black community because of Dodson's flamboyant demeanor, choice of clothing, and outspokenness; others feared the news clip and resulting music video also overshadowed Dodson's act of heroism in placing more attention on his internet stardom than the fact that there was still an attempted rapist loose in the community. Likewise, the same criticism applied to DEAD GIVEAWAY, the Gregory Brothers video previously discussed in this chapter; rather than from his heroic act, much of the fame and attention Ramsey has received has come as a result of songs created from YouTube clips from his initial interview. In much the same way, Shaft, Sweet Sweetback, and many others are heroes (or anti-heroes) within the blaxploitation genre, yet their acts of bravery and heroism are regularly overshadowed by the fact that their characters were thought to embody negative racial stereotypes. In an article for the online newspaper *The Daily Dot* titled "Are 'hilarious black neighbor' videos a modern minstrel show?," Fidel Martinez describes the viral news clips used to make the auto-tuned music videos discussed in this chapter:

> These sound bites were cherry-picked by the Internet users for their own amusement. What's disconcerting is that the Internet zeros in on phrases that employ elements of African American Vernacular English (Dodson's pronunciation of the word "everybody") or hint at a low levels [*sic*] of education (Brown's usage of a double negative) to serve as the punchline. These are the jokes the Internet has decided we need to be laughing at—and they're all about being black, poor and living in the ghetto.[18]

Not only is the focus of these videos centered on the perceived ignorance of their subjects, this perception—based solely on presumption and stereotypes—is also the foundation for the their intended humorous aesthetic.

Some scholars even go so far as to compare Dodson's video "performance" to the character of Zip Coon in blackface minstrel shows of the nineteenth century. Zip Coon was one of a few "classic" stereotyped Black characters, described by J. Stanley Lemons as, "a preposterous, citified dandy. In the minstrel show, he was easily recognized in his bright, loud, exaggerated clothes . . . He was a high-stepping strutter with a mismatched vocabulary. He put on airs, acted elegant, but was betrayed by his pompous speech filled with malapropisms."[19] Media theorist Angela Agloro makes Dodson's resemblance to Zip Coon explicit, writing that in the way he was dressed, and certainly based on the confident, yet colorful and non-standard manner in which he spoke, Dodson is "donning of the symbolic blackface mask in order to have visibility, bring attention to his sister's attempted rape, and make a profit. Dodson's actions mirror the history of coon songs, where professional opportunities for Black performers and composers were rare . . . In similar fashion, the minstrel show was the primary vehicle for America's first African American performing artists to find success."[20]

This comparison with minstrel shows can be extended to other "hilarious black neighbors" in other similar music videos; for instance, the Gregory Brothers' DEAD GIVEAWAY could be read as caricaturing Charles Ramsey as Buck, a character in minstrel shows famous for his preoccupation with white women, particularly due to the fact that the video begins with the pre-chorus wherein Ramsey is "singing" the phrase "I knew something was wrong when I pretty little white girl ran into a black man's arms."[21] Not only does the bandana Sweet Brown is wearing in AIN'T NOBODY GOT TIME FOR THAT physically resemble that of the Mammy archetype from minstrelsy and early films, such as Hattie McDaniel's character in *Gone with the Wind* (1939), but other less-obvious attributes also suggest that Brown is portrayed as a Mammy in the videos made using her interview. Mammy characters are usually older, non-sexualized, and as a result, non-threatening to white people; compared to characters in other music videos (with the exception of Cher, Madonna, and a few others), Sweet Brown is more mature and closer to middle age, and although she's wearing a colorful halter top, her body is mostly hidden from view, and she is not cast in a sexualized light (see Figure 1.3). Further, much like other Mammies, Sweet Brown was well known, in part, for her endearing yet frank, "no-nonsense" manner of speaking; recounting her escape from a fire at her apartment complex in Oklahoma City, Brown said:

> Well, I woke up to get me a cold pop, and then I thought somebody was barbequing. I said, "Oh Lord Jesus, it's a fire!" Then I ran out! I didn't grab no

Figure 1.3 Media representations of the Mammy archetype (l–r: Sweet Brown, Hattie McDaniel as Mammy in *Gone with the Wind* (1939), and Nancy Green as Aunt Jemima). (Screenshot of Brown by the author.)

> shoes or nothin,' Jesus! I ran for my life! And then the smoke got me. I got bronchitis! Ain't nobody got time for that![22]

In addition to Sweet Brown's depiction as a Mammy character, other questionable or confusing images appear within the video, including B.B. King playing the guitar; Carlton from *The Fresh Prince of Bel-Air* (1990–1996) dancing and singing into a drumstick; clips of other viral videos such as YouTube user Costas' "All the single ladies: Fat guy dancing to 'All the single ladies' by Beyonce," and Hasan Baba's "Apache Dance;" a still image of Don King and Antonine Dodson barbequing; video footage of a charismatic church service; and clips of an outdoor concert featuring Judy Collins and the Harlem Boys Choir from 1993. Toward the end of the video, during the bridge of the song, a different image of Jesus appears as Sweet Brown sings the name "Jesus." In addition to traditional icons, other, more dubious, images of Jesus appear, such as one in which Jesus is wearing large sunglasses, one in which Jesus's head is replaced with a dinosaur head, another with Jesus hugging a dinosaur, and a final image that replaces Jesus altogether with famously religious American football player Tim Tebow.

In their MOMMY & DADDY SONG (2010), the Gregory Brothers sample the voice of a toddler who walked in on her parents making love and turn her recollection of the event into an R&B song, a "slow jam," most suitable for the late-night "Quiet Storm" radio format. As an adult male, presumably her father, films her, she is interviewed:

MAN: "Who—who you say was naked?"
GIRL: "Daddy and mommy"
MAN: "And what happened?"

GIRL ("songified"):

"Mommy said 'Ah-Ah-Ahhhhh!'
Daddy said 'Ah-Ah-Ahhhhh!'
And Daddy screamed like a girl, like 'Oo Oo!'
Mommy screamed like a girl, like 'Ah ah!'
Both of them screamed like 'Ah-Ah-Ah-Ah-Ahhhhhhhhh!"[23]

The girl's naïvety and her subjugation to being filmed while she recounts what could have been a traumatizing incident in witnessing her parents engaging in a sex act—not to mention the entertainment value drawn from this video by the original video maker and later by the Gregory Brothers—is quite similar to "pickaninny" caricatures. The picaninny archetype was used to represent children in minstrelsy as the child version of the "coon" archetype; they were always uneducated and poor, usually nameless and disheveled, they spoke with stereotypical dialect, and were sometimes troublingly sexualized, even hypersexualized: boy pickaninnies were frequently depicted with their penis stuck in precarious places (such as a fence or bitten by an animal), and girls were sometimes depicted as visibly-pregnant toddlers. The child in this video is shown with slightly unkempt hair that is in the process of falling out of its braids, swinging a small cat toy by the tail as she sings.

At the end of MOMMY & DADDY SONG, in a section of the video titled "Evan's Musings" (beginning near the two-minute mark), Evan Gregory discusses why they made the video, saying:

> We were trying to read your minds, and we got blurry images of cute kids and also R. Kelly [Here, a picture of a Black infant is shown on the left side of the screen that is quickly replaced with a picture of singer-songwriter R. Kelly]. It was obvious you were all lookin' for a booty jam sung by a precocious toddler, so this one goes out to all the parents what's [*sic*] got babies and still makin' babies. [As Evan Gregory dedicates this song to parents who still have sex, an image of the baby reappears with R. Kelly's head superimposed on her body].

During "Evan's Musings," the band is performing their own, self-described "hastily prepared cover," with Sarah Gregory singing lead, Evan playing the keyboard and singing the chorus with Sarah, and Andrew Gregory playing bass and Michael Gregory playing quiet rimshots on a snare drum while both provide backup harmonies.

The cultural phenomenon of casting Black subjects into stereotypical roles for humor or profit is also reminiscent of another, equally controversial form of aesthetic labor that I briefly mentioned earlier: the blaxploitation films of the 1970s, wherein Hollywood producers took profitable film archetypes and plugged in

Black stars to various degrees of success and failure. Most simplistically, A&C Black Publishers' *Dictionary of Media Studies* defines *blaxploitation* as "a style of film-making popular in the 1970s in which black people were represented as stereotypes."[24] Writing in the *Encyclopedia of Black Studies*, Stephanie Yarbough provides a more nuanced definition of blaxploitation films, describing them as:

> A series of films released between 1969 and 1974 that featured a primarily black cast and whose narratives focused on the contemporary black urban experience. Grounded in the action-adventure genre, these films were usually low-budget Hollywood productions geared toward the black youth market.[25]

Blaxploitation is a useful term for demarcating and describing the handful of films made during this particular period to "exploit" a specifically Black demographic; however, the term is also used to identify films that misrepresent Black culture in aesthetically and/or socio-politically and often included gratuitous sex and violence. On the one hand, many view blaxploitation films as a "recoding" of Blackness in cinema—an opportunity to replace the macho white hero with an equally masculine and sexualized Black hero for young Black men to look up to. Writing about the influence blaxploitation film had on hip-hop culture, Nelson George describes the aesthetic of these films:

> Never in the history of American cinema had there been so many aggressive, I-don't-give-a-damn black folks on screen. That is so crucial. Blaxploitation movies reserved little space for the singing of Negro spirituals, turning the other cheek, or chaste kisses. In fact, characters who possessed these qualities were often the brunt of much-appreciated derision. In blaxploitation black people shoot back with big guns, strut to bold jams, and have sweaty, bed-rocking sex.[26]

Even very prominent Black figures, such as professional football player-turned-actor Jim Brown and writer and *Shaft* director Gordon Parks Sr., defended blaxploitation films at the time they were made. Parks wrote, "The so-called black intellectuals' outcry against black films has been blown far out of proportion. It is curious that some black people, egged on by some whites, will use such destructive measures against black endeavors."[27] Others saw the rise of a culture of blaxploitation outside of the films embodied in Black empowerment groups such as the Black Panthers.

Black men and women were, and still are, largely excluded from many prominent roles in the film industry. Mark Reid argues that even with representation *on screen*, blaxploitation films do not adequately represent the Black artistic voice because they were typically conceived, produced, and distributed within a framework wherein Black men and women were sorely under-represented and from which they had historically been almost completely excluded. He writes:

> Having established the fact that there was a young black audience receptive to thoughts about violence, it should have been possible to create black action films that appealed to this audience while satisfying a black aesthetic. The commercial black action films of the 1970s, however, never reached this ideal because they were not independent productions or because black independent producers relied on major distributors.[28]

Even with any redemptive qualities, such as seemingly positive representations of Black heroes, Black people in positions of political power, and Black agency that gave people of color a voice in cultural industries, there are many who agree that the genre of blaxploitation film marks "the film industry's targeting [of] the black audience with a specific product line of cheaply made, black-cast films shaped with the 'exploitation' strategies Hollywood routinely used to make the majority of its films."[29] In even stronger terms, Black studies scholar Cedric Robinson believes:

> Blaxploitation was a degraded cinema: it degraded the industry which prostituted itself to political and market exigencies and constructed the genre of an urban jungle; it degraded the Black actors, writers, and directors who proved more affectionate to money than to the Black lower classes they caricatured; it degraded its audiences who were subjected to mockery of the aspirations of Black liberationists.[30]

In fact, the perceived ills of blaxploitation films (particularly the prevalent sexual content, drug use, and graphic violence) drew the ire of groups such as the National Association for the Advancement of Colored People (NAACP), the Southern Christian Leadership Conference, and the Congress of Racial Equality, who together formed the Coalition Against Blaxploitation (CAB). The backlash against blaxploitation films even resulted in violent protests, including an instance wherein the car of Richard Zimbert, AIP vice president, was set ablaze while parked in the studio's parking lot by an unnamed Black militant group. Because of the controversy surrounding these films, Hollywood made fewer blaxploitation features and stopped altogether the production of films in the genre by the end of 1975.

I want to explore some of the connections that can be drawn between these videos, music videos from more familiar media, and blaxploitation films, hopefully addressing some of the positive and negative memetic material, or "units of cultural transmission," that are shared among both genres, and discuss similarities in the aesthetic labor invested in producing both types of visual media. The first and most glaring issue is the representation of alterity in these music videos; are they positive representations that Black youth can look up to, or are they caricatures purposefully chosen for humor and/or derision? The most famous of these videos—BED INTRUDER SONG!!! (now on iTunes)—was created by the Gregory Brothers using news footage from July 28, 2010, from Northern Alabama NBC affiliate WAFF-48. The video featured Antoine Dodson, a young Black man who was being interviewed after a man broke into the Dodson's home and attempted to assault his sister Kelly as she slept. In the interview, Dodson exclaims: "Well, obviously we have a RAPIST in Lincoln Park. He's climbing in your windows, he's snatching your people up, trying to rape them. So y'all need to hide your kids, hide your wife, and hide your husband 'cause they're raping everybody out here."[31]

Once the news clip was uploaded to YouTube by user "Z01D111" the next day, it became viral through Internet outlets such as *Reddit*, *Buzzfeed*, *Best Week Ever*, and others, and was parodied by others who dressed as Dodson and asked out versions of his interview. The video became astronomically more "viral" when the Gregory Brothers released their auto-tuned version on July 30, 2010. The "Bed Intruder Song" became the twenty-fifth most purchased song on the main iTunes charts, selling 10,571 copies during the first two days it was available, rising to No. 3 on the iTunes R&B charts and No. 15 on the pop charts, and No. 89 on the Billboard Hot 100; it was also the most-watched YouTube video of 2010 (with over 121 million views as of this month).[32] The song was discussed on many network and cable news programs and popular culture outlets; it was released as downloadable content (DLC) for the video game *Rock Band* 3, and it has been covered by many other musicians, including the North Carolina A&T Blue and Gold Marching Machine and the Ohio State Marching Band.

One of the first of many bloggers to address the issue of Dodson's exploitation, professor and scholar Pontente Susurro, writes on her blog *Like a Whisper* that the Gregory Brothers are ignoring the serious issue of rape and exploiting the suffering of a Black family for a laugh. In a powerful critique, she criticizes American liberals and feminist bloggers, writing:

> In the midst of this institutional racism are the actions of three groups that cannot be ignored:
>
> 1. the viewers and listeners who openly mocked Dodson, completely ignoring the rape survivor narrative embedded in this story
> 2. the white middle class hipster-nerd comedy troupe that made money off the rape and attempted rape of poor black women and girls and the one man willing to stand up for them

3. the mainstream feminist blogs and feminist communities who have remained largely silent on Dodson's sister despite the core issue of rape.[33]

Explaining further, Susurro later writes:

> Once again, liberal, middle class, white hipster-nerds also failed to act on the tenets they claim to be central to their very beings, ie social justice, in the face of the opportunity to be "clever." Thus three white men, and one white woman, cut and remixed Dodson's interview in order to point and laugh at the uneducated black man in crisis. His crisis at not being able to get help for his sister, his sister's attempted rape, and the targeting of poor black women and girls were either edited out or remixed in order to highlight the "hilarity" of blackness and poverty and for some, gender transgression. Dodson and his sister's story were pimped out by white liberals for a few bucks a pop on itunes [*sic*] precisely because they fit all of the stereotypes of blackness that liberals are quick to criticize in the mouths of conservatives but embrace as "clever" in their own . . . So what is the lesson of Antione [*sic*] Dodson and his sister. For many people, it will always be that poor "black people are funny", "white people are clever", "'girlie men' are funny", and the spectacle of blackness is really a benefit in disguise because after all the Dodsons are out of the projects.[34]

While I later discuss the fact that Antoine Dodson did eventually share the profits of the song with the Gregory Brothers, many still see his representation in the Gregory Brothers' music video as one of exploitation for humor and profit. Others quickly come to the defense of the Gregory Brothers, arguing that they also have many more videos that feature "hilarious white neighbors;" however, these videos, too, smack of exploitation as many of the white subjects in Gregory Brothers videos are potentially those who suffer from mental illness or other similar disability. For example, DOUBLE RAINBOW SONG!! (2010), BACKIN UP SONG (2010), CAN'T HUG EVERY CAT—A SONG ABOUT LOVING CATS (2011), and SMASH, SMASH, SMASH (2013) are some of the Gregory Brothers' most-viewed music videos, and all capitalize on the apparent "craziness" of the video's subjects.

The Gregory Brothers have tried to frame their use of Dodson's voice as a positive portrayal of the man and his bravery. In an interview for the *New York Times*, David Itzkoff writes:

> The Gregory Brothers were circumspect when they spoke with me about Dodson. Michael said he appreciated Dodson not as a caricature but as a charismatic personality who brought a lightness to what would otherwise have been a frightening set of circumstances. Andrew agreed, saying that Dodson was "just full of energy and really mad, but he's just so naturally witty, he's coming

> up with these turns of phrase on the spur of the moment." When he first saw Dodson's interview, he said, "I'd never seen such an amazing combination of righteous anger and dead seriousness, about something so serious, mixed with humor so successfully."[35]

Other journalists seem to echo the sentiment, claiming that the Gregory Brothers somehow redeem the loss of journalistic integrity that would prevent the news clips from showing in the first place and that these representations through music overlook the dicey racial issues they sometimes raise. NPR columnist Andy Carvin writes:

> There were two things that struck me about these musical responses. First of all, the performers actually have some talent—and in some cases, a lot of talent. They put serious energy into crafting their own version of the ATTN song, sending the meme into new musical directions. Secondly, you can't help but notice the multicultural nature of their videos. People of various racial backgrounds happily jumped into the meme. The initial TV news video was racially polarizing, but the Gregory Brother's [*sic*] injection of music and humor into it led to a broad public response that's been surprisingly colorblind.[36]

In the same article, artist, activist, and meme specialist Kenyatta Cheese of KnowYourMeme.com is quoted:

> There's a history of local news media exploiting under-represented communities for a quick story . . . And yes, I can hear the black community's anxiety about representation in the media coming from my own head—I'm African American and Chinese. But these issues are about the audience's perception. While there will always be a small percentage of the public who is laughing at him, it's hard to not empathize with Antoine because he is so sincere.[37]

These statements, and many others like them, beg the question: Can any sign of exploitation be overlooked or excused as long as these music videos give "sincere" Black voices a platform to express themselves—much the same way blaxploitation films were supposed to give Black filmmakers and other industry professionals a chance to express themselves through this media outlet?

Several characters in blaxploitation films are well-known for their memorable, and usually cheesy, catchphrases, movie posters, and other memorabilia. Christie Love's trademark was "You're under arrest, sugar," Cleopatra Jones was famous for saying "You better put that down before I make you eat it," Black Belt Jones' tagline was "I'm gonna make you sweat one way . . . and then the other," and

Youngblood Priest is most famous for saying, "Can you dig it?" The characters featured in the initial viral news videos often say things during their interviews that become well-known catchphrases in popular culture. These phrases then become titles and/or hooks within their auto-tuned re-configurations. In her interview, Sweet Brown uttered several catchphrases for which she is famous, including "I Got Bronchitis," "Oh, Lord Jesus it's a fire," and "Ain't nobody got time for that." These catchphrases were heavily marketed on T-shirts and other merchandise, and Sweet Brown herself made several television appearances in which she uses variations of these phrases, including a commercial for Tulsa-area business Shortline Dental in which she says, "Well, I woke up to go get me a cold pop, and then I realized my tooth was hurtin.' Then I said, 'O Lord Jesus, it's a toothache!' Ain't nobody got time for that!" After this business is able to make a same-day appointment, Brown remarks with a smile, "Now, I got time for that;" at the end of the commercial's jingle, someone sings "Shortline Dental," and Brown reappears, saying "Everybody got time for that." Similarly, in a commercial for 1-800-2SellHomes, Brown appears with company spokesperson Paulette Kingston:

SWEET BROWN: "Paulette, you want a cold pop?"
PAULETTE KINGSTON: "Sweet Brown, we're shooting a TV commercial"
SWEET BROWN: "OK"
PAULETTE: "You know you don't want to fix up your home"
SWEET: "Ain't nobody got time for that"
PAULETTE: "You know you don't want to have an open house"
SWEET: (more emphatically) "Ain't NOBODY got time for that"
PAULETTE: "Sell your home, call . . . "
BOTH: "1-800-2SellHomes"
PAULETTE: "If we buy your home, we close quick, and we buy in any condition"
SWEET: "Even if there's a fire, Paulette?"
PAULETTE: "Even if it had a fire, Sweet Brown."
SWEET: "Call 1-800-2SellHomes. It's Sweet Brown Approved."[38]

Whether Sweet Brown is milking her Internet fame for all it is worth or she is being exploited, a substantial amount of cultural capital (and I would imagine some capital in monetary form, as well) was wrung from Brown's catchphrases. Catchphrases from Antoine Dodson's interview also appeared on T-shirts, mugs, wristbands, cigarette lighters, and an assortment of other merchandise. From the website www.bedintrudercostume.com, one can order the self-proclaimed collector's edition "Bed Intruder Costume (Antoine's Revenge!)." Aside from cashing in on his likeness, Dodson's catchphrases are also used for marketing purposes across the website; the costume's descriptions read,

"Obvvioouuusllyyyy, [*sic*] this is the Official Antoine Dodson Costume! So first hide ya kids, hide ya wife [*sic*] and order it today!" There were also several other unauthorized Antoine Dodson Halloween costumes available online that, like the more official version, included a black wig, red bandana, a black "A shirt," and rolled-up newspaper, usually sold for around $25. In response to one iteration of unauthorized costumes, Dodson posted a link to the online retailer's website and commented, "These people down here, are raping me and my family for real! they [*sic*] don't have my permission to be selling this costume."[39]

Why are we drawn to these phrases? Is it due to the way Sweet Brown delivers them with such excitement? Does it have anything to do with our own comfort level regarding linguistic code-switching between African American English and Standard English? In many transcripts of the videos, and in the creation of merchandise and Internet memes, people use both forms of English interchangeably, but African American English transliterations are chosen in instances wherein emphasizing the "ghetto-ness" of the speaking subject might be more lucrative or appealing to youth. Also, despite the fact that these catchphrases often fall in the middle of the interview, they become the centerpiece of the viral music video, so careful and creative video editing (in addition to the creative audio editing that we have already discussed) is required to extract each phrase from the original news footage and loop it into the music video at the correct speed at the appropriate time. This type of editing calls to question the ethics of re-contextualizing, or more appropriately, de-contextualizing the speech act of the speaking subjects as their syntax is chopped up and rearranged to emphasize its more marketable, exploitative features.

Blaxploitation films capitalized on difference: these films were raw and rude in comparison to most white films of the time; they appealed to audiences, even white audiences, because they were radical spectacles, highlighting the differences between "us" and "them." Traditional music videos also capitalize on difference: music videos are often hyperreal or surreal glimpses into the lavish life of the artist singing. In addition to the lyrics, even the visual images in hip hop videos in particular focus on the money, the cars, the women, and so on that the rapper has and other rappers (and the audience) do not. Difference in these viral music videos is demonstrated on two levels; at the first, more obvious level, the Gregory Brothers inject themselves into some of these videos, their palpable differences in race and class made more apparent by the fact that they are frequently wearing suits, playing characters that signify their roles as "gate-keepers" or "authority figures," for example, as a second or third news anchor involved in these interviews.[40]

These differences, including the fact that the Gregory Brothers are white and the subjects of their music videos are Black, do not *necessarily* point to racism or exploitation. While they are arguably most famous for their videos that feature Black people, they also have several viral videos with high view counts that feature "crazy white neighbors" and politicians, too. Most often difference is found, not in the music video itself, but within the context in which the video is created, distributed, and consumed. A sinister example of this focus on difference can be seen in the "Obama Phone Remixes," wherein Michelle Dowery is caught on camera explaining that she supports Barak Obama's re-election for president in 2012, saying "Everybody in Cleveland [unintelligible] minority got Obama phone! Keep Obama in president, you know? He gave us a phone [*sic*]." The video became an instant success due to its proliferation among conservative, right-wing websites and radio shows. Pundits such as Rush Limbaugh openly mocked her, saying, "She knows how to get this free Obama phone. She knows everything about it. She may not know who George Washington is or Abraham Lincoln, but she knows how to get an Obama phone, and she knows that Romney sucks, and she ends up at a Romney rally . . . That's not Saturday Night Live. This is a real Obama voter. That's not a comedy skit. That happened. That happened yesterday in Bedford, Ohio. Your average Obama voter."[41]

Most derivative music videos do not auto-tune Dowery's voice; rather creators add a backbeat and overlay her voice and loop it to make her appear to "rap," or they insert clips of her voice into pre-existing songs. For example, "The David Madeira Show," a conservative radio show in Scranton, PA, incorporated Dowery's voice into a version of Raffi and Michael Creber's "Bananaphone" (1994). Commenting on Elspeth Reeve's article "Just How Racist Is the 'Obama Phone' Video?" user "cobra9clysm" asks, "Just how mentally impaired do you have to be to suggest that recording while a person makes non-racist comments of her own accord could possibly be racist?" Does the content of the video need to be racist in order for the video to be considered racist, or is context sufficient evidence? In creating these music videos, who is responsible for the ethical consequences of derivative videos and the meta-meme as a whole?

The nature of the media outlets and cultural milieu through which the "Obama Phone" video spread the quickest draws sharp attention to the misrepresentation, marginalization, and use of racial and class differences to exclude and harm Black people. As a consequence, many of these particular music videos can be considered blatantly racist. But what about the other videos discussed in this chapter? They are *racial*, but can they be labeled *racist*? Even though the aim of this chapter (and, in fact, this book) is not to answer this question, I do hope it brings to light some of the reasons why this question is hard to answer, despite the countless times and myriad ways in which the question has already been answered in newspaper editorials, political commentary, and blogs across the Internet. Therefore, I want to focus the rest of this chapter on re-examining the ethics of participatory culture and the ideology it cultivates, paying particular attention to issues surrounding race, ethnicity, and even representations of mental illness in online music videos.

Remixes, Race, and Exploitation

Understandably, each of the topics hitherto discussed raises many ethical questions in regard to these music videos. For example, does the fact that the Gregory Brothers share some of the profit they make from these songs with the videos' subjects somehow redeem this process? What about derivative works? The Gregory Brothers ask viewers to perform and record covers of their hit songs; what happens to the voice of the "other" as these videos become memes and the songs' lyrics are further separated from their original sources? If these clips, songs, and music videos are appropriated and re-appropriated with more sinister designs, who is ultimately responsible for the ethical consequences? What effect do these viral videos have on the Black community, and how are these videos shaping conversations about the curation of ethnicity and race on the Internet, notions of fictive kinship, social justice, class, mental illness, and other issues? In this final section, rather than answer these questions outright, I hope to situate some of them within a critical framework suitable for further analyses in the future.

Taking full advantage of their Internet celebrity, Brown and Dodson in particular have capitalized on their fifteen minutes of fame; soon after his interview went viral, Dodson launched a Kickstarter campaign to raise money for his own reality show, a website, and merchandise that featured his likeness and catchphrases from the video. Similarly, after her video went viral, Sweet Brown became a successful entrepreneur, having made dozens of television and commercial appearances, voice-overs, and her own line of barbecue sauce, and is herself planning a new reality show. Arguably, these examples of personal success are largely due to a greater focus on the individual, and the charisma and charm of the people portrayed in each video led to the viral success of these videos in the first place. However, does the fact that these two people were able to somehow marginally profit from these videos excuse the Gregory Brothers and others for re-appropriating someone else's voice for their own financial gain as if sharing some of the money could serve as a reparation of sorts? In describing Dodson's case, visual studies scholar Corella Di Fede problematizes this notion, writing, "representations of race, and accusations of exploitation, are recuperated as ultimately economically 'positive' because they are framed within a narrative of Dodson's rise to fame."[42] There has been some attempt by the Gregory Brothers to share their success with a few of the subjects of their videos. They reached out to Antoine Dodson, agreeing to split the income from the sale of the "Bed Intruder Song" on iTunes (mainly because the song would be removed from iTunes due to laws protecting Dodson's intellectual property rights); with his share of the money, Dodson, who was a struggling community college student, was able to purchase a new home and move his family out of the dangerous neighborhood that had originally put them in the spotlight. Does this success excuse the Gregory Brothers and others for re-appropriating someone else's voice for their own financial gain? Reich's *Come Out* was originally part of a benefit concert at Town Hall in New York City to raise money for the Harlem Six (including Hamm and five other young Black men), so they could afford a re-trial with lawyers of their own choosing and possibly be acquitted of the murder charges they faced as a result of the riots. Even with the purest of intentions, are these artists exempt from the blame that results from the ideological violence done to these individuals through these music works? Does authorial intent excuse any perpetuation of racial stereotypes through these videos? Are the creators of this type of content like the Hollywood studios that produced blaxploitation films, seeking to make a buck at the expense of many Black people, rewarding only a few Black people in the process?

While it is important to guard against essentialism, presuming that these videos elicit the same reaction from all people in the African American community, or that these videos will even have the same negative effects on all Black people, it is crucially necessary to take into account the added element of "fictive kinships" that comes into play when considering the reasons for such strong reactions against these music videos. Although the term "fictive kinship" has been used by ethnographers and other social scientists since the 1980s, the term has been re-introduced by politics and international affairs scholar, television host, and political commentator Melissa Harris-Perry; in her book, *Sister Citizen: Shame, Stereotypes, and Black Women in America*, she defines the term and associates it to the experience of Black women, writing:

> Stories of black excellence are particularly powerful for countering derogatory racial images because African Americans have historically relied on "fictive kinship" ties. The term *fictive kinship* refers to connections between members of a group who are unrelated by blood or marriage but who nonetheless share reciprocal social or economic relationships . . . I draw on the deep tradition of black fictive kinship when I refer to black women as "sisters." This imagined community of familial ties underscores a voluntary sense of shared identity that maps onto the historical construction of race. Fictive kinship makes the accomplishments of African Americans relevant to unrelated black individuals. There is a sense in which we are all family.[43]

While fictive kinship has a particularly strong power to unite members of a racial group and to uplift in instances of celebration and achievement, the same fictive kinship is also used, at times, as a powerful source of shame. Harris-Perry writes:

> Racial shaming is made particularly insidious by the element of fictive kinship . . . fictive kinship also makes African Americans more vulnerable to collective shame. If it is possible for one person's good actions to serve as a "credit to the race," then one person's bad actions may "shame the race" . . . Ethnic and racial groups differ in shame proneness: for African Americans, shame is not exclusively focused on personal inadequacies but is equally affected by social and interpersonal concerns.[44]

Although the style and fashion of blaxploitation films were embraced by many young people during the 1970s, one of the genre's loftiest goals and its biggest impact on Black culture was to get more Black youth involved in filmmaking. While these viral music videos do not share the same objective, per se, they do, by their very nature, invite viewers to participate in the creative process by making videos that mimic the style, culture, or ideals represented within the video. One of the hallmarks of participatory culture that is demonstrated very well with these viral music videos is the tendency for viewers to create their own parodies and remixes of viral material as a way to express their own creativity as prosumers of emerging media. Video and audio recording and editing have both become relatively cheap and easy enough that the creative process has been greatly democratized, allowing willing users to participate in this aesthetic labor. Participants not only use software and hardware (that often comes free and built into their computers), but many also engage in transmedia practices, using their mobile phones to either record video or audio, or to use smartphone applications. Of particular relevance is the "Songify" app, created by Smule for the Gregory Brothers, which, much like its precursor, the "I Am T-Pain" app, allows users to auto-tune their own voices in real-time. This app is advertised at the end of most of the videos on the Gregory Brothers' YouTube channel. When the Gregory Brothers released the BED INTRUDER video, they also released a lead sheet that included the lyrics and chords for their version of the song so viewers could more easily create their own video covers.

As fans and other viewers responded to the call for covers and remixes, astoundingly diverse material was posted. For example, one of the more notable covers of BED INTRUDER SONG!!! is Mike Penny's cover, played on the Tsugaru Shamisen, a stringed instrument from Northern Japan; adding an additional layer of cultural complexity, Penny himself is a red-headed white man. There is also a better-known "power-punk" cover, produced by Paramore singer Hayley Williams, Jordan Pundik from New Found Glory, and Ethan Luck, drummer for

Reliant K; all three are famous, white music industry celebrities. Of course, there is a danger that various types of epistemological damage are done when white people, especially white celebrities, co-opt a *cause célèbre* that itself is arguably already the result of co-opting subaltern voices. This is especially true in the case of Mike Penny in his use of a Japanese instrument to play a cover of a white band's song that was created by manipulating a Black man's voice that is at once both a serendipitous multi-cultural confluence facilitated by music and an example of acute, yet inconspicuous cultural hegemony affecting two ethnic groups at once.

2

China Dolls and Polynesian Beefcakes

Asians and Pacific Islanders in Music Videos

"I Think I'm Turning Japanese"

Not long after World War II, a wave of Japanophilia began to wash over the West as the export of Japanese media and culture dramatically increased over the course of the late twentieth century. In the 1950s, Akira Kurosawa's samurai films (or *chanbara*) were shown in American and European cinemas as an action-packed complement to Westerns, with many Spaghetti Westerns even taking their plot directly from these movies. Likewise, Americanized versions of *kaiju*, or media featuring strange beasts or giant monsters, such as Godzilla, took their place alongside Western science fiction. Western children were introduced to Japanese anime overdubbed in English, such as *Speed Racer* (1966–1968) and *Kimba the White Lion* (1965–1966), which appeared intermixed among their regular Saturday morning cartoons. In the 1970s, martial arts films became increasingly popular in the West, stoking further interest in East Asia more generally.

Throughout the 1980s (and well into the 1990s), globalization, improving trade relationships with Japan, and a booming Japanese economy turned this wave of Japanophilia into a tsunami as Japanese-made arcade games and video game consoles, media featuring giant *mecha* robots (especially *Transformers* and *Power Rangers*), and ninja-themed cartoons and video games (such as *Teenage Mutant Ninja Turtles*) permeated nearly every corner of Western youth culture. Around this same time, many pop, disco, and New Wave bands took inspiration from Japan and its culture; (including one band even taking its name from the country); several songs were inspired by Tokyo in particular, including "Tokyo" (Donna Summer, 1983), "Tokyo Nights" (Bee Gees, 1989), "Tokyo" (Flock of Seagulls, 1982), "Tokyo" (Thompson Twins, 1985), "Sunrise in Tokyo" (Tokyo Blade, 1983), "Love from Tokyo" (Rita Coolidge, 1984, which was the theme to the James Bond film, *Octopussy*, 1983), and "My Private Tokyo" (Vicious Pink Phenomena, 1982).

Many visual elements from Japanese pop culture found their way into music videos, sometimes even sprinkled in seemingly indiscriminately to give a video a general sense of "Japaneseness," and oftentimes in a harmful, stereotypical way.

Audiovisual Alterity. Michael L. Austin, Oxford University Press. © Oxford University Press 2024.
DOI: 10.1093/oso/9780190277789.003.0003

For example, I THINK I'M TURNING JAPANESE (1980) by the Vapors includes a geisha; a couple of samurai and a samurai sword for the band's lead singer, David Fenton, to wave around; and shoji (room dividers made of translucent sheets of paper on a lattice frame). The video even opens with a red circle representing the one on a Japanese flag which, as we will see, is a common visual element among music videos with Japanese themes from this period. Fenton also pulls back the corner of his eyes to signify that he is "turning Japanese," a racist gesture now widely seen as particularly offensive.[1]

Similarly ham-fisted attempts to represent other Asian and Pacific Island cultures can be seen in music videos from at least the 1970s through the present day. Aside from occasionally appearing in supporting roles, often as stereotypical stock characters, AAPI faces, that is, people with Asian, Asian American, or Pacific Islander ancestry or cultural heritage, were rarely seen in popular music videos or on music television for many years. Even after the "Korean Wave" began to bring K-pop acts such as Psy, BTS, and Blackpink to the attention of Western audiences in the early 2010s, AAPIs are still conspicuously absent from contemporary music videos. In this chapter, I examine some of the controversies surrounding the misuse of Asian aesthetics in Western music videos by non-Asian artists both through genuine, however misguided, interest in Asian culture and through unfortunate misappropriations and misrepresentations of members of the AAPI community. The chapter begins with a discussion of the fraught history of the AAPI community in the West, and the United States in particular, including the historical roots of a number of negative stereotypes found in various audiovisual media; conversely, it also addresses so-called "positive" stereotypes, such as the "model minority" myth, which is often used to excuse or explain away discrimination and misrepresentation of the AAPI community. As with other chapters, this one concludes with a brief discussion of music videos created by Asians and Pacific Islanders in which they represent themselves and their experiences and celebrate their own culture.

"Yellow Peril": The Myth of the Dangerous Asian in Western Culture

To understand the root of many of the Orientalist, othering stereotypes used to represent Asians and Pacific Islanders in music videos, it is important to first understand the complicated history of immigration to the United States by various parts of the AAPI community from which these stereotypes were borne. For Asians and Pacific Islanders, immigration to the United States has almost always been a matter of race and class. In the 1800s, China became more open to trade with the West, and treaties, such as the Burlingame Treaty of 1868, were designed to facilitate fair trade between the US and China, and to guarantee fair treatment of Chinese workers in America. As a result, Chinese laborers, pejoratively called "coolies," immigrated as indentured servants to the United States in waves throughout the late nineteenth century, working primarily as miners in the California Gold Rush and builders of western sections of the Transcontinental Railroad for a much lower wage than natural-born American workers. Because these workers were not white, they were unable to naturalize as citizens of the United States. The *Naturalization Act of 1790* reserved naturalization as a United States citizen only for "free white persons." Other acts such as the *Naturalization Act of 1870* and the *Indian Citizenship Act of 1924* extended naturalization rights to non-white residents of the US (African Americans and Native Americans, respectively) but still excluded East and Southeast Asians. Race-based prohibitions on immigration to the United States would not end for Asians until at least the 1950s.

The first Chinese immigrants to California were described as "'the most worthy of our newly adopted citizens,' 'our most orderly and industrious citizens, 'the best immigrants in California.'... 'thrifty,' 'sober,' 'tractable,' 'inoffensive,' 'law-abiding'; and they showed 'an all-round ability' and an 'adaptability' beyond praise."[2] But due to several factors, such as the bursting of the gold speculation bubble, economic instability during the economic Panic of 1873 and the resulting "Long Depression," and the completion of the Transcontinental Railroad in 1869 and the subsequent displacement of the workers who were building it, the remaining jobs in manufacturing and various service trades became increasingly scarce (especially in agriculture as a result of two successive years of drought in 1869 and 1870), pitting white workers against the remaining Chinese immigrants. As the competition for jobs became more bitter, Chinese immigrants were characterized in far less commendable ways and even demonized as:

> "a distinct people," "unassimilable," "keeping to their own customs and laws." They "did not settle in America"; they "carried back gold to their homes"; they "went back to China." Their mere presence "lowered the plane of living"; they "shut out white labor." They were "clannish," "dangerous" because of their secret societies, "criminal," "secretive in their actions," "debased and servile," "deceitful and vicious," "inferior from a mental and moral point of view, immeasurably lower than the Indians, for instance." They smuggled opium" and "spread the use of it," and their Chinatowns were "full of prostitution and gambling." They were "filthy and loathsome in their habits" and their "unsanitary quarters made the neighbourhood (sic) uninhabitable." They were "undesirable as workers and as residents of the country" . . . Every aspect of the

invaders became obnoxious and irritating. Their yellow skin was unpleasant; their slant eyes bespoke slyness; their conversation among themselves frightful jabbering.[3]

This prejudice against Asian immigrants was even expressed by other minority groups. Although African Americans in the Eastern United States proclaimed solidarity with the plight of Chinese workers in California, those who were more local saw the immigrants as an immediate threat to their own tenuous status as full citizens. The Black press reinforced stereotypes that framed Chinese immigrants as "filthy, immoral and licentious—according to our notions of such things" and even objected to the fact that their children were educated together in segregated schools with "idolatrous heathens."[4]

This fearful and prejudicial treatment of Chinese immigrants by imagining them as dangerous or threatening is known as "Yellow Peril." As discussed in the introduction to this book, Edward Said argued in *Orientalism* that Western society has long perceived "the East" or "the Orient" as "the other," and through this othering, the Occidental world has been able to "manage—even produce—the Orient politically, sociologically, militarily, ideologically, scientifically, and imaginatively during the post-Enlightenment period."[5] According to comparative literature scholar Gina Marchetti, Yellow Peril is a fear of Asians "rooted in medieval fears of Genghis Khan and Mongolian invasions of Europe," that serves to "other" Asians by combining a "racist terror of alien cultures, sexual anxieties, and the belief that the West will be overpowered and enveloped by the irresistible, dark, occult forces of the East."[6] These prejudicial mischaracterizations of Asian immigrants form the bases of many of the dehumanizing, economic, social, gender and sexual stereotypes used to represent the AAPI community that we see in popular films, television, video games, and of course, music videos. Yellow Peril relegates Asians to the role of the "perpetual foreigner" who will never be able to successfully assimilate into Western culture, always the "other," always speaking with an accent, eating "weird" food, being unable to drive, and so on, no matter how hard they have tried to acculturate themselves or assimilate.

In the absence of any formal immigration policy to address the threat of Yellow Peril, tax laws were imposed in California to limit the number of Chinese workers arriving in the state and to drive out many who were already there. A Foreign Miners' Tax was imposed in 1850, triggering the deportation of miners from Mexico and Chile, but exempting any "free white person," such as the English, Canadian, or German miners who were also part of the Gold Rush. Although it was repealed the next year, a new version was passed in 1852 specifically targeting Chinese miners. The law required any miner without US citizenship to pay $3 each month for the right to mine in the state, and the amount rose yearly in an effort to make the tax even more onerous. The money collected from Chinese miners during this period constituted one-quarter to one-half of California's state revenue.[7] In 1862, California also collected a "police tax" of $2.50 per month from Chinese immigrants over the age of eighteen who did not mine or produce rice, sugar, tea, or coffee—crops which were not grown in California at the time. They also instituted the Commutation Tax Act, which required shipowners to pay $500 for every foreigner onboard, but the tax could be commuted with the payment of a $5 fee from each Chinese passenger. Nevertheless, Chinese immigrants still came to the United States, so members of Congress passed legislation to impose limits on immigration from Asia, including the Page Act of 1875, which prohibited Asian women who might be prostitutes from immigrating to the United States, and the Fifteen Passenger Bill of 1879, which only allowed ships from China to carry up to fifteen passengers. In August 1880, President Rutherford B. Hayes sent a group of lawmakers to China, led by James Burrill Angell to renegotiate the Burlingame Treaty of 1868 in an effort to further limit immigration. Congress soon passed the Chinese Exclusion Act of 1882, the first law in the United States to deny immigration to a specific ethnic group. It permitted white-collar professionals, tourists, and students from China to visit the United States for a short period of time, but laborers of any kind were prevented from entering the country. At first, Chinese immigrants currently in the country were not affected, but subsequent acts and additions to the law prevented those who left from re-entering. The Chinese Exclusion Act was extended for ten years in 1892, becoming permanent in 1904. The Immigration Act, 39 Stat. 874 (February 5, 1917) created the "Asian Barred Zone," a geographical region that included all of Asia, Eastern Russia, and parts of the Middle East, from which no immigration was allowed.

As part of the Treaty of Paris (1898) that ended the Spanish-American War, control of the Philippines was ceded to the United States. Stoking fears that Asian immigrants, particularly Filipinos, were unfairly taking the jobs of hard-working, more deserving Americans. Samuel Gompers, president of the American Federation of Labor, gave a speech in October 1898 titled "Imperialism—Its Dangers and Wrongs" in which he expressed concern about the United States' annexation of the Philippines. He was not worried about the well-being of Filipinos or their right to govern themselves, but instead used overtly anti-Asian rhetoric to fan the flames of Yellow Peril and warn against the danger that was sure to follow the impending influx of Asian workers:

> If the Philippines are annexed what is to prevent the Chinese, the Negritos and the Malays coming to our country? How can we prevent the Chinese coolies from going to the Philippines and from there swarm into the United States and engulf our people and our civilization? If these new islands are to become ours, it will be either under the form of Territories or States. Can we hope to close

> the floodgates of immigration from the hordes of Chinese and the semi-savage races coming from what will then be part of our own country?[8]

Because the Philippines was an American colony at the time, Filipinos were still allowed to immigrate to the US mainland at the time, but because they were not white, they were not allowed to become American citizens. The Tydings-McDuffy Act of 1934 barred Filipinos from entering the United States in exchange for their country's independence within ten years (which did not happen until 1946).

In his inaugural address in 1905, US President Theodore Roosevelt sought to ease tensions and reassure the American public that the immigration laws in place at the time were sufficient to keep immigration from Asia at a minimum, making a distinction between the dangerous "coolie" class and the more desirable white-collar Chinese immigrants:

> The questions arising in connection with Chinese immigration stand by themselves. The conditions in China are such that the entire Chinese coolie class, that is, the class of Chinese laborers, skilled and unskilled, legitimately come under the head of undesirable immigrants to this country, because of their numbers, the low wages for which they work, and their low standard of living. Not only is it to the interest of this country to keep them out, but the Chinese authorities do not desire that they should be admitted. At present their entrance is prohibited by laws amply adequate to accomplish this purpose . . . But in the effort to carry out the policy of excluding Chinese laborers, Chinese coolies, grave injustice and wrong have been done by this Nation to the people of China, and therefore ultimately to this Nation itself. Chinese students, business and professional men of all kinds--not only merchants, but bankers, doctors, manufacturers, professors, travelers, and the like--should be encouraged to come here, and treated on precisely the same footing that we treat students, business men, travelers, and the like of other nations.

Early twentieth-century court cases made clear that citizenship in the United States was reserved exclusively for white people of European ancestry and, as a result of the Civil War, Black men. In Takao Ozawa v. United States, 260 U.S. 178 (1922), the Supreme Court of the United States ruled that Takao Ozawa, a Japanese-born immigrant living in the United States, was ineligible for naturalization, despite his claim that Japanese people are "free white persons," because, "[T]he intention [of the naturalization acts from 1790 on] was to confer the privilege of citizenship upon that class of persons whom the fathers knew as white, and to deny it to all who could not be so classified," and that "white" actually was intended to mean "Caucasian" (Southerland 1922).[9] The next year, in US v. Bhagat Singh Thind, 261 U.S. 204 (1923), the court sought to exclude Asians from naturalized US citizenship by defining who qualifies as "Caucasian," relegating Asians to the status of the perpetual foreigner. Although Thind, an Indian Sikh, defined himself as a "high caste Aryan, of full Indian blood" and was thus literally an Indo-European Caucasian, the Supreme Court ruled that "Caucasian" really meant "white" in the common sense, and because Indians had intermarried too freely with other races, assimilation into American society was too unlikely. In his opinion, Associate Justice George Sutherland wrote:

> The children of English, French, German, Italian, Scandinavian, and other European parentage, quickly merge into the mass of our population and lose the distinctive hallmarks of their European origin. On the other hand, it cannot be doubted that the children born in this country of Hindu parents would retain indefinitely the clear evidence of their ancestry. It is very far from our thought to suggest the slightest question of racial superiority or inferiority. What we suggest is merely racial difference, and it is of such character and extent that the great body of our people instinctively recognize it and reject the thought of assimilation.[10]

Soon after these cases, Congress passed the Immigration Act of 1924 (also known as the Johnson-Reed Act and the Asian Exclusion Act), which banned Asians from immigrating to the United States and set quotas on the number of Catholic Europeans, Arabs, and Jews who came to the country.

After the bombing of the US naval base at Pearl Harbor, Hawaii by the Imperial Japanese Navy Air Service on December 7, 1941, the perception of Asian Americans and Asian immigrants—especially those who were Japanese—plummeted among white Americans, leading President Franklin Roosevelt to issue Executive Order 9066, which dictated the internment of nearly 120,000 people of Japanese descent in concentration camps on American soil.[11] During World War II, Hollywood was especially keen to portray both Japanese Americans and Japanese people living abroad as dangerous, "fanatical near-savages, sneaky, dirty fighters."[12] Writing about the illusory threat posed by the Japanese in the American imagination, cultural critic Eugene Franklin Wong explains:

> The otherwise inhuman characteristics of early Asians in America were integrated into the Asian enemy, the competitor, the unfair and degrading threat to white labor, the culturally peculiar aliens whose low standard of living paralleled their own low value on human life, and the secretive Japanese farmer who was under his coveralls a barbaric samurai ready at a moment's notice to spearhead an invasion of white, Christian America.[13]

This can be especially true of Pacific Islanders or other native people groups from the Pacific Rim who are often portrayed as exotic savages, headhunters, or cannibals in hundreds of years of colonial literature. Yellow Peril came to represent all "Oriental" people, as Chinese, Japanese, Korean, and any other non-white person from Asia and the Pacific Islands were lumped into one monolithic group.

Yellow Peril often extended beyond representations of people and onto the places they live and work, and we carry vestiges of these prejudicial perceptions into the present. In an attempt to escape prejudicial treatment in the Western United States, Chinese immigrants began to settle elsewhere, and in urban centers, Chinatowns sprang up to provide refuge in which Chinese workers could open restaurants, stores, laundries and tailor shops, and other businesses that did not necessarily threaten the surrounding white establishments. Unfortunately, Yellow Peril followed the Chinese Eastward, and Chinatowns are often seen as an especially seedy part of a city's underbelly, run by dynastic criminal families and unscrupulous businessmen. Even Asian restaurants and Asian-run convenience stores are sometimes represented as fronts for backroom opium dens and gambling parlors. These restaurants and stores are even viewed as being dangerous and foreign in their own right, unable to maintain basic standards of cleanliness or food safety, serving headless ducks that had been hanging in the window and other food loaded with carcinogenic MSG.[14] Writing in his autobiography about his boyhood in a small New Jersey town in the early 1900s, Robert Lawson, white illustrator of the famous children's book *The Story of Ferdinand* (1936), recounts his distorted childhood impression of Chinese restaurants and culinary customs, writing:

> We knew that they lived entirely on a horrible dish called chopsooey which was composed of rats, mice, cats, and puppydogs. We knew that the long pigtail that they wore at the time was their most cherished possession and . . . if any foolish little white boy were to lay profane hands on one and give it a yank, the Chink would reach under the counter, draw out a razor-sharp cleaver which he kept there in readiness, and cut off your head as quick as a wink . . . [Some older boys] were reputed to have flung open the doors of various laundries and tossed in dead cats, rats, or mice, escaping the dreaded cleavers by only a hair's breadth.[15]

In other words, Chinese spaces were framed as horrific sites where cute animals and pets were eaten and savage foreigners lying in wait for an opportunity to chop up white children.

Mistreatment and misrepresentations of Asians and Pacific Islanders extended throughout the twentieth century and into the twenty-first. Prior to

World War II, Western imaginations were sparked by depictions of islands in the South Pacific, especially due to the deposition of the Hawaiian monarchy by American and European plantation owners in 1893, Hawaii's consequential occupation as a US territory in 1898, and America's occupation of the Philippines in 1989. However, as Americans who served in the Pacific theater returned from World War II, they brought with them myths, misunderstandings, and fetishes about the peoples and cultures of East Asia and the Pacific Islands. In the 1950s and 1960s, "Tiki" bars and exotica music helped to blend Oceania, Southeast Asia, Hawaii, and many other parts of the Polynesian world into one fantastical Orientalized pseudo-culture as visual, sonic, and cultural elements from a very wide variety of people groups were amalgamated into consumable cocktails and records. Further US military involvement in Asia, namely the Korean War (1950–1953) and the Vietnam War (1955–1975), also helped to introduce Americans to the Korean martial art Taekwondo, Muay Thai, a style of kickboxing from Thailand, and the exaggerated and over-the-top action, sound effects, and music of "Chopsocky," or kung fu action films produced in Hong Kong featuring martial artists such as Bruce Lee and Lo Lieh that became popular in the West in the 1960s to early 1980s further contributed to an Orientalized and distorted view of the East. Despite these representational failures, these films did have some redeeming qualities that were particularly appealing to BIPOC audiences:

> kung fu films offered the only nonwhite heroes, . . . to audiences alienated by mainstream film and often by mainstream culture. This was the genre of the underdog, the underdog of colour, often fighting against colonialist enemies, white culture, or the Japanese. The lone, often unarmed combatant fighting a foe with greater economic clout who represented the status quo provides an obvious but nonetheless real connection between kung fu films and black audiences.[16]

When refugees fled to the US after the Vietnam War, they faced routine discrimination and hate, including an attack on Vietnamese fishermen by the Klu Klux Klan in Galveston, Texas in 1979. On June 19, 1982, Vincent Chin, a Chinese American, was beaten to death in Detroit, Michigan by two auto workers who scapegoated Chin for massive lay offs in the American auto industry that were occurring at that time due to the high oil prices of the 1970s and the introduction of Japanese cars into the US market in 1981. Japanaphobia, sometimes called "Japan Panic," can also be found in media from this period in films such as *Back to the Future II* (1989) and *RoboCop 3* (1993), wherein Americans of the future work under controlling Japanese bosses, reflecting Western discomfort with Japan's growing economic and technological influence.

To this day, Asians are still depicted as "perpetual foreigners," stereotypically cast in Western media as being "fresh off the boat," slotted into specific occupations within entertainment media based on their country of origin and, as we will discuss in more detail later in this chapter, their gender. Typically, if they are not a ninja or some other type of martial artist, scientist/doctor, or musician (and almost exclusively a violinist or pianist), Japanese and Chinese men are often portrayed as businessmen. This is a stark contrast to and disturbing development from the generally positive view of East Asian businessmen as described by sociologist Ezra Vogel in his first book, *Japan's New Middle Class* (1963), in which he introduced the West to the new, white-collar "salaryman" and the emergence of a new type of Japanese family structure after World War II. In his second book, *Japan as Number One*, published in 1979, Vogle extolled the virtues of Japanese business culture and what American businesses could learn from it. Indian men are often represented as cab drivers or convenience store owners, and Chinese and Korean men frequently run a grocery store or restaurant.

Women were also victims of the Yellow Peril hysteria. Out of fear of a growing Asian population, immigration to the United States by women was heavily regulated and rarely allowed. In 1870, females made up 7.2% of the total Chinese population in the US, and the number decreased to 3.6% by 1890.[17] Immigration of Chinese women to the United States was first limited using laws that barred actual or alleged prostitutes of foreign origin from entering the country. The Page Law of 1875 further restricted the entry of Chinese, Japanese, and Mongolian contract laborers, female prostitutes (real or imagined), and felons. Laws passed in 1903, 1907, and 1917 gave immigration officials even more power to deport women suspected of being prostitutes, and because "the stereotypical view . . . that all Chinese women were prostitutes was still widespread, it meant that no Chinese woman, regardless of her social standing, was safe from harassment."[18] Further, Chinese women were a female embodiment of Yellow Peril, allegedly bringing with them to America "especially virulent strains of venereal disease, introduced opium addiction, and enticed young white boys to a life of sin. In short, Chinese prostitutes were seen as potent instruments for the debasement of white manhood, health, morality, and family life."[19] Thus, when they are depicted in Western media, if they are not the perpetually foreign war bride of a white soldier, Asian women often find themselves in one of three jobs: subservient restaurant or laundry worker, overbearing stay-at-home mom, or prostitute.

Anti-Asian sentiment flared yet again in popular culture when the COVID-19 pandemic was first reported as having originated in Wuhan, China in late December 2019. A combination of fear, ignorance, and hate led conservative pundits and politicians in the United States, including Donald Trump who was serving as US president at the time, to give the virus Sinophobic nicknames, such as the "Chinese virus" and "Kung Flu," and play into racist tropes that frame Asians as being sneaky and incompetent and who eat meat from unconventional sources. This rhetoric contributed to an increase in racist and xenophobic views and hate speech toward the AAPI community, regardless of their actual heritage or national origin, and a dramatic increase in the number of hate crimes, including physical attacks, that the AAPI community experienced.[20]

The "Chinaman Lick" and Look in Music Videos

As you can see, racist and xenophobic attitudes about the AAPI community run deep in Western culture, and its enduring legacy continues to influence the ways in which we visually and sonically represent this community in media, even in music videos. Perhaps the most well-known and easily recognizable sonic stereotype related to race or ethnicity is what is known as the "oriental riff," "East Asian riff," or "Chinaman lick" (Figure 2.1).

The idiosyncratic rhythm of this riff first appears in a stage show titled *The Grand Chinese Spectacle of Aladdin or The Wonderful Lamp*, by S.S. Steele and T. Comer, published in 1847, itself an example of late nineteenth- and early twentieth-century Orientalism in which Middle Eastern folk tales were set in Chinese settings. This riff, and many variations with striking rhythmic, melodic, and/or harmonic similarities, appears in a wide range of media as a symbolic representation of East Asia. Since the 1930s, the lick has been included in the scores for cartoons, films, TV shows, and video games.[21] Famous examples include two televised "Young People's" Concerts presented by Leonard Bernstein and the New York Philharmonic Orchestra, in which he erroneously refers to this lick as "old Chinese music" and "Chinese folk music;" Disney's animated film *The Aristocats* (1970), in which a very stereotypical Siamese cat, drawn with squinty eyes, large front teeth, and whiskers that mimic a Fu Manchu mustache, plays it on a piano using chopsticks as he sings nonsense sentences, such as "Shanghai, Hong Kong, egg foo yong [sic] / fortune cookie always wrong;" and when players fight the character Hoy Quarlow in the video game *Super Punch-Out!!* (Nintendo, 1994).[22]

Figure 2.1 The "oriental riff."

The riff appears in popular music throughout this same period, first appearing in a music video in the live performance video recorded for Jamaica-born British singer Carl Douglas's "Kung Fu Fighting" (1974), which heavily features the riff. In KUNG FU FIGHTING, visual elements within the video, especially Douglas's sartorial and choreographic choices, are as inauthentic to the practice of kung fu as the "oriental riff" is to actual Chinese musical practice, and like the riff, these elements serve only as vague, stereotypical references to the actual martial art or meditative discipline and the Chinese culture from which they come. Rather than wearing a *yī-fu* or other uniform typically worn by kung fu practitioners, Douglas wears what appears to be a silky red karate *gi* with large white characters (i.e., Sinograms) around the bottom and along the black collar that is tied at the waist with a black belt (a garment that could easily be mistaken for a smoking jacket), loose white pants with a large black Chinese character on the leg, and a large red headband. Throughout the video, Douglas adds choreographed "karate chops," kicks, and other martial arts-inspired movements among his dance moves to enact various lyrics of the song, for example:

> There were funky Chinamen from funky Chinatown /
> They were chopping them up [stylized downward "chop" motion at waist level with right hand that is raised up to eye level at the word "up"] /
> They were chopping them down [stylized downward "chop" motion past left thigh with left hand at the word "down"]

Despite its apparent cultural insensitivity, "Kung Fu Fighting" became an instant disco hit, and after hitting No. 1 on the UK charts the single was distributed by Century Records in the United States; there, the song was played on heavy rotation on R&B and disco radio stations and reached No .1 on both US *Billboard* Hot 100 and *Billboard* Hot Soul Singles and was certified "Gold" by the RIAA in 1974.

The Scottish singer, Aneka, reached No. 1 on several European charts in the summer of 1981 with her song "Japanese Boy." Like "Kung Fu Fighting," "Japanese Boy" begins with variations of the "oriental riff," recognizable by their use of planing parallel fourths and fifths along a pentatonic scale. They are played here on synthesizers using a number of different timbres, first over calming synth pads, and later over a driving disco bass line. Unlike "Kung Fu Fighting," which only includes the riff as a lick that appears in the song's accompaniment during the chorus, the melodic contour of large segments of the verses and chorus of "Japanese Boy" follows the same melodic contour of the riff established in the song's introduction. JAPANESE BOY (1981) is also a performance video, with Aneka performing dressed as a geisha for an audience in what looks to be a dance club.[23] Although her purple and turquoise kimono appears to be at least somewhat authentic, her hairstyle is not, as it is cut into a bob with bangs and long sides, and she plays into tropes about East Asian hairstyles by adding crossed chopsticks that protrude from a small bun on the top of her head. This particular sartorial trope of essentializing Asian identity or culture through geisha costuming can be found in a number of music videos, even in more recent ones, such as Madonna's NOTHING REALLY MATTERS (2009), Nicki Minaj's YOUR LOVE (2010), and Coldplay's PRINCESS OF CHINA (2012), ft. Rihanna.

JAPANESE BOY opens with a red-tinted screen and a bright yellow circle in the middle, an image that bears a striking similarity to the standard of the Japanese Emperor (a red flag with a golden circular chrysanthemum in its center). In the background, you can see faint images of carvings depicting Japanese characters. Although she does not move much throughout the video, Aneka sways back and forth while slowly rotating, sometimes holding her hands together in front of her chest, while at other times she moves her hands and arms outwardly as if to mimic the gestures geisha might use during *mai*, a type of Japanese folk or theater dance that features the use of hand gestures to tell a story.

China Dolls and Dragon Ladies: Gendered and Sexual Stereotypes of the AAPI Community in Music Videos

One of the most well-known and most often used tropes related to women in the AAPI community is the "China doll." This trope is also known as the "Butterfly," "Celestial lady," "Geisha girl," and "Lotus blossom," and centers around racial and sexual stereotypes of Asian women that frame them as exotic, delicate, subservient, and eager to please. These portrayals of Asian women not only fetishize them and construct them as objects of sexual desire but also often project on them an inability to sexually resist white men. Because whiteness and white masculinity are depicted as the best, most desirable qualities in a mate, surpassing the masculinity of all other races, female Asian characters fall in love with white men (usually at first glance) and offer themselves up for the romantic and sexual pleasure of white men. In 1834, Afong Moy, known as the "Chinese Lady," came to the United States from China as an exotic curiosity and living museum tableau, igniting American fantasies and fetishes about mysterious Asian women.[24] In *Full Metal Jacket* (1987), English-Chinese actress Papillon Soo Soo plays a Vietnamese prostitute who approaches white American GIs with the now-infamous and clichéd pickup line from the film: ". . . me so horny! Me love you long time!" In *The World of Suzie Wong* (1960), the title role also serves as the stock character of "hooker with a golden heart." Although Robert Lomax decides not to hire Suzie because he cannot afford her services, she shows a hidden level of depth and integrity by being emotionally attracted to him despite his rejection of her.

One of the earliest prominent music videos to feature the China doll trope is David Bowie's CHINA GIRL (1983). In an interview with Kurt Loder for *Rolling Stone* in 1983, Bowie explained how he wanted to use the video for his singles, "Let's Dance" (1983) and "China Girl" (1983), to serve as a form of social commentary:

> Very simple, very direct . . . And the message that they have is very simple—it's wrong to be racist! . . . But I see no reason to fuck about with that message, you see? I thought, "Let's try to use the video format as a platform for some kind of social observation, and not just waste it on trotting out and trying to enhance the public image of the singer involved.["] I mean, these *are* little movies, and some movies can have a point, so why not try to *make* some point.[25]

Although the underlying message of CHINA GIRL (1983) is designed to critique anti-Asian racism and Britain's long history of exploitation in China, the video relies heavily on the China doll trope and all of its associated baggage, depicting the Asian women featured in the video as being exotic, hyperfeminine, hypersexual, and somewhat subservient, often in the service Bowie, a white man.[26]

The video begins with images of ocean waves crashing on a beach in slow motion. An image of a woman dressed as a porcelain doll emerges as a version of the "oriental riff" is heard, played on electric guitar and synthesizers. When the drum kit comes in, barbed wire appears across the screen, indicating that the doll is either locked up, perhaps as a prisoner of China's communist regime or is otherwise off-limits.[27] Bowie soon appears on screen, dressed in a sleek gray suit and yellow necktie, singing into a sleek gray microphone; the only instrumentalists visible in the video, although blurry, is playing an upright bass in the middle distance. Viewers then see a split screen: on one side, an image of Bowie, his entire body above his knees visible, singing on the left side of the screen against a wall covered in vaguely Asian-themed wallpaper printed with mere suggestions of yellow and green leaves; on the other side, the face of an Asian woman, Chinese-New Zealander Geeling Ching (neé Ng), being stroked by a hand that is presumably Bowie's. After the video suddenly shifts to a scene in which a woman is running through a desert wearing a Maoist work uniform and carrying a red flag, the side-by-side scene returns. Here, we see Ching playfully make fun of Bowie's nose by pressing hers upward, laughing and sticking out her tongue as reassurance that her criticism is in jest. We then see Bowie's head and bare shoulders; just as Ching teased Bowie about his facial features, here Bowie uses his fingers to "slant" his eyes to mimic the characteristic "almond" eye shape created by an epicanthic fold of the upper eyelid that is common among some AAPI communities. To reassure the woman that he, too, is only joking, he quickly and aggressively wiggles the slanting of his eyes up and down, and then tilts his head and offers a consoling smile to his doll.

In a later sepia-colored scene in CHINA GIRL, we see the couple on a date in a Chinese restaurant. As Bowie attempts to use chopsticks, he dumps noodles out of his bowl and Ching exasperatedly laughs at him while still maintaining a demure, coy demeanor. A little later, we see Ching cover her face with her hands, instantly transforming into a china doll, dressed in an elaborate traditional gown and tiara, standing perfectly still with her face painted white and her arms by her side and the palms of her hands facing forward. Bowie grabs her by the shoulders and kisses her as the camera rotates around the couple multiple times. The kiss seemingly gives life both to the "doll" and to the video: throughout the duration of the kiss, color slowly replaces the sepia tint of the video, and as the kiss ends, Ching's eyes slowly open and a smile spreads across her face as if she had been awakened.

In the final scenes of the video, Bowie and Ching stand facing each other on opposite sides of the frame. Here, the China doll trope is exchanged for the "Dragon Lady" stereotype. A mixture of the *Femme Fatale* trope and Yellow Peril, the Dragon Lady stereotype shares some of the sexual attractiveness qualities associated with the China doll stereotype but with an added physical, emotional, or social aggression or domineering attitude.[28] Dragon Ladies are also portrayed as being cunning, untrustworthy, often cheap or miserly, and mysterious. As Bowie sings, "And when I get excited / My little China girl, she says / 'Oh, baby, just you shut your mouth.' / She says, 'Shh . . . ,'" Ching mouths the words as if she were actually saying them, lifting her finger to shush him and brandishing a long, talon-like fingernail. A superimposed image of Ching wearing her traditional gown and tiara and holding two flaming torches then appears, and she proceeds to "breathe fire" by spitting a flammable liquid through the flames. The video ends with the couple making love in the nude on a beach with waves lapping against their bodies. They are startled and look up at someone towering over them—it is Ching who has again transformed, this time into an angry woman with a bad perm and lots of makeup, who forcefully wipes her lips with the back of her clenched fist as the barbed wire graphics similar to those from the beginning of the video reappear over her face, denoting that this Dragon Lady is off limits and/or dangerous. We hear the "oriental riff" return as the music and visuals fade.

Other music videos that employ the China doll stereotype do so with even less care and concern than Bowie's CHINA GIRL. In January 2023, Gwen Stefani was interviewed by journalist Jesa Marie Calaor for *Allure Magazine* to discuss the launch of "GXVE Beauty," Stefani's new line of vegan cosmetics, and to discuss the success and cultural impact of her "Harajuku Lovers" fragrance collection. Launched back in 2008, this had been inspired by four Japanese and Japanese American backup dancers who were hired to accompany Stefani on her 2004 "Harajuku Lovers Tour" to promote her debut solo album, *Love. Angel. Music. Baby.* (Interscope, 2004). Harajuku Girls are mentioned several times on the album, and one song, "Harajuku Girls," is specifically about them. Stefani's entourage of Harajuku Girls appear in several music videos created for singles from *Love. Angel. Music. Baby.*, including WHAT YOU WAITING FOR? (2004), RICH GIRL (2004), HOLLABACK GIRL (2005), LUXURIOUS (2005), and CRASH (2006); they are also featured in WIND IT UP (2006), THE SWEET ESCAPE (2006), and NOW THAT YOU GOT IT (2007). Three of the dancers appear in No Doubt's 2012 video SETTLE DOWN, and two appear in Stefani's 2021 video, LET ME REINTRODUCE MYSELF. In the 2023 *Allure* interview, Stefani recounts how her father's job at Yamaha required him to take business trips to Japan and how he introduced her to the Harajuku street fashion that inspired her aesthetic: "That was my Japanese influence and that was a culture that was so rich with tradition, yet so futuristic [with] so much attention to art and detail and discipline and it was fascinating to me."[29] After explaining how her father's fanciful stories of the Harajuku district's street performers and fashionistas led to her own trips to the district as an adult, Stefani shockingly claimed to be a part of that culture: "I said, 'My God, I'm Japanese and I didn't know it.' I am, you know."[30]

Unsurprisingly, Stefani, whose parents are Italian American and Irish American, has faced several accusations of cultural appropriation over the last two decades, but perhaps the most criticism comes as a result of her inclusion of the Harajuku Girls in her tour and videos, none of whom seemed to be allowed to speak during public appearances with Stefani. Korean American comedian Margaret Cho wrote in a 2005 blog post:

> I mean, racial stereotypes are really cute sometimes, and I don't want to bum everyone out by pointing out the minstrel show. I think it is totally acceptable to enjoy the Harajuku girls, because there are not that many other Asian people out there in the media really, so we have to take whatever we can get . . . At least it is a measure of visibility, which is much better than invisibility. I am so sick of not existing, that I would settle for following any white person around with an umbrella just so I could say I was there.[31]

In 2005, Slate.com's Mihi Ahn wrote even more critically about Gwen Stefani's silent entourage of Harajuku Girls:

> Stefani fawns over Harajuku style in her lyrics, but her appropriation of this subculture makes about as much sense as the Gap selling Anarchy T-shirts;

> she's swallowed a subversive youth culture in Japan and barfed up another image of submissive giggling Asian women. While aping a style that's supposed to be about individuality and personal expression, Stefani ends up being the only one who stands out.[32]

Whether or not one agrees with Ahn's accusation that Stefani is using Asian women as props (an accusation Stefani vehemently denies), it is hard not to agree with Ahn's assertion that Stefani has adopted Harajuku style and culture to be conspicuous rather than to fit or join a wider community. Stefani's stock answer for this type of criticism and accusations of cultural appropriation is perhaps most fully fleshed out in her interview with Nolan Feeny for *Time Magazine* in 2014:

> There's always going to be two sides to everything. For me, everything that I did with the Harajuku Girls was just a pure compliment and being a fan. You can't be a fan of somebody else? Or another culture? Of course you can. Of course you can celebrate other cultures. That's what Japanese culture and American culture have done. It's like I say in the song ["Harajuku Girls"]: it's a ping-pong match. We do something American, they take it and they flip it and make it so Japanese and so cool. And we take it back and go, "Whoa, that's so cool!" That's so beautiful. It's a beautiful thing in the world, how our cultures come together. I don't feel like I did anything but share that love. You can look at it from a negative point of view if you want to, but get off my cloud. Because, seriously, that was all meant out of love.[33]

Of course, being a "super fan" of a particular culture or cultural output never gives a person the right to claim to be a part of that culture, especially when the most tangible representation of that supposed appreciation, the Harajuku Girls in Stefani's videos, are essentially rendered voiceless, forbidden to speak in the videos or in public appearances. Rather, Stefani appropriated the Harajuku street style as a central part of her reinvention as a solo artist, appropriating Japaneseness and commodifying Orientalized fashion, images, and people, in order to embody an exotic femininity we associate with various cultures but without the negative baggage that usually accompanies this embodiment. This is something she is able to do as a white Italian and Irish American that people of color often cannot. Stefani continued to actively exploit this virtually consequence-free exotic feminine embodiment for nearly a decade.[34]

Stefani's music video WHAT YOU WAITING FOR? is inspired by Lewis Caroll's fantasy novels *Alice's Adventures in Wonderland* (1865) and *Through the Looking-Glass* (1871) as its inspiration, with Stefani playing the role of the novels' main character, Alice, as well as the Red Queen and White Queen. In this video, the

Harajuku Girls are cast as several other characters within the classic stories, namely, the White Rabbit, who is dressed very fashionably and in typical Harajuku style, with white and pink puffs on her head serving as rabbit ears. Harajuku Girls also play the roles of various participants in the Mad Hatter's tea party. The video begins and ends in (and often returns to) a recording studio in the "real world" and—except for a moment at the very end of the video when Stefani performs a peculiar dance move and they lightly giggle and demurely cover their mouths in modesty (each dressed in especially fashionable versions of a school girl uniform)—the Harajuku Girls otherwise sit silently, stone-faced, and perfectly still on a ledge against the studio window. Although the representation here is subtle, the Harajuku Girls are effectively Japanese "China dolls"—in their still silence, they wait submissively for permission to speak or more (or to be moved by Stefani), and once they do move and utter a sound, their coquettish, giggling in schoolgirl uniforms is both infantilizing and sexualizing.[35] Perhaps the most troubling representation within the video is the appearance of an Asian figure seen playing the role of the Caterpillar, who is dressed in clothing from a very wide range of cultures: flowing black robes, red plaid pants, what appears to be a long bearskin cap (similar to those worn by British grenadiers), a headscarf with a small skull and white cross on the forehead, and what look to be traditional japamala prayer beads (used in the practice of a number of Indian religions). The Caterpillar is smoking a hookah, a smoking instrument from the Middle East and North Africa, and blows what appears to be the Mandarin Chinese symbol for love, 愛, in Stefani's direction. Here, the bizarre mixture of "Eastern" cultures—*few if any of which are Japanese*—seems especially Orientalist and "othering."

The China doll trope is present in each of Stefani's videos that includes the Harajuku girls. It is even clearer in RICH GIRL, which opens with four Asian school girls (i.e., the Harajuku Girls as children) playing with literal dolls and a toy pirate ship. In this video, the adult Harajuku Girls are featured dancing behind Stefani dressed as seventeenth-century prostitutes in various locations on a life-sized pirate ship. Within the song's lyrics, Stefani discusses the Harajuku girls as if they were literal dolls, blank slates for her to name and dress as she pleases, singing:

> I'd get me four Harajuku girls to (uh huh) /
> Inspire me and they'd come to my rescue /
> I'd dress them wicked, I'd give them names (yeah) /
> Love, Angel, Music, Baby /
> Hurry up and come and save me. /

In WIND IT UP, a video inspired by the Rodgers and Hammerstein musical, *The Sound of Music* (1959), the Harajuku Girls and other dancers act as if they are toys that Stefani winds up with a giant gold key. At the beginning of HOLLABACK GIRL, the Harajuku Girls are dressed in clothing typical of West Coast hip-hop culture, giving viewers the impression that they might be dolls that Stefani can dress in any way she pleases; later, they appear in various cheerleading and drill team outfits, another common version of the sexualized schoolgirl trope. Similarly, LUXURIOUS features the Harajuku Girls dressed as "Cholas," a Chicano/a and Latinx subculture originating from Los Angeles, and in NOW THAT YOU GOT IT, they wear Jamaican tracksuits and other Caribbean clothing and hairstyles, both of which smack of cultural appropriation and playing "dress up." Throughout many of these videos, Stefani also appropriates the clothing and hairstyles of many other communities and cultures, providing further evidence that she considers these significant cultural elements to be things with which she can experiment and play and that she is free to appropriate for the sake of fashion.

In 2014, Avril Lavigne also appealed to her love for Japanese culture when faced with accusations of racism resulting from the use of racist tropes and clichés in her video, HELLO KITTY (2014). At first glance, the upbeat pop song itself does not appear to point directly to any of the overt musical tropes that we have seen in other videos in this chapter; however, the chorus's melody does use the pentatonic scale and uses the same rhythmic figures of the "oriental riff," although the first three measures of the chorus of "Hello Kitty" (2013) uses the rhythm of the first measure of the "oriental riff" in retrograde (reverse), while the rhythm of the fourth measure matches that of the last measure of the riff perfectly (Figure 2.2).

Like Stefani, Lavigne adopts the fashion sensibilities of the Harajuku district of Tokyo, but she focuses on a particular aesthetic sensibility found in some facets of Harajuku fashion and culture called *kawaii* (かわいい), meaning "lovely," "adorable," or "cute." People described as *kawaii* are seen as cute, charming, and childlike, while *kawaii* objects are colorful (and often pastel) and appeal to childlike sensibilities. Leila Madge defines *kawaii* (translated simply as cute) or *kawaisa* (cuteness) as follows:

> In short, *kawaisa* carries more than one connotation. On the one hand, the term can be one of approval because *kawaii* behavior is generally considered to be innocent and thus natural or honest rather than socially contrived. On the

Figure 2.2 The "oriental riff" in the first four measures of the chorus of Avril Lavigne's "Hello Kitty" (2013).

> other hand, insofar as there is a connotation of a lacking—lack of reserve, responsibility, adulthood, etc.—the term can be received ambivalently, especially when a young female calls an older male in a position of authority "kawaii." The potential for (re)defining behaviors in terms of "lovability," which is itself a somewhat ambiguous term, rather than power or status, is also an important part of the proliferation of the term in the 1980s.[36]

In addition to fashion, this aesthetic can be found in Japanese toys (for example, Sanrio's "Hello Kitty," from which this song takes its inspiration), media, handwriting style, and even mannerisms. Lavigne wears a pink skirt adorned with pastel blue cupcakes and has pastel streaks of color in her blonde hair, while her disinterested backup dancers wear identical pastel blue shorts over pink tights, with pink suspenders, white shirts, and white headbands. Throughout the video, Lavigne visits several locations full of plush *kawaii* cupcakes and candy, and in other scenes, she uses a *kawaii* pink Fujifilm Instax camera.

In a statement to ABC News Radio, Lavigne's representative responded to these misrepresentations as if there were a simple misunderstanding of her intent, stating that the video "is an homage to all things she loves about Japan . . . food, fashion, fun!"[37] Replying on Twitter, Lavigne made a similar argument: "RACIST??? LOLOLOL!!! I love Japanese culture and I spend half of my time in Japan. I flew to Tokyo to shoot this video . . . "[38] Like Stefani, Lavigne refers both to the time she spends in Japan and her love of the culture as justification for appropriating Japanese culture and aesthetics for use in her video. The use of *kawaii* aesthetics in particular also invokes the China doll trope: aside from the fact that Sanrio's "Hello Kitty" often takes the form of a doll, Lavigne's clothing alludes to the fact that she is either a doll herself or is childlike and would play with dolls. And much like Stefani's videos, the Asian backup dancers in HELLO KITTY read as voiceless, emotionless dolls waiting for the lead singer to play with them.

Perhaps the most egregious abuse of the China doll trope in a music video can be found in rock band Day Above Ground's ASIAN GIRLZ (2013). The video opens with a close-up of the lips, legs, and feet of Vietnamese American actress and model Levy Tran, who is bathing in a deep, claw-footed bathtub. The title of the music video, the featured actor credit for Tran, and the band's name appear on screen, written in a "Mandarin" font—a culturally inauthentic typeface created in America that belongs to a group of fonts known as "chop suey types" and has been used for over one hundred years to symbolically represent Asia and the East in print.[39] As the music begins, simple chords played on an acoustic guitar are accentuated with the "oriental riff," and the video seemingly goes back in time, showing Tran arriving home, flipping on a light switch, placing her keys and purse on a table, and walking over to uncover a bird cage containing the shrunken members of Day Above Ground who are playing their instruments. As soon as the cover is removed, Tran gleefully smiles and runs her tongue across her teeth as the band begins to sing the song's chorus: "Asian girl / she's my Asian girl / you're my Asian girl." Tran backs away from the cage and begins to slowly and provocatively dance and remove her clothes in a performance for the caged band. During the first verse, Tran dances in her bra as she undresses even further while the band's lead singer Joe Anselm sings particularly vile and sexist lyrics laden with racist stereotypes that fetishize Asian women in an especially disrespectful way:

> I love your sticky rice / Butt fucking all night /
> Korean barbecue / Bitch, I love you /
> I love your creamy yellow thighs / Ooh your slanted eyes /
> It's the Year of the Dragon / Ninja pussy I'm stabbin'

In subsequent verses and the song's bridge, Anselm seems to list any Asian stereotype that comes to mind, singing disparagingly about Asian superstitions, the fact that many Asian cultures celebrate the Lunar New Year (and the fact it often occurs in February), shark soup, and so on. He also insinuates that Tran's father is rich because he drives a Mercedes, playing into the stereotype that Asians are good at business or are otherwise financially successful, and he suggests that her mother either works at or frequents an Asian nail parlor. He even implies that his love interest is in the country illegally; in fact, the band even threatens to make Tran a victim of human sex trafficking ("come sit on my lap / or we'll send you back"), and they comment that she's aging so well (yet another stereotype about Asians) that they are unsure whether she is seventeen or twenty-three years old, assuring her that it ultimately does not matter to them if she is underage. The song ends with an instrumental interlude and one more iteration of the chorus during which Tran carries the birdcage into the bathroom. As she sits in the bathtub, covered in bubbles and surrounded by candles, she opens the door to the cage. The miniature band then strips down to their underwear and dives into the bathtub with Tran. We see each band member swimming around Tran's legs in the bathwater. Here Tran rubs Marcello Lalopua, the band's bassist, on her shoulder and between her breasts as if he were a bar of soap. As Anselm swims between Tran's legs and toward her vagina, we reach the point in time from the beginning of the video, putting the beginning bath scene into context.

Near the end of the video, we see alternating clips of the band playing their instruments and drying off with towels alternating with scenes in which crowds of people cheer as the band gives shout-outs to parts of the Los Angeles metropolitan area with significant Asian populations, such as Alhambra, "J-Town" (the Little Tokyo Historical District) "K-Town" (Koreatown in central LA), and

Temple City. The video concludes with Anselm and Drew Drumm, the band's rap vocalist, shouting a list of random Asian things (Toyota, Spicy Tuna Sashimi, Sailor Moon, Tibet, Bruce Lee, etc.), including some that are patently racist and stereotypical, such as "Fried Lice" and "Fa ra ra ra ra ra ra ra ra" (a reference from the 1983 film *A Christmas Story*), reinforcing the stereotype that Asian immigrants mix up the pronunciation of the letters "L" and "R."

As the video ends, Tran continues to dance for the band, now dressed and wearing a short cocktail dress and a long blond wig as glowing neon Maneki-neko ("beckoning cat" or "waving lucky cat"), garden gnomes, and Day Above Ground logos surround her. Throughout ASIAN GIRLZ, polaroid photo montages featuring Tran wearing the same wig and going on dates with each of the members of the band further reinforce the China doll stereotype by framing Tran as an object of sexual desire who is eager to please each band member. In a surprise ending after the conclusion of the song, we see Tran approaching a shelf of garden gnomes from which she removes a bottle labeled "Shrinking Potion;" here, the "Tiger Lady" trope is employed as the plot twist reveals that although she is the object of their sexual desire, Tran is actually the aggressor, and she shrunk the band to keep them as pets, sex toys, and so on.

The public backlash resulting from the release of ASIAN GIRLZ was swift and relatively severe. Within a week of the video's initial release on YouTube, it had received over 1 million views and 12,000 mostly negative comments. Phil Yu, founder and editor of the blog, *Angry Asian Man*, even dubbed the video "pretty much the worst thing ever made."[40] LA's House of Blues canceled a scheduled gig at which the band was meant to play because of the public outcry on the venue's Facebook page and a Change.org petition that was launched, and Tran apologized profusely on social media for taking part in the video.[41] At the time, the band also offered a half-hearted apology of their own, but they almost immediately backtracked in an interview for *Huffington Post* with journalist Derrick Clifton in which Anselm argued the song couldn't be racist "because no one in the band is racist."[42] He even went so far as to claim that they could not be racist because their band is "multicultural" and includes an Asian member:

> The guy in the bow-tie, our cutie bass player, was born in Indonesia, and he steals the show!! Please don't take this tongue-in-cheek tribute to some of the most gorgeous women on the planet too seriously!! You'll ruin the fun of it all!! Thanks for watching, seriously!![43]

When asked how the band's relationships with Asian women inspired the lyrics, Anselm provided a rather rambling excuse that began with the argument that the song is about "being accepting of another culture because you love a culture" and ended with a claim that the song is actually a satirical observation making fun of white men with fetishes for Asian women and the stereotypes that they associate with Asian women. Worse still, he goes on to claim later in the interview that critics misunderstood their point and they are, in fact, worshipping Levy as "this ideal Asian goddess," thus further fetishizing her himself.[44]

Nerd, Guru, Eunic: Emasculating Asian Men in Music Videos

Negative stereotypes and tropes about Asian men also exist, and as with the tropes used to represent Asian women, they too have sexual undertones. Counterintuitively, limiting the number of Chinese women who were allowed to immigrate to the United States in the nineteenth and early twentieth centuries left fewer possible romantic and marriage partners for the Chinese men working in the US, leaving white women in what Americans of the time considered to be a precarious position. Gary Hoppenstand contends that sexualized Yellow Peril, that is, the threat of possible rape of a white woman by an Asian man, often serves as a metaphor for the impending danger the Orient poses and the Occidental need for protectionism. Discussing Yellow Peril stereotypes in media, he writes:

> The threat of rape, the rape of white society, dominated the action of the yellow formula. The British or American hero, during the course of his battle against the yellow peril, overcame numerous traps and obstacles in order to save his civilization, and the primary symbol of that civilization: the white woman. Stories featuring yellow peril were arguments for racial purity. Certainly, the potential union of the Oriental and white implied at best a form of beastly sodomy, and, at worst, a Satanic marriage. The yellow peril stereotype easily became incorporated into Christian mythology, and the Oriental assumed the role of the devil or demon. The Oriental rape of the white woman signified a spiritual damnation for the woman, and at the larger level, white society.

Despite the fact that this threat was imagined, exaggerated, and based largely on racist stereotypes, Americans attempted to protect white women from the mythic, dangerous, sexual Asian man by symbolically emasculating him. Asian men in television programs and films are often seen working in more effeminate "women's jobs," such as running a convenience store, restaurant, or dry cleaners. If they are not altogether asexualized, they are portrayed as being awkward nerds who have trouble speaking to women, such as the character Raj Koothrappali on *The Big Bang Theory* (CBS, 2007–2019), who is so frightened by attractive women he is completely unable to speak to them. Jokes are often made at the expense of Asian men about the small size of their penis, giving the impression that even if women were attracted to them, they would not be able to sexually satisfy them—or at least not as well as white men.

Having been symbolically emasculated or domesticated and rendered sexually powerless, Asians are often relegated to roles in which they only support the main character, rather than featuring as a star themselves. Romantic relationships between white and Asian actors were not featured very often, even before the 1930s Hays Code, which expressly banned any on-screen representations of interracial couples or interracial sex. Even now, well into the twenty-first century, not much has changed. To add insult to injury, there have been several relatively recent incidents wherein directors have cast white actors to play roles as Asian, such as casting white actress Tilda Swinton to play "the Ancient One" in the film *Doctor Strange* (2016) or Emma Stone's selection to play a surfer of native Hawaiian, Chinese, and Swedish heritage in *Aloha* (2015). When they are cast, Asian men often play two roles as supporting characters: that of a wise mentor or a trusty sidekick. The sensei, or teacher or master, is usually portrayed as an older character who exists within the story to impart knowledge or skills to a younger, usually white, character. Many martial arts films have such a character who is a master of his craft and who is tasked with teaching the main character of the story how to fight. Here, not altogether unlike the "Magical Negro" trope, the trope of Asian Guru/Sage can sometimes mix with the Perpetual Foreigner stereotype, and rather than kindly shepherding their young white protégé, the Guru often lives a secluded life and can be seen as especially demanding, unnecessarily cruel, or rude, unaware of the inherent expectations of a nurturing student-teacher relationship. They also teach using mysterious language and pseudo-Confucian proverbs, rather than choosing to confer wisdom on white characters in a culturally relevant way. For example, in the film *The Karate Kid* (1984), Mr. Miyagi served as guru for Daniel, subversively teaching him karate by having him do seemingly menial chores. Only later does Daniel find out that "wax on, wax off" is not only about waxing the car but that the movements he performs while doing the waxing are also a fundamental martial art technique. Further, media content creators often attribute Asian senseis, other Asians generally, and the entire continent of Asia with mysterious and magical properties. White characters are taught by their guru to find supernatural power from within either explicitly through meditation, or more subtly, as with the Indian characters in *Eat, Pray, Love* (2010). White characters can also be seen buying magic potions from Asian herbalists, as was the case in the film *Alice* (1990).

Well-known Asian sidekicks in Western media include Katana (*Suicide Squad*, 2016), Sulu (*Star Trek*, especially the 2009 film), Kato (*The Green Hornet*, 2011), Russell (*Up*, 2009), Wang Chi (*Big Trouble in Little China*, 1986), Short Round (*Indiana Jones and the Temple of Doom*, 1984), among many others. Only in recent years in action films such as Marvel's *Shang-Chi and the Legend of the Ten*

Rings (2021), *Snake Eyes: G.I. Joe Origins* (2021), and *Dune* (2021) have Asian men been cast in leading roles in action films that were not considered to be primarily martial arts films (although martial arts still feature quite prominently in many of these films).

Even fewer films, TV shows, and other media feature Asian or Pacific Islanders as the object of romantic or sexual desire, especially for white female protagonists. In *Romeo Must Die* (2000), a film loosely based on Shakespeare's *Romeo and Juliet*, the male protagonist and male love interest is Han Sing, a Chinese man, who only hugs his female co-star at the end of the film because "mainstream America, for the most part, gets uncomfortable with seeing an Asian man portrayed in a sexual light."[45] And there is some empirical data to support this claim. Studies indicate that among all races/ethnicities and genders, Asian males are least likely to be part of a romantic relationship in adolescence and young adulthood, and have a later average sexual debut than their White, Black, and Hispanic counterparts.[46] This marginalization has become so ingrained within Western culture that it has become part of our cultural psyche; in a 2011 study, Asian males were perceived as being "less attractive" and "less masculine" than both white and Black males, and when compared to white males, the more "Asian-looking" a man is, the less attractive he is perceived to be.[47] These prevailing perceptions have established what sociologist C. Winter Han calls a "highly racialized hierarchy of desire" at the bottom of which both straight and gay Asian men often find themselves.[48]

Bucking this trend, Asian men do appear as love interests in a few recent music videos. Taylor Swift's video WILLOW (2020) features Taeok Lee, a Korean American who previously toured with Swift during her 2013 "Red" tour, as her love interest. A continuation of her CARDIGAN (2020) video, WILLOW sees Swift follow a magical golden string into the back of a piano in her cabin and emerges in a fantasy world where she sees a reflection of herself and Lee in a pool of water. In the following scene, we see her and Lee playing with the golden string as children inside a tent. Swift emerges from the tent as an adult and suddenly finds herself inside a glass box playing a lute; Lee approaches and the two look at each other longingly. They each raise a hand to press together, although the glass prevents them from actually touching. Swift escapes through a hole under a trap door, and she suddenly stumbles upon a group of people performing a ritualistic dance around a fire in a snowy forest before following the golden string and continuing on her journey. As she walks away, Lee removes his mask, revealing himself to be one of the ritual's participants. Reaching the end of the golden string, Swift emerges from the piano at the place where she began. As she looks up from the string, Lee is there to meet her. The two hold up a hand as they did before, but this time, they are able to interlock their fingers, finally putting the words of the song's chorus into practice: "Begging for you to take my hand / Wreck my plans

/ That's my man." Notably, rather than sharing an overtly romantic embrace or even a kiss, they simply stand several inches apart and smile at each other. The video ends as the two walk out of the cabin door holding hands. So, although Lee is featured as a love interest in the video, expressions of this love are still very limited. While it is in no way emasculating, this gesture does suggest that anything beyond interracial handholding would be considered unsuitable for Swift's audience.

Similarly, Doja Cat's surreal KISS ME MORE, ft. SZA (2021), includes an Asian male subject as the main object of female desire, but as with Swift's video, a limited amount of physical contact is featured in the video. The main male character in this video is Alex Landi, an American actor and model, most famous for his role as Dr. Nico Kim on ABC's medical drama, *Grey's Anatomy*, who is of Korean and Italian descent. The video opens just after the crash landing of a space shuttle on a pink desert planet, with an astronaut walking toward the camera while removing his helmet. Through radio static, we hear that the astronaut's mission is to observe the planet "Her" as Kim sets off on his quest, wandering aimlessly through the pink sand dunes. Clearly exhausted, he stumbles upon a canoe floating in a stream of water, and we soon see him paddling upstream in it. Along his journey, he passes women (Doja Cat and SZA) who are so large in comparison to him that they seem to be part of the landscape. At around 3:02, the music stops and the audio is replaced with a suspenseful soundscape reminiscent of a horror film trailer as Kim reaches a giant stone mouth at the end of the stream. Before continuing toward the lips, he reaches into a tree on the bank of the stream and picks an exotic, pink alien fruit to eat. Likely designed to symbolize cunnilingus, Kim bites into the fruit and blue juice runs down his chin. The stone mouth then opens, emitting a bright light, and as he enters, he seems to become disoriented. When he awakens, we see Kim, now shirtless and a little sweaty, wearing satin pants and lying in an empty pink room on a bed with pink satin sheets. As he sits up in the bed, the music begins again, and we see Doja Cat sitting to his left, kissing his shoulder and caressing the back of his head and neck while SZA sits to his right, running her finger sensually along his right shoulder. We later see Doja Cat lick her finger and run it down Kim's abdomen, but as she does so, her hand remains off-screen. As the song ends, both women shove Kim down onto the bed, but they instantly disappear and we again see him lying alone. He looks with concern at his hand as it begins to glitch and flicker, and his entire body soon does the same and disappears.

In a plot twist, Kim reawakens yet again, this time in a glass tube, suspended in pink liquid and attached at the head to a number of cables and tubes. As he notices his space suit on the ground outside of the tube, we hear the initial radio message from the beginning of the video, this time without the static and radio malfunction: "Your mission is to observe and study the planet Her only. Do not engage with the local inhabitants! Warning, do not engage with the local inhabitants!" We then see Doja Cat and SZA sitting on a couch playing a video game in which their avatar is an astronaut paddling a canoe down the same stream we saw Kim navigate earlier in the video. After seeing this interaction, along with a number of other men suspended in similar containers along the back of the room, viewers are led to the conclusion that these women have previously captured other men and have now captured Kim, and they have hooked him up to the video game console in order to control him within the game.

In the last few scenes of KISS ME MORE, we see the use of several tropes often used to represent Asian men in contemporary Western media. First, although Kim is obviously a sex symbol and object of desire, any physical interaction with him is either off-screen or innocuous, even though the song's lyrics are quite sexually explicit. Beyond being an object of desire, we also see a variation of the China doll trope used to represent Asian women both as Kim is displayed in a glass tube, rendered powerless and collected among other men, and as he becomes a plaything for the women in the form of a video game avatar. At the end of the final scene, Doja Cat asks SZA, "Why am I strangely attracted to this being? Where is he from?" Incredulous, she wonders why she would be attracted to a human man, a not-so-subtle (but likely unintentional) reference to the stereotype that women find Asian men less attractive when compared to men of other races. They then discuss the fact that he is from a planet, spelled E-A-R-T-H, about which they have never heard before and the name of which they struggle to pronounce, reducing Kim to the stereotype of the "perpetual foreigner" and recasting the racist trope that frames Asian names, places, foods, and so on as being nearly impossible to pronounce correctly and too foreign to be worth much care or consideration.

The "perpetual foreigner" trope is also featured in another "alien" themed music video: Nicki Minaj's STARSHIPS (2012). This video begins with a starship flying low near the surface of the ocean as it approaches a tropical island, scanning for life—or a party. In addition to several tourists, all of whom also look like models lounging around on cliffs of volcanic rock, we see a group of tattoo-covered Pacific Islander men in neon orange loincloths, puka shell necklaces, and bowler hats serving as local "tribesmen" who seem to have been performing a ritual to summon the alien ship. Notably, the racial, ethnic, or cultural identity of these men is never specified at any time throughout the video. Nicki Minaj suddenly appears on the beach in a neon pink bikini and long, neon green hair. These tribesmen later carry Minaj on a reflective metallic litter borne on their shoulders, giving viewers the impression that these men worship her as a goddess of sorts. Even later in the video, these men are seen performing a "haka," a ceremonial group dance performed by members of the indigenous Māori culture of New Zealand (Aotearoa); together with the designs of their tattoos, it becomes clear that these men are Māori, but in this video, they are "perpetual foreigners," a tribe of exotic muscle-bound savages or witch doctors with power to summon beautiful aliens from space. At nightfall, we see a different group of Pacific Islander "tribesmen," whose ethnic or cultural identity is also unacknowledged, each twirling a fire staff on the cliff of a volcano near Minaj and other models who are illuminated with blacklight and neon body paint, as lava flows in the distance. Throughout the video, both groups of exotic "tribesmen" are portrayed as both primitive and mystic, and as such, they seem to worship Minaj and serve at her pleasure. As the video ends, they appear to have become "domesticated" or "civilized" as they join the white models and tourists in a dance party, accepted to participate, but only by dancing like everyone else, a mode of performance in which their previous cultural expressions play no role.

Whether consciously or not, these negative tropes about Asian male love interests can even be found in music videos by artists from the AAPI community. Joseph Vincent (Encarnacion) is a Filipino-American guitarist from Los Angeles, California who became relatively well-known for the cover songs he uploaded to YouTube, and as a result, he has appeared twice on NBC's *The Ellen DeGeneres Show*. In his video, IF YOU STAY (2011), Vincent plays the role of the stereotypical "shy Asian nerd," albeit a very stylish and handsome one, wearing a loose black necktie, diamond earrings, and spikey hair, who seems to find it difficult to talk to women. Filmed in the library at Biola University, a non-denominational Christian university in La Mirada, CA, the video opens with Vincent sitting among *World Almanacs* and other reference books listening to music on earbuds as he spots his crush, a young white woman, browsing for books further down the aisle. The act of taking off the earbuds sets Vincent in motion, who glides through the library playing his guitar and singing. From this point in the video, it appears that the rest of the video is shot in one take, with the primary focus of the video on Vincent, and the occasional panning of the camera to show Vincent's love interest at one point and the band's drummer and some background extras in another. In the final moments of the video, the camera pans back toward Vincent as he appears to have worked up the nerve to speak to the young woman. We see him walking through a darkened section of the library toward her, now without his guitar. But just as he almost gets close enough to speak to her, her white boyfriend walks up seemingly out of nowhere, reaches around her waist and hugs her, leaving Vincent laughing and embarrassed just a few feet away.

The Myth of the Model Minority

Restrictions on the naturalization of Asian immigrants to the United States were slowly lifted after World War II. Chinese immigrants were given the right to naturalize in 1943, thanks, in part, to China's role as a US ally in the Pacific theater during the war. Filipinos were allowed to naturalize in 1945, and the Immigration and Nationality Act of June 27, 1952 (also called the McCarran-Walter Act of 1952) abolished race-oriented regulations of naturalization. Japanese and Korean Americans were first allowed to naturalize under this law, but only in small quotas. By the mid-1960s, political and cultural changes eased white America's feelings of Yellow Peril, exchanging stereotypes of dangerous Asians for equally damaging stereotypes that framed Asian immigrants and Asian Americans as mild-mannered, family-focused, hard-working citizens that other minority groups should emulate. The Immigration and Naturalization Act of 1965 abolished the existing quota system established by immigration policies, established just after World War I, which mainly attracted immigrants from Europe. Also known as the Hart-Celler Act, this new policy was viewed as a means to attract skilled laborers to the United States workforce and to reunite immigrants with members of their families from Latin America, Africa, the Middle East, and Asia—locations from which immigration had been severely limited or altogether forbidden. It also provided solace to refugees, who could now flee to the US from violence and oppression in their home country; almost immediately, refugees from Vietnam, Cambodia, and other Southeast Asian countries that had previously been disallowed to immigrate to the United States fled to the US to escape the Vietnam War and other armed conflicts in progress at the time.

Several contemporary articles were published that transformed the way white Americans viewed their Asian neighbors. The first was a *New York Times* article published in January 1966, titled "Success Story, Japanese-American Style," written by the sociologist William Petersen and in which he describes how hard work and conscientious citizenship propelled Japanese Americans from the wartime camps of twenty years prior to achieving the American dream with astonishing speed, writing, "By any criterion of good citizenship that we choose, the Japanese Americans are better than any other group in our society, including native-born whites."[49] Other articles, such as "Success Story of One Minority Group in the U.S.," published in *U.S. News & World Report* in December of 1966, and *Newsweek*'s 1971 article, "Success Story: Outwhiting the Whites," fermented the myth that Chinese immigrants to the US and their children had done so well in assimilating with the dominant white culture to have become even more successful than white people.[50] Without bothering to make a conscious effort to distinguish between the experiences of various other groups of Asian immigrants, the stereotype was extended to Korean, Vietnamese, and other Asian immigrants. Lumping all Asians together into one group functions as a form of erasure for Asians with less access to education and high-earning employment, especially when the myth of the "model minority" is used to explain away any hardships or institutionalized racism or discrimination they may face that contributes to, or even causes, these hardships.

Furthermore, coming at the height of the Civil Rights Movement, this myth has been used to reinforce harmful stereotypes about other racial groups in America regarding their intellectual ability and work ethic, providing opponents of the movement with a means to discredit advocates and protesters and dismiss their demands for racial justice and equal treatment. The myth of the model minority reinforces the false assumption that if Asians are able to lift themselves by their bootstraps to overcome systematic racism to achieve the American dream—and even surpass white Americans in doing so—racism isn't an actual problem (at least not anymore), and therefore, members of other racial groups would be able to achieve just as much if they were smart enough or were not so lazy.

Admittedly, it is hard to dispel the myth of the model minority when many of the positive stereotypes upon which it is built seem to be accurate. Asians are the fastest-growing, highest-earning, and most educated racial and ethnic group in the United States.[51] However, although some of these positive characteristics may be true for some Asian ethnic groups, such as Indian, Filipino, and Japanese Americans, the opposite is true for other subgroups, such as Huong, Bhutanese, Cambodian, and Burmese Americans, who experience high poverty rates and low education rates. In fact, according to a July 2018 report by the Pew Research Center, income equality in the US is now greatest among Asians, with Asian Americans in the top-earning 10% having incomes 10.7 times greater than the incomes of Asian Americans in the bottom-earning 10%.[52] The same report goes on to explain that although Asian Americans are the highest-earning racial and ethnic group in the United States, this status is not shared by all members of this group. While the top-earning 10% of Asian Americans earn 13% more than the top-earning 10% of European Americans, the bottom-earning 10% of Asian Americans have not been able to keep up with this trend: although they earned 8% more than the bottom-earning 10% of white Americans in 1970, the bottom-earning 10% of Asian Americans now make 17% less.[53]

Despite the fact that Asians are represented relatively well in high-earning fields such as science, engineering, and medicine, they often do not reach positions of authority, power, or popularity in business, government, media, or professional sports, a phenomenon known as the "bamboo ceiling."[54] The myth of the model minority is also used in contemporary contexts as a means to deny the existence of white privilege and as propaganda to support the dismantling of affirmative action policies, especially in higher education. Traces of Yellow Peril can be seen in depictions of the threatening model minority who is such a good student, musician, citizen, and so on, that he or she is unfairly awarded admission into an Ivy League university ahead of a more deserving white student.

K-pop's BTS are unarguably one the most successful musical groups in the world, and their global success places them in a prime position to serve as Model Minorities when it comes to discussing positive stereotypes and representation in popular music videos. They are especially popular online: In 2021, BTS held the Guinness World Records for being the most-followed music group on both Instagram and TikTok (including the fastest time to reach one million followers on the app), and for having the most average retweets on Twitter; for being the most streamed group on Spotify; for having the most viewers for the premiere of a music video on YouTube; having the most streamed track on Spotify in the first twenty-four hours; and for selling the most tickets for a livestreamed concert.[55] As of August 2023, among the twenty-seven BTS songs that have charted on the *Billboard* Hot 100, ten have reached the Top 10, and six have been No. 1 hits.[56] But the ability of supergroups like BTS to be able to succeed in Western markets in such a spectacular way does not necessarily indicate that AAPI artists are universally accepted by Western audiences. *Splinter News* staff writer Isha Aran notes that while K-pop is currently

> giving America a glimpse at what immensely popular stars of Asian descent could look like, it isn't contributing to Asian American success. In fact, in some ways it's inadvertently undermining it. As K-pop becomes more successful in the U.S., there is a chance that it will define what "Asian music" sounds like in America, which will only box Asian Americans in even more.[57]

There are Asian American artists who have written songs and created music videos in order to directly confront or contradict the model minority myth. Immigrating to the United States at the age of seventeen, Indonesian Chinese rapper Brian Imanuel Soewarno first became popular with his viral, RIAA Gold-certified trap hit, "Dat $tick" (2016), initially released on Soundcloud under the stage name Rich Chigga. The lyrics of "Dat $tick" include references to shooting police officers, gang violence, living in poverty, publicly embarrassing an ex-lover, and so on, but the lyrics do not come from his own lived experience; in an interview in which he explains both the meaning and the source of his lyrics, Imanuel freely admits, "When I was making the song, I really did not know what I was doing." He continues:

> I was kind of listening to all this trap music and when they're talking about scary shit, I just love it so much. So I was like, 'I kind of wanna recreate this. I wanna do something. I wanna have some scary ass lines.' And I didn't realize what that could do and how people would feel about that, because I don't live any of this shit. I'm not with the shit.[58]

In DAT $TICK (2016), Soewarno redemptively appropriates negative stereotypes and tropes found in hip-hop music videos to subvert expectations related to the model minority. In this video, he and the other Asian members of his "crew" are seen imitating a number of controversial or anti-social hip-hop tropes, such as "pouring one out for the homies" (i.e., pouring beer or liquor on the ground in tribute to a dead or incarcerated friend or fellow gang member) and waving pistols around. However, this performance is also quite ironic and tongue-in-cheek as Soewarno appears in the video dressed in the style of a model minority, wearing a pink, buttoned-up polo shirt, khaki shorts, and a Reebok fanny pack, driving a minivan, and living in a nice, upper-middle-class home.

Under a new stage name, Rich Brian, Soewarno later released a more serious song, "Yellow," ft. Bekon (2019), to share his experience as an immigrant to the United States. Unlike "model minorities" from Japan, China, South Korea and other, more "developed" Asian countries, Soewarno grew up in Jakarta, Indonesia, and despite the fact that his father was a lawyer, he never had access to a formal education, instead working as a child in his parents' café and learning English by watching YouTube videos, many of which were hip hop music videos.[59] In the song, Soewarno makes references to alcoholism, suicide, and other struggles he faced as an immigrant; in the song's chorus, he sings, "Don't fight the feeling 'cause I'm yellow," a reference to Asian identity. In an interview with journalist Eric Diep for *Complex Magazine*, Soewarno explains:

> It's about Asian identity and in a more general sense, I wrote the song to let other Asians know that they can do what they want. Everything is possible. That's not something that you really think about, but if you don't have a role model to that . . . I'm not saying I am the role model or whatever. It's tough, you know?[60]

The video YELLOW (2019) begins with scenes from a suburban neighborhood where a house party is taking place, but Soewarno, representing a perpetual foreigner, is not invited and watches through a window from a house across the street, bathed in yellow light. Although he is standing, he is wrapped from head to toe in plastic or cling wrap, including over his face, which moves as he breathes, representing the way he felt when he moved to the US: "I'm fucked up and I'm suffocating. That's initially how I felt at the time. I felt like every time I hit a wall. I came to America when I was 17. And that's when I felt like, 'OK, what's next?' "[61]

As he breaks free from the plastic, his increasing confidence is palpable, but in a surreal twist, a hand emerges from his mouth, over the top of his head, and under the skin of his neck, clearly symbolizing the internal pressures he feels about making a name for himself and representing his country and race well. He finally breaks free from these pressures, too, jumping through the glass window and landing in his front yard as the house, along with all of the suffocating pressure inside it, burns behind him. Toward the end of the video, viewers see a number of fast-motion vignettes depicting scenes in Soewarno's life in which he struggles to overcome hardships and succeed in the music industry. Despite the fact that YELLOW is designed to dispel the model minority myth by showing how Rich Brian's experience was far from ideal, he does still hope to serve as a role model for other young immigrants:

> I want kids from all over the world to feel like they can make it no matter where they're from . . . I see myself in the same boat that many have travelled in before in hopes of reaching something better. This song is for the past, present, and future generations who brave new worlds with nothing guaranteed.

The likelihood that the message of this song is reaching young audience members is quite high; as of August of 2023, YELLOW has been viewed on YouTube nearly 20.5 million times.[62]

3

Digital Natives and Cultural Tourists

Indigenous Peoples in Music Videos

Within the last decade, the representation of Native Americans in popular culture has received increased media attention, namely through the controversy surrounding the Washington Redskins American football team name (renamed the Washington Commanders in 2022), several water rights disputes and oil pipeline projects on tribal territory, and horrific reports of the treatment that Indigenous children have faced in the Canadian child welfare system. Native American history and culture are often packaged and sold in museums as limited, encapsulated experiences that, at best, portray these cultures as friendly, gullible suckers whose kindness directly led to them becoming downtrodden victims of European settler colonists and the diseases they brought with them to the "New World." When they are not presented as victims, depictions of Indigenous cultures in the media are also often framed as "us against them" through uses of the "Cowboys and Indians" trope of Western films and television shows that reinforce racial stereotypes and xenophobia. Stereotypes about Native cultures and a general sense of unawareness or lack of empathy for these cultures are so ingrained in our culture that insensitive idioms and phrases, such as "low man on the totem pole," "circle the wagons," "hold down the fort," "sitting Indian style," "Indian summer," and references to someone "going off the reservation" often go unnoticed in our day-to-day lives.

This chapter discusses the issues surrounding the depiction of Native Peoples in music videos, especially the use of "redface" in music videos, including instances in which non-Native people adopt Indigenous dress and customs, and reinforce racist stereotypes with the inclusion of tropes that frame Indigenous people as "Indian princesses," "noble savages," "barbarians," "drunkards," or "sexy squaws" in music videos. It likely comes as no surprise that these modern-day stereotypes relating to Indigenous communities are a direct result of settler colonialism in which Europeans came to North and South America and many other places around the world, and through genocide, forced relocation, and various other forms of oppression, occupied and exploited the land on which these communities lived and worked for generations. Many of these stereotypes continue to prop up the hegemonic power of settler colonialism to this day and have roots in how we have historically understood Indigenous cultures. Indigenous

Audiovisual Alterity. Michael L. Austin, Oxford University Press. © Oxford University Press 2024.
DOI: 10.1093/oso/9780190277789.003.0004

Studies scholar David Stirrup writes that it has become "a truism almost beyond repetition that Native Americans have been of endless fascination to Europeans since explorers, from Columbus onward, located an archetype for the self-reflexive musings of sixteenth- and seventeenth-century intellectuals on the nature of Europe's civilization(s)."[1] Canadian historian Daniel Frances argues that "the Indian is the invention of the European," writing:

> The Indian began as a White man's mistake, and became a White man's fantasy. Through the prism of White hopes, fears and prejudices, Indigenous Americans would be seen to have lost contact with reality and to have become "Indians"; that is, anything non-Natives wanted them to be.[2]

The representation of Native Americans within our various forms of media has been as troubling as our nation's real-life relationships with the myriad native communities across North America. Throughout this chapter, we will see that cultural appropriation and other issues relating to insensitivity toward Native cultures in music videos is a perennial issue that continues into the present, and not only is it an issue for artists in the United States and Canada, but rather, it persists in a wide variety of genres around the world. However, in instances of "counter-appropriation" or "redemptive appropriation," members of Indigenous cultures also adopt tropes from the dominant settler colonist culture as a subversive way to more accurately represent themselves and their communities. It is important to keep in mind that although I refer to a wide variety of nations, people groups, tribes, and communities using broad terms such as Indigenous, First Nations, or Native communities, these terms do not encompass the great diversity of cultures, religions, languages, and perspectives among the members of these groups. Stereotypes about these groups are so persistent in our culture that there is a tendency to reduce the multitude of multifaceted Indigenous cultures to one overarching "Indian" culture with a singular language whose culture is on the brink of extinction; on the contrary, the members of these groups and their cultures and subcultures are thriving, as we will see throughout this chapter.[3]

I'm an Indian, Too

Despite the myriad ills of colonialism, decades of wars and genocide, continued disregard for Native sovereignty and rights to land, and geographic, economic, educational, and cultural marginalization, the dominant culture in the United States now seemingly purports to hold Native Americans in high esteem. However, this high esteem is often used as a cover for even further hegemony and cultural domination. Paradoxically, one can find some cultural caché in being able to claim native heritage. Shari Huhndorf writes, "Over the last century, going native has become a cherished American tradition, an important—even necessary—means of defining European-American identities and histories. In its various forms, going native articulates and attempts to resolve widespread ambivalence about modernity as well as anxieties about the terrible violence marking the nation's origins."[4] Journalist Gregory Smithers notes that claiming Indigenous heritage is a way for white Americans to communicate and authenticate a particular type of white Southern identity. In the 1840s and 1850s, large numbers of white Southerners began to claim that they were descendants of a Cherokee "princess" (despite the fact that such a role never existed among the various tribes of the Cherokee Nation) due to the obsession with social status that existed in the American South during the nineteenth century. Those who claimed a royal native ancestor "were legitimating the antiquity of their native-born status as sons or daughters of the South, as well as establishing their determination to defend their rights against an aggressive federal government, as they imagined the Cherokees had done."[5]

Periodically, claims of Indigenous descent or assimilation into a Native community appear in music, and as one might expect, these claims are often hamfisted and laden with negative stereotypes. In Irving Berlin's musical *Annie Get Your Gun*, the title character sings the stereotype-laden and highly offensive song, "I'm an Indian, Too," to celebrate the fact that she was adopted into the Sioux tribe by Sitting Bull. In their video I'M AN INDIAN, TOO (2012), the 1491s, a Native American sketch comedy group, critique the contemporary trend of appropriating Native American art, fashion, and culture.[6] In it, the 1491s adopt the disco cover of "I'm an Indian, Too" (1979) by Don Armando's Second Avenue Rhumba Band as the video's music track, setting the racially insensitive lyrics as the backdrop against which Ryan RedCorn (a member of the Osage Nation and one of the group's members) dances.[7] Wearing a warbonnet and a towel as a loincloth, RedCorn has the word "HiPSTER" (*sic*) written across his bare chest, and he dances absurdly with visitors at the Santa Fe Indian Market, a popular tourist destination. The video is interspersed with various still images of examples of appropriation of Native cultures ("sexy squaw" Halloween costumes, sports team mascots, romance novel covers, etc.), and features other "live" instances of appropriation, including RedCorn dancing with young white women (one of whom is wearing a cheap Indian costume headdress) and a young man wearing a tank top featuring a skull in Navajo print.

There is a sense of nostalgic innocence in thinking back to the 1950s and 1960s when little boys would dress up to play "Cowboys and Indians," reenacting their favorite Western-themed television show or movie. Play is another way in which our culture permits white people to "racially trespass" and assume the traits and aesthetics of marginalized communities without having to experience the day-to-day ramifications of living with a marginalized identity. Media Studies and Asian-American Studies scholar Lisa Nakamura writes about the ways in which video games afford white players to participate in "identity tourism," assuming avatars that allow them to appropriate a non-white racial identity in a way that is "recreational, exotic, and exciting," without having to experience any of the "risks associated with being a racial minority in real life."[8]

So what's the big deal with playing dress up, especially if you are dressing up as a person who belongs to a culture you claim to admire? In an interview for *Jezebel*, Jennifer Weston, member of the Hunkpapa Lakota and Standing Rock Sioux nations and former Endangered Languages Program Manager at Cultural Survival (a non-profit organization that advocates for the human rights of Indigenous people), eloquently sums up the damage this type of misappropriation can cause:

> When modern Natives see half-naked chicks strutting around on runways or street corners completely devoid of knowledge of our real cultures and religions, AND misrepresenting and misappropriating these sacred symbolic articles, we must demand respect for our religious practices. Such misrepresentations sexualize, commodify, and pervert our traditions—and impart to children of all cultures and backgrounds that it's perfectly acceptable to "play dress up" as a Native person, without regard for our ceremonial practices that have persisted here for millennia despite historic violence, and recent legal acts that literally outlawed our religions until 1978! Our ancestors and our parents survive attempted genocide (for their lands) and severe discriminations (for our languages and spirituality. So to pretend that we're fictional characters vs. real people from real cultures is not only offensive, and racist, it's a vicious act suppressing our lived realities as Native peoples, and an appropriation of our very identities.[9]

And just as we see these stereotypes and instances of "racial tourism" in television, film, video games, and other media, they also appear in music videos. An early example of this Indigenous cosplay is Cher's HALF-BREED (1973), a recorded performance filmed as part of *The Sonny & Cher Comedy Hour* (CBS, 1971–1974). In the video, Cher is wearing a costume designed by world-famous designer Bob Mackie that is based purely on stereotypes and sexualized tropes of Indigenous peoples, and includes a Plains-style war bonnet, a sexy version of a hair pipe breastplate, and a Vegas-style glittery loincloth. Although the song "Half Breed" is about the plight of a woman who is not accepted by her community because she is half white and half Cherokee, none of the elements of Mackie's costume are based on actual Cherokee regalia. The video begins with flames surrounding a totem pole, a sacred artifact to First Nations and

Indigenous communities in the Pacific Northwest (not the Cherokee Nation) as stereotypical war drums are heard in the background. Although a *People Magazine* article claims that Cher herself is the daughter of a mother "with Irish, English, German and Cherokee bloodlines, and a father . . . whose parents left Armenia after an ethnic-cleansing campaign conducted by the Ottoman Turks," there is no proof that Cher or her family have any formal or other recognized affiliation with the Cherokee Nation.[10] As late as 2017, Cher continued to perform "Half Breed" in public, with backup dancers wearing similarly insensitive costumes. Defenders still claim that Cher did not write the song herself and that "maybe, just maybe, it's less about Cher appropriating an identity and more about her assuming a character, telling a story."[11] However, the story she was telling through music—however fictitious or autobiographical—did not at all match the visual story she told in a culturally insensitive costume while sitting on a stationary white horse.

Another case of this type of racial trespassing can be seen in Tim McGraw's INDIAN OUTLAW (1994), although the harm is more clear in the music and lyrics than in the video's imagery. In a review for *Billboard Magazine*, critic Larry Flick wrote that the song "is positively stuffed with lyrical and musical Native American cliches, from tomtoms to wigwams to peace pipes. If this one becomes a hit, it'll set relations back 200 years."[12] Several radio stations around the country received complaints from Indigenous communities and decided to ban it from the airwaves. When asked for his reaction to the objections that some tribal communities had raised regarding his song, McGraw explains away their concern, claiming:

> You're concerned any time somebody doesn't like something you do, but you're never going to please everybody . . . A lot of times a song or something like the "tomahawk chop" isn't the real issue, but a means to an ends [*sic*] (for the protesters), a way to be heard.[13]

However, activist WaBun-Inini, president of the Minneapolis-based National Coalition of Racism in Sports and the Media and a national representative for the American Indian Movement was not pleased with McGraw's flippant response:

> I have no doubt that the intentions were not to be offensive . . . But if somebody told me something I did was offensive, I would apologize and not do it anymore. Now the ones who are doing the offending try to dictate to us what should be acceptable. That's boorish arrogance.

As was also the case with Cher's "Half-Breed," the song itself begins with stereotypical "Indian" musical tropes: minor key, open fifths, driving beat played on tom-tom drums, and melodic material based on (or in this case harmonizing with) a minor pentatonic scale.[14]

This riff, shown in Figure 3.1 and played on steel guitar, is reminiscent of the music that accompanies the "tomahawk chop," a celebratory gesture popular at sporting events among supporters of teams with Native American mascots or team names, such as the Atlanta Braves (professional baseball), Kansas City Chiefs (professional football), and the Florida State University Seminoles (various NCAA Division I college sports). Fans move their forearm up and down in a chopping motion, simulating a racist caricature of Native Americans in which they symbolically "scalp" their opponents. This movement is often accompanied by a song, shown in Figure 3.2, that is sung by the crowd which, like the "oriental riff" discussed in Chapter 2, is also racist and quite stereotypical. The music itself has roots in music composed for FSU's marching band to perform at football games in the 1960s, titled "Massacre," and a tune called "War Chant" used by the Florida State and the University of Illinois marching bands in the 1970s. These tunes were based on even earlier songs from the turn of the twentieth century that were themselves inspired, but not really informed, by the work of white ethnomusicologists working to collect and catalog Native American musical traditions.[15]

As shown in Figure 3.3, a more closely related variation of the "tomahawk chop" appears within "Indian Outlaw," heard at the end of an upbeat interlude between the chorus and the beginning of the third verse played on electric guitar and Hammond organ.

Figure 3.1 "Indian Outlaw" (1994) by Tim McGraw, mm. 1–4, steel guitar riff.

Figure 3.2 The "tomahawk chop" riff (transposed).

Figure 3.3 The "tomahawk chop" riff variation in McGraw's "Indian Outlaw" (1994).

Here, diminution of the rhythm of the original "tomahawk chop" is used to match the quick step of the dance break in which it is found while retaining the somber "war chant" aesthetic the riff mimics and appears to mock.

The representation of Native Americans within the lyrics of "Indian Outlaw" is equally callous. Claiming to be "half Cherokee and Choctaw," McGraw appears to be another example of white Americans claiming (without proof) that they are descendants of Cherokee ancestors. When facing criticism at the time of the song's release, he publicly claimed without providing any proof that his "maternal great-great-great-grandmother" was Cherokee.[16] Other reckless uses of stereotypes and tropes insulting to Native Americans in the song's lyrics include lines such as:

> You can find me in my wigwam / I'll be beatin' on my tom-tom /
> Pull out the pipe and smoke you some / Hey and pass it around

and:

> They all gather 'round my teepee / Late at night tryin' to catch a peek at me /
> In nothin' but my buffalo briefs / I got them standin' in line

The song ends with a reference to both the stoicism and bloodlust stereotypically associated with Native Americans, with McGraw singing that Cherokee people are "so proud to live / so proud to die," a quote from the chorus of "Indian Reservation" (1970) by Paul Revere & the Raiders.

While the misrepresentation of Native Americans within the song's lyrics is clear, the visual representation of Native Americans within the video is much less prominent, almost to the point of being unnoticeable. Much of INDIAN OUTLAW features McGraw performing in a dance club where he is standing on a round, mirrored stage as individuals and couples dance around him. In other scenes, McGraw is seen riding an Indian (brand) Motorcycle and playing pool while wearing an Avirex Choctaw Football Team leather varsity jacket, which features the portrait of a Native American wearing a war bonnet on the back. In 2015, McGraw released INDIAN OUTLAW (OFFICIAL LYRIC VIDEO) to coincide with the release of his retrospective compilation album, *Tim McGraw—35 Biggest Hits* (2015). This video includes additional visual references to Native Americans. Edited clips of the dance club scenes from the original INDIAN OUTLAW video play in the background while the song's lyrics appear as stylized animations on screen. Lyrical references to McGraw's "Indian Outlaw" persona are written in a stylized font used on the wanted posters seen in Western films, and the font used within the video for the other song lyrics matches this "Wild West" aesthetic. Occasionally, stereotypically Native American-themed graphics will appear, such as a flint-tipped arrow shot across the screen between words or eagle feathers sweeping lyrics away.

In early 1996, country music singer-songwriter Pam Tillis released THE RIVER AND THE HIGHWAY (1996), the focus of which is a heterosexual Indigenous couple from the Pacific Northwest. The video opens with a spoken monologue delivered by a stereotypical Native Elder or "sage," who explains that two people who come together may have different personalities and perspectives, but even though they have been independent, they sometimes meet at a particular point in life to travel together and support one another. In the video, the male protagonist is a log truck driver and represents "the highway" as he is emotionally unmoving, and Tillis explains in the lyrics that "he's headed for a single destination / he doesn't care what's standing in his path." He is stoic, a character trait that appears in stereotypical tropes for both "Noble Savages" and men in general who feel emotion but also face perceived expectations that they must put on a brave face. In contrast, the woman in the video is an artist and more of a restless, free spirit who represents "the river." Within the video, she is seen hitchhiking and drawing in a sketchbook on a bridge that overlooks white river rapids, and she is described in the song as someone who "follows the path of least resistance / . . . / She twists and turns with no regard to distance / She never comes to a stop."

There are several visual and cultural markers of indigeneity within THE RIVER AND THE HIGHWAY, but unfortunately, they do not point unfamiliar or uneducated viewers to a particular Indigenous nation or tribe. With the exception of bone necklaces (of unspecified cultural provenance), neither of the video's protagonists are wearing clothing that is generally identifiable as being particularly "Native," wearing denim jackets, jeans, and other casual Western wear quite common throughout North America. However, Tillis herself wears several Native or "Native-esque" items of clothing, including a large hair pipe breastplate (typically associated with Indigenous communities from the North American Plains), long beaded earrings, and lots of leather fringe. Several times throughout THE RIVER AND THE HIGHWAY, Tillis is shown performing in front of totem poles, which are carved wooden monuments created by several First Nations of the Pacific Northwest. The video ends with a scene in which the protagonists meet with the elder whose sage advice began the video in a plank house, a type of shelter constructed from cedar planks that is also emblematic of Native communities in the Pacific Northwest. As a native Floridian, Tillis certainly appears to be a tourist of sorts in these scenes; although she occasionally claimed Cherokee heritage at concerts, she would also quip, "My Indian name is Running Mascara," undermining any real claim to this cultural heritage, and she seemingly has no connections to First Nations of the Pacific Northwest.[17]

Aegyo Indians

The sexualization, commodification, and perversion of Indigenous traditions and aesthetics have also gone global. Take South Korea for example: after the Japanese colonization of the Korean Peninsula ended in 1945, the area was divided into two states: the communist North Korea and the anti-communist South Korea, occupied by the Soviet Union and the United States, respectively. Although the US relinquished its military administration of the territory it occupied to the newly formed South Korean government after three years, it continued to exert cultural influence in the country throughout the Korean War (1950–1953) and maintains significant influence today. Although many Koreans were previously introduced to Western hymns and folk tunes by Christian missionaries, Western troops exposed South Koreans to many styles of Western popular music through performances at USO shows and via radio broadcasts on the American Forces Korea Network. Strategic integration of films, television programming, and now the Internet provide a steady stream of Western ideals and American culture into South Korea. This cultural integration (rather than territorial imperialism) has been the American strategy to keep the constant threat of communism that lay just across the DMZ at bay.

In the last decade, K-pop has exploded into an enormously popular worldwide phenomenon, making a spectacular splash in US markets beginning with Psy's "Gangnam Style" in 2012. However, K-pop music videos and other related media are rife with instances of cultural appropriation and insensitivity. Communications scholar Gil-Soo Han describes the decades-long legacy of "blackface" in Korean media, recounting how blackface portrayals of African Americans by Koreans in television and film have become a marker of "nouveau-riche racism" and expression of ethnocentric nationalism, both of which rise from a mixture of brutal treatment based on skin color and ethnic identity during Japanese colonialism and interactions with Black American soldiers during the Korean War, with many of these negative perceptions and representations of African Americans being directly reinforced in globalized media coming from the West.[18] As we will see in this section, "redface," that is, the act of wearing makeup or clothing or otherwise impersonating Native Americans, First Nations, or other Indigenous cultures, is a similar problem in contemporary K-pop.

The United States was not the only foreign power to significantly shape popular culture in South Korea. Even though the Japanese colonization ended with World War II, Japan still exerted cultural influence over the peninsula, despite a regulation called the *Law for Punishing Anti-National Deeds*, enacted in 1945, which banned all media from Japan. Japanese culture was still a hot commodity, nonetheless; according to Roald Maliangkay,

> Although Japanese cultural products were banned until 1998, manga, anime and Japanese fashion magazines had long circulated on the Korean market, becoming readily available by the mid-1990s. This allowed them to make an impact on Korean aesthetics long before the start of the Korean Wave, the huge success of Korean popular entertainment overseas since the late 1990s.[19]

Aegyo (애교) is a Korean term used to describe a "cute" aesthetic (similar to Japan's *kawaii*) and denotes the childlike and submissive attitudes and behavior of K-pop stars. This term is also used to call out affected, saccharine, and over-the-top cuteness, and applies equally to male and female "idols" (or K-pop stars). Music critic Jon Caramancia sums up this aesthetic in a *New York Times* review of SM Town Live (a K-pop concert at Madison Square Garden in 2011) titled "Korean Pop Machine, Running on Innocence and Hair Gel," writing:

> Girls' Generation gave perhaps the best representation of K-pop's coy, shiny values in keeping with a chaste night that satisfied demand, but not desire. (It was an inversion of the traditional American formula; in this country young female singers are often more sexualized than their male counterparts.)
>
> Male and female performers shared the stage here only a couple of times, rarely getting even in the ballpark of innuendo. In one set piece two lovers serenaded each other from across the stage . . . In between acts the screens showed virginal commercials about friendship and commitment to performance; during the sets they displayed fantastically colored graphics, sometimes childlike, sometimes Warholian, but never less than cheerful.[20]

K-pop idol groups and their songs are built around "concepts," or specific themes that inform the group's identity and the aesthetics of their concerts, interviews and other appearances, and their music videos. The "Native American chic" aesthetic and other misappropriations of Indigenous culture in fashion and interior design are at best naïve conceptual mistakes, and at worst, poor choices used to propagate racist stereotypes about native cultures. Due to the pressure to develop unique concepts for groups and their songs, "Native American chic" appears from time to time in K-pop videos as a way to appeal to both American nostalgia and some forms of childhood play, specifically, "playing Indian" through the use of elements from a variety of Indigenous cultures with a cute, *aegyo* twist (however unfortunate and/or offensive).

Dressing as a Native American has long been a symbolic part of European-American history (for better or worse), stretching back to the Boston Tea Party when the Sons of Liberty co-opted the regalia of the Mohawk Nation as a symbol of American-ness and freedom when they attacked merchant ships in Boston Harbor and famously destroyed a tea shipment from the East India Company to protest the British *Tea Act of 1773*. In recent years, as American culture has become more critical of cultural appropriation, there has been much more public conversation and controversy surrounding the use of Native Americans as mascots for sports teams, sexy Halloween costumes and fraternity parties with "Native American" themes, and New Age appropriations of Indigenous spirituality.

As is the case with traditional or ceremonial fashion, hairstyles, and textiles of many other minority groups, the clothing, weaving patterns, and other ornamental designs of Indigenous communities in the United States have been appropriated by fashion designers eager to incorporate Native aesthetics into their own work with little or no regard for their cultural or religious significance. According to Karen Kramer, The Stuart W. and Elizabeth F. Pratt Curator of Native American and Oceanic Art and Culture at the Peabody Essex Museum in Salem, MA argues that designers

> appropriate Indian style for their own purposes . . . often [using] it to assert a kind of "true" Americanness, or to stand for reductionist concepts like "freedom" or "authenticity." Their garments may be handsomely executed; they may raise the profile or prestige of Native aesthetics. But when symbols of Native culture are deployed by people who don't understand their meaning, it's like a game of "telephone," where the message comes garbled. After all, the "America" these designs now represent is the same one that has oppressed its Indigenous people for so long.[21]

In this sartorial game of "telephone," culture is replaced with costume, and objects of significant religious or cultural value—even the community's name and other markers of their identity—are reduced to mere accessories in service of capitalism and colonialism. Likewise, "Native American chic" has become an unfortunate buzzword in the fashion industry as designers adopt native patterns, styles, and clothing as their own. Nicole Richie's "House of Harlow" line sold $225 moccasins in the early 2010s. Karlie Kloss famously wore a floor-length headdress and a bikini at Victoria's Secret Fashion Show in 2012 and Pharrell Williams wore one on the cover of *Elle UK*. This trend is also rampant in American popular music: Outkast's performance of "Hey Ya" at the 2004 Grammy Awards, Ke$ha's 2010 performance on *American Idol*, Ted Nugent's performance at many of his concerts, and Gwen Stefani's music video for "Looking Hot" (2012) are a few of many instances of pop stars misappropriating aboriginal regalia for style, giving little to no thought about substance. Further, in 2012, the Navajo Nation filed a trademark case against fast-fashion outlet Urban Outfitters, which sold more than twenty items using the Nation's unique textile aesthetics and "Navajo" in the name of their products, including a "Navajo Hipster Panty." Before settling the case out of court, lawyers for Urban Outfitters argued that their use of the name "Navajo" qualifies as fair use because it has "acquired a descriptive meaning within the fashion and accessory market . . . the fashion industry has adopted 'Navajo' to describe a type of style or print."[22] The divorce of the Navajo Nation and its cultural output led the company to believe that they were free to slap Navajo designs onto any item, including underwear, and trade in whatever cultural capital the Navajo Nation's name might carry among American consumers interested in the "Native American chic" aesthetic. In 2015, the designer of Dsquared2's Fall 2015 Ready-to-Wear line, Dean Caten, described the collection as if "a suitcase of clothes and jewels from Old Europe had fallen out of a plane over the icy tundra and been taken up by an Inuit tribe, who had incorporated the finery into their own tribal duds."[23] Writing about the collection, journalist Tim Blanks pushes Indigenous/First Nations communities even further toward the margins, fetishizing them and writing about the clothing's "erotic cross-cultural clash in the attenuated sass of women wearing tribal tattoos (body stockings), vast tundral pelts, and tasseled Napoleonic bullion braiding." He clearly separates the European style from the uncivilized Natives by claiming that "corset dresses, virginal draped nightdresses, and hyper-tailored little jackets spoke of high-flown civilization, while a hooded fur parka, a poncho, and a fringed blanket skirt were life on the ground."[24]

Traces of culturally appropriative "Native American chic" can be found throughout a number of K-pop music videos. For example, several elements of After School RED's IN THE NIGHT SKY (2011) incorporate this aesthetic: the choice to shoot this video in the desert, the "cowgirls vs. Indians" theme of the video, the turquoise guitar that appears in an early scene in the video, the bracelets and leather jewelry worn by many of the band members, and especially the headdresses and headbands worn by the "Native" faction. At the end of the video, the cowgirls and Indians get past their differences and do a rain dance around a bonfire, playing into the "Friendly Indian" or "Noble Savage" trope in which Indigenous community members are seen taking the proverbial high ground and overlook atrocities committed against them, and instead, befriend and support colonizers.

All singers in IN THE NIGHT SKY are "bagel girls," or [베이 (baby face) 글 (glamor body) 녀 (girl)], a "Konglish" (a mixture of Korean and English) *portmanteau* that describes a young female who is admired for her ***ba***by face and ***gl***amorous body; and despite their suggestive dance moves, they preserve their pretence of innocence by insisting in the song's lyrics that they only cry about their heartbreak in secret, and when they think about their lost love and get angry, they want to curse but refrain from doing so because it only hurts their own mouth. In this way, they also play into the "Indian Maiden" or "Sexy Squaw" tropes, which are as much hyper-sexualized and fetishized objects of desire as pillars of the community.

T-ara's YAYAYA (야야야) (2012) also includes aspects of the *aegyo* aesthetic in their misappropriation of native dress and customs and adoption of Western stereotypes of Native Americans and other Indigenous cultures. Although the narrative thread of the video is quite thin, it begins with a pilot, played by actor and musician No Min-woo, a Korean "flower boy" (or a male with feminine features and who is seen to naturally exude *aegyo*) flying a prop plane in a storm which crashes on a desert island. When he awakes, the pilot finds himself on a sandy beach, surrounded by members of T-ara. Here, the group's members assume the "Savage" trope as they capture and tie the pilot to a stake, suggesting they may be cannibals who plan to eat him. Adopting a variation of the "Sexy Squaw" trope—the "*Cute* Squaw" (although certainly still sexy as this variation is couched in a fetishization of playful, naïve girls)—members of T-ara are wearing very colorful "Native-inspired" clothing, with Navajo prints, beaded jewelry, and feathered headbands. Many of the group's members are also wearing "warpaint," with some group members wearing stripes under a single eye, and others with stars or other "cute" symbols; band member Park So-yeon's warpaint even includes a Star of David and a tear. Part of the *aegyo* present in their dance involves patting their mouths with their hands, an apparent appropriation of the Western misrepresentation of the vocal ululation practiced by some Indigenous American nations (Figure 3.4).

This sound can be heard over "tribal" drumbeats at the beginning of the song when they first capture the pilot, and its accompanying mouth-patting choreography can also be seen later during several iterations of the chorus when the group sings the lyrics "Let me see ya la la la la" and "Ah ah ah ah, go it, go it / Ah ah ah ah, do it, do it."

Figure 3.4 Mouth-patting in T-ara's YAYAYA (2012). (Screenshot by the author.)

Explaining the meaning of the lyrics, the song's producer E-Tribe evokes the tribal "Witch Doctor" trope:

> I used the hook technique to turn the song into a sort of riddle. I wanted the unique expressions to arouse the curiosity of listeners . . . I wanted to express the unique music through lyrics that sounded like *a spell.* Please don't misunderstand it and just enjoy the exciting music.[25]

Throughout the video, each member of the group takes a turn interacting with the pilot individually; for example, one gives him a drink, another brushes his hair, and yet another fans him and places a pillow behind his head to make him more comfortable before giving him a hug. The video ends as another man, coded as being less attractive than the pilot, wakes up on the beach and sees the attention the pilot is receiving at the hands of his doting captors; however, when he is tied to the stake and offers the group a kiss, they shriek and run away.

The scenery is perhaps the most striking use of "Native American chic" within YAYAYA. In his book, *Globalization and Popular Music in South Korea*, ethnomusicologist Michael Fuhr argues that although performance settings in K-pop music videos can often be abstract, conceptual, and super-modern, some are a "schematic representation of a familiar type of site" that is artificial in its appearance but is based on a place in the real world.[26] Fuhr goes on to explain that in order to appeal to American audiences, K-pop video directors sometimes include settings from "the historical repertoire of American popular culture," such as Motown, American football games, 1950s diners, and 1970s discos, so it comes as no surprise that the "spatial imaginaries" of YAYAYA would include vague, over-the-top, and arguably racist visual references to Native Americans.[27] The pole to which the pilot is tied is surrounded by teepees with colorful stripes and patterns from the fiber arts of the Navajo Nation and West Africa. In dance scenes, the group is surrounded by surfboards covered in colorful Navajo patterns while the floor is covered in black and white designs that point to origins in the arts of Indigenous communities in the Pacific Northwest. In what seems to be the interior of the teepees, viewers see walls covered in dashiki, floral, leopard, and zebra prints as well as Hawaiian "Aloha shirt" print. In other scenes with an even more abstract setting, the group dances between two giant disks composed of concentric circles, some of which are bright, solid colors, and others which are dashiki designs. In each case, there is a clear conflation of the "tribal" imaginary as so many aesthetic elements from a number of West African and Indigenous North American and Pacific Island cultures are haphazardly adopted purely for style and without due consideration or attribution.

The misappropriation of Indigenous aesthetics in MC Mong's INDIAN BOY, FT. JANG GEN EE AND B.I (2009) is even more flagrant in comparison to IN THE

NIGHT SKY and YAYAYA. The video begins with cliché "jungle" animal sounds, such as lion roars, elephant trumpets, monkey screams (and even an inexplicable wolf howl) as rapper and featured artist Jang Geun Ee peeks out from the jungle brush using binoculars and wearing a pith helmet with a yellow feather sticking out of it. As the song begins, "tribal" drumbeats are heard, performed both by on-screen "Natives" and the percussion line of a marching band while Jang Geun Ee, MC Mong, and others chant "oo ga cha cha / oo ga cha cha," yet another reference to the "Witch Doctor" trope. There is a clear similarity among these "nonsense" lyrics and those in the 1958 novelty song "Witch Doctor" by Ross Bagdasrian ("Ooh ee ooh ah ah ting tang walla walla bing bang"), and especially Blue Swede's 1974 hit cover of "Hooked on a Feeling" ("Ooga-Chaka, Ooga-Ooga"). The members of Blue Swede were inspired to include these syllables by English singer-songwriter Jonathan King's cover of the song in 1971, himself inspired by American rock and roll singer Johnny Preston's "Running Bear" (1959), a song full of racist musical caricatures of Native Americans.[28]

Later in the song, MC Mong refers to himself as "Jeranimong" (a *portmanteau* of his own name and that of the famous Apache warrior Geronimo) as he makes arrows while wearing a war bonnet and warpaint, creating a strange juxtaposition with the jungle setting of the video; later in the video, he and Jang Geun Ee are ambushed by another "Savage native" character (also played by MC Mong) wearing an Aztec-style headdress, including in a desert scene, despite the fact that the Aztec Empire was located in a primarily sub-tropical climate.[29] This "Savage" trope returns when twelve-year-old B.I concludes his featured rap break, he wraps his arms and legs around a pole to be carried off by MC Mong and Jan Geun Ee as if he were captured by cannibals.

In dance scenes, MC Mong, Jang Geun Ee, featured artist B.I, and other dancers wear headbands with single feathers and fuller war bonnets. In various parts of the video, dancers dance in stereotypical circles, and like T-ara in YAYAYA, ululate using their hands. When singing "Indian Boy" in each chorus, MC Mong places his index and middle fingers of both hands under each eye to mimic warpaint for "Indian" (a hand sign that reads as *aegyo*) and then flexes his biceps to represent "Boy." Even in instances that are not blatantly appropriative, there are still visual cues; for example, as he sits on the bleachers in the marching band drum major's uniform, he represents the band's "chief" (the feather plume signifying the war bonnet).

How are we to interpret the "redface" in these videos? On the one hand, strong American influence in South Korean media can be seen as media imperialism, an attempt to conquer and control South Korean popular culture through the homogenization of cultural artifacts, thereby shaping the ideology, desires, and identities of South Korean consumers, and the misappropriations of Native culture and artifacts are simply manifestations of this hegemony. In a way, these videos are colonial by several orders of magnitude, repressing Native American culture through media designed to repress native Korean culture through the acceptance of Western/American culture, all in order to repel the influence of communism and Japanese imperialism. Considering the troubling prevalence of both blackface and redface in K-pop music videos in recent years, it seems as if K-pop artists and video directors have found some of the worst parts of Western media and made them the conceptual linchpin in some of their music videos.

On the other hand, some see the popular appropriation of Native American art and artifacts as "cultural appreciation," or what Henry Jenkins calls "pop cosmopolitanism," referring to "the ways that the transcultural flow of popular culture inspires new forms of global consciousness and cultural competency."[30] Both of these arguments can be seen in online fan forums and the comment sections of YouTube videos and other social media. Global K-pop fans famously use media technologies both to find community among fans of the genre and particular groups, idols, or other aspects of K-pop fandom, and to engage in net activism and affect social justice—as happened, for example, when they flooded servers to thwart police suppression of peaceful Black Lives Matter protests in Dallas, Texas in 2020.[31] And while topics related to cultural appropriation and sensitivity are often featured in online forums, K-pop fans who also identify as BIPOC can often feel ignored, bulldozed, threatened, or altogether silenced when their own identities are up for discussion and fans ferociously defend the actions of their favorite idol or group, especially when these actions are harmful. In a groundbreaking study investigating the perceptions of their interactions with other fans online when discussing instances of cultural appropriation in K-pop, media studies scholar Kristin April Kim interviewed a number of Black and Native American K-pop fans and found that these fans are often mistreated online by other fans. Kim found that legitimate criticism of cultural appropriation in K-pop can be met with "severe backlash, particularly exacerbating the marginalization faced by Native American fans who encountered underrepresentation and limited support."[32] Alex Reid, K-pop's first Black idol and a member of the group BP Rania from 2015 to 2017, suggests that Korea's historically insular culture makes it hard for groups to understand the implications of some of the decisions they make when it comes to representation and appropriation of other cultures, but with pressure from a global fan base they have no choice but to improve. In an interview with *Dazed*, Reid said, "As K-pop gets so much more popular [entertainment companies] will realize the consumers, their fans, are of different cultures than just East Asian cultures, and they're going to realize they have to appeal to that market."[33] If their goals are not purely financial and they truly hope to embody increased cultural consciousness and competency with their music and music videos, many K-pop groups *and their fans* still seem to have a long way to go.

"Hear My Cry": Indigeneity and Self-Representation in Music Videos

Describing the ethics of representation within media and in scholarly contexts, Ella Shohat writes, "Each filmic or academic utterance must be analyzed not only in terms of who represents but also in terms of who is being represented for what purpose, at which historical moment, for which location, using which strategies, and in what tone of address."[34] As we have seen throughout this chapter and in other chapters, the power to represent others usually lies in the hands of those in the dominant culture. When Stuart Hall published his essay, "The Whites of Their Eyes: Racist Ideologies and the Media" in 1981, he argued that media serves as the principal form of ideological dissemination of social representation, describing to audiences "how the world is and why it works as it is said and shown to work."[35] Within these media, representation of the "other" has always been the "burden" of white media producers who are tempted to essentialize race and ethnicity, creating and reinforcing stereotypes as natural. Hall reiterates: "The 'white eye' is always outside the frame—but seeing and positioning everything within it."[36] The democratizing power of social media has afforded subaltern communities the opportunity to represent themselves to global audiences, shouldering the "burden" of their own representation, and bypassing and surpassing (to varying degrees of success) traditional hegemonic power structures.

As we have seen in previous chapters, appropriation isn't always necessarily a bad thing, especially when appropriative acts are used as rhetorical tools for the benefit of marginalized communities to enact resistance. In this form of appropriation—what I call "redemptive appropriation"—members of subaltern groups appropriate rhetoric or artifacts from the dominant culture and use them, ascribe redeeming qualities to them, or otherwise "rescue" them, in order to construct and express their own narratives and ideology. In her essay, "Counterhegemonic Acts: Appropriation as a Feminist Rhetorical Strategy," Helene A. Shugart describes ways in which

> members of various disenfranchised social groups . . . claim and utilize labels conventionally applied by their oppressors in a derogatory manner as a way of challenging their original meaning. Some lesbians and gay men, for example, refer to themselves as *dykes* and *faggots*, respectively; some African Americans defiantly refer to themselves as *niggers*; and some women celebrate their identities as *whores* and *bitches*.[37]

Describing the media post-production process, curator and art critic Nicholas Bourriaud explains how redemptive appropriation can also be a direct maneuver against power structures, writing, "It is a matter of seizing all the codes of culture, all the forms of everyday life, the works of global patrimony and making them function. To learn how to use forms . . . is above all to know how to make them one's own, to inhabit them."[38]

Lately, Native communities have had a few successes in terms of positive representation, and even recognition for these representations, in mainstream popular music culture and in reaching mainstream audiences. In fact, in 2001, the Recording Academy of the United States established a Grammy Award to recognize the "Best Native American Music Album" within the "American Roots" field; for the past twenty years, the Native American Music Awards have been recognizing the talent of Indigenous artists on their own terms. Native artists have been creating music videos that represent their struggles and successes for decades, sometimes in the form of videos in which the musical genre and aesthetics of hip-hop have been appropriated by younger generations within Indigenous communities who feel a sense of solidarity and kinship with urban, Black hip-hop artists. In "Toward a Hip-Hop Aesthetic: A Manifesto," rapper Danny Hoch advocates for hip-hop's potential power as a medium:

> Hip-hop art, when it is bad, is often embraced by the mainstream as the entirety of the talent and voice of the hip-hop generation. When it is good, outsiders and insiders alike misunderstand it for reasons of politics and fear. Bad hip-hop art is invariably inarticulate, unpolished, amateurish, juvenile. Good hip-hop art is highly articulate, coded, transcendent, revolutionary, communicative, empowering.[39]

By including Indigenous instruments, dance, costumes, and more, many Indigenous youth realize this potential and find ways to successfully represent themselves both collectively as a generation and through the individual stories of their own lived experiences in the context of their own tribal affiliations, family, geographic location, and so on, often in direct, defiant opposition to the continuing legacies of settler colonialism. Other videos demonstrate artists' dual affiliation with their native roots and their integration into the dominant culture through the use of hip-hop—a genre that, over the last fifty years, has moved from the margins of popular music, into the mainstream, and to the forefront of American musical culture.

Without access to major record labels and their ability to churn out quality music videos, many Indigenous youth make their own videos and share them on social media sites, such as YouTube and TikTok. Among the varied ways in which Indigenous communities are formed both within real and virtual spaces, cultural citizenship is facilitated by participation on social media. Discussing community formation online, William Uricchio writes:

> Community, freed from any necessary relationship to the nation-state, and participation, in the sense of active, then, are two prerequisites for the enactment of cultural citizenship . . . And it is in this context that I want to assert that certain forms of . . . participatory culture . . . in fact constitute sites of cultural citizenship. I refer here particularly to collaborative communities, sites of collective activity that exist thanks only to the creative contributions, sharing, and active participation of their members.[40]

By extension, I argue that there is relative freedom from the hegemony of traditional media found on the Internet, especially on social media; the way it facilitates participation and fosters participatory culture(s) allows for the emergence of cultural citizenship in which almost any willing participant can feasibly take a part. Communications scholars Jean Burgess and Joshua Green explain how YouTube affords this opportunity to develop digital citizenship:

> YouTube is a potential site of cosmopolitan cultural citizenship—a space in which individuals can represent their identities and perspectives, engage with the self-representation of others, and encounter cultural difference.[41]

So not only are Indigenous communities able to represent their own identities and perspectives through YouTube, but they are also able, through the participatory nature of social media, to use the site as a means to interface with other communities with which they identify, in this case, Black hip-hop culture. Indigenous cultures in other parts of the globe have also realized this potential in hop-hop well beyond an African American context, using it as a means of resistance and community building. Tony Mitchell writes that hip-hop is:

> a linguistically, socially, and politically dynamic process which results in complex modes of indigenization and syncretism. The global indigenization of rap and hip-hop . . . has become a highly adaptable vehicle for the expression of Indigenous resistance vernaculars, their local politics, and . . . the "moral geographies" of different parts of the world.[42]

Some Indigenous hip-hop artists see a direct link between life on "the rez" and life in "the ghetto;" for example, Flex, an Ojibwe hip-hop artist discusses the growing appeal that hip-hop is experiencing in Native communities because of the fictive kinship Indigenous youth feel with African Americans:

> Some of us have been doing it for years, but we really just got on the radar. Because it's so new, we're kind of where African Americans were with hip-hop 30 years ago, when it was about the message. These are intelligent people, they

> see how the world is run, they come from low-income areas with a lot of poverty and abuse, carrying shame, fear, and guilt along with them, and this is how they express themselves, this is how they let that stuff go.[43]

Through their appropriation of hip-hop, which has become one of the most dominant genres within the global capitalist juggernaut that is the US music industry, younger members of Native American communities and First Nations are finding their place, their culture, and each other.

Adopting many of the sampling and looping techniques of contemporary hip-hop MCs and turntablists, Apsáalooke Nation member Christian Parrish Takes the Gun, who lives on the Crow Indian Reservation in Montana and works under the stage name "Supaman," has been active as a hip-hop artist for nearly twenty years. In an interview with NPR, he says, "Native Americans grasp that culture of hip-hop because of the struggle. Hip-hop was talking about the ghetto life, poverty, crime, drugs, alcohol, teen pregnancy; all that crazy stuff that happens in the ghetto is similar to the reservation life. We can relate to that."[44] And his comparison is understandable: Native American reservations comprise some of the most poverty-stricken regions in the United States and Canada, and on these reservations, citizens face high rates of drug and alcohol abuse, crime, suicide, and high school dropout. Supaman confesses that he was not always able to see hip-hop's potential for good or social change. He recalls:

> It was just nonsense, it was just dumb. It was like gangsta rap, or something. The way hip-hop influenced me in my earlier years is in a negative way. I mean, I hate to say that, but it's true. We would play the part, you know. We were wannabees, trying to be, like, these rappers on the rez. So we started doing the crime, robbing, went into the house and traded the merchandise and then got weed from the merchandise, and then started selling.[45]

Supaman began touring with a record label from Seattle (with whom he eventually decided against signing), leaving his wife and baby at home. After a religious experience in his hotel room with a Gideon Bible, Parish began to produce Christian hip-hop and later socially conscious hip-hop that appealed to a broader audience. Supaman is most famous for a performance of his PRAYER LOOP SONG (2014), which was recorded live in the news studio of the *Billings Gazette* and released on the *Gazette*'s YouTube channel. After being featured by MTV's "Iggy Blog as the Artist of the Week" (March 2014), the video now has over 3.5 million views.[46] This exposure through social media launched Supaman as perhaps the best-known Native American hip-hop artist.

Hip-hop artist, Gates Scholar, and Sicangu Lakota Oyate member Frank Waln discovered hip-hop when he was twelve years old. Walking with his mother through the Rosebud Indian Reservation in South Dakota where they lived, he found a scratched Eminem CD in a ditch. In an interview with journalist Dawn Turner Trice the *Chicago Tribune*, Waln reflects, "I knew hip-hop resonated with the youth on my rez, but I never had a personal experience with it until that moment . . . It changed my life."[47] Many of Waln's songs deal with the fight of Native Americans against what he calls "symbolic annihilation," and he often recounts ways in which Native Americans are exploited or misappropriated in media, mirroring the same kinds of struggles described in socially progressive hip-hop in the Black community. On his 2012 single, "Hear My Cry," he raps:

> I was born red, stained with the blood of genocide /
> Now all mascots the only way that I'm identified /
> Blackhawk, Red Skin, the image of our dead men /
> Dressed in the headdress / my people it's depressing.

Waln attended Columbia College in Chicago to study audio arts and acoustics, and now he "describes himself as an activist who uses music and other art forms to improve the community.[48] Often collaborating with other artists and community members, Waln writes, records, and produces all of his own content, and says he is unwilling to give away creative control to a traditional label. Instead, "he relies exclusively on word-of-mouth and social media like Facebook, Twitter, SoundCloud and Instagram to market his music."[49]

Produced in conjunction with Outlast Film Camp (now Outlast Arts and Education), an organization that provides film and media arts education to Indigenous and Black youth from rural communities in South Dakota, Waln released his video WOKIKSUYE (2018) in honor of Indigenous Peoples Day, a redemptive appropriation of the national holiday established in the United States to celebrate Christopher Columbus' colonization of the New World each year on October 8. Using Waln's song, "Wokiksuye" (2018) as the video's track, the youth participating in the camp created all of the visual elements of the video. According to Waln, "They did the makeup, picked the locations, everything . . . Every shot and scene is their way of showing the world what life on the rez is really like."[50] Waln also explains the Lakota words used throughout the song, including its title:

> The song's title and hook are, in Lakota, "Wokiksuye," which means "remembrance,". . . "Wokiksuye Mi Oyate" means "remembrance of my nation"; "Wokiksuye Mi Tiwahe" means "remembrance of my family." It's really important to remember who you are, where you came from, and those who came before you.[51]

The video features children and teenagers wearing both traditional and Western clothing, sometimes at the same time, demonstrating the two worlds which many of them straddle every day; for example, the video opens with a young girl dancing in a traditional beaded turquoise dress while wearing a "Hello Kitty" necklace around her neck.

The hip-hop duo Snotty Nose Rez Kids (SNRK), Quinton "Yung Trybez" Nyce and Darren "Young D" Metz are members from the Haisla Nation and originally from Kitamaat Village, British Columbia, who take a more iconoclastic position with their lyrics and videos—evident even in the name under which they perform. As American Studies scholar Stefan Benz explains:

> By selecting the phrase "Snotty Nose Rez Kids" as their *nom de plume*, as the title of the album and its first song, the two rappers arguably assume a performative stance that is anti-capitalist. The phrase identifies a two-sided performative stance of adolescent deviancy and of the grief that they see defining Indigenous experience.[52]

In BOUJEE NATIVES (2019), SNRK adopt the hip-hop music video trope of extravagant displays of aspirational wealth, but rather than flashing gold chains and grills, fancy cars, stacks of money, sneakers, and other items stereotypically associated with the genre, they instead brag about cultural riches from their own Native community: turquoise bracelets, large-brimmed hats, custom beaded necklaces, new cedar and sage, and holding knowledge in their braids. After a montage of clips in which the members of SNRK put on rings, necklaces, and hats and prepare a cup of coffee, Nyce, Metz, and other young people sit around a table and enjoy a meal of salmon, fry bread, mussels, and other foods associated with First Nations in the Pacific Northwest. The only other scene in the video takes place outdoors at night around a campfire. SNRK describe their crew, taking special care to make sure to highlight those who represent their community well: "I got carvers, weavers, beaders and designers on my team / I got braiders hella famous that I'm signing to my team," and a few bars later: "I know ballers, I know chiefs, I know riders from the east / I know educated natives down to picket in the streets." In an interview with journalist Tamara Ikenberg, Nyce notes:

> Everyone in that video represents something in our community that we come from here in Vancouver and they're all artists . . . We were just messing around and all that, having fun with it. When we talk about rich kids, we talk about the seafood that comes from their territory . . . When we say boujee Native, we're not talking about glitz and glamour. We're talking about land defenders, chiefs that we respect, elders . . . We're talking about knowledge people.[53]

They also adopt and subvert other hip-hop tropes in the song's lyrics. They call their love interest "my indigi-queen," stating that "My wifey be the wolf and I'm the wolf that's from the sea / And she no Pocahontas, more like Buffy Saint Marie," referring to the legendary Canadian American singer-songwriter, social activist, and member of the Piapot Cree Nation. Several times throughout the song, they mention the term "Neechie," meaning "my friend" in the Ojibwe language, and they even use the phrase "Neechie, please." The use of this particular Indigenous "n-word" is a nod to the phrase "N*gga, please," which is both the title of a 1999 album by American rapper Ol' Dirty Bastard and an expression of annoyance used in some Black communities that has been redemptively appropriated from a racial slur that was (and unfortunately, often still is) used against them.

SNRK's video HOT PLANET (2022) focuses on the growing crisis of global warming and the role that settler colonists are playing in exacerbating the issue. In an interview with Nick Krewen for *The Toronto Star*, Metz explains how the song has a double meaning: "It's about climate change . . . It's about us f--ing up the planet. But at the same time, we're paralleling it with our careers and how we're hot at the same time. It's a negative and a positive."[54] This dual meaning is clear in the song's lyrics, such as "I'm hotter than the grease when my grandma make her bannock / We're hotter than the planet, we never couldn't never planned it."[55] They also directly address settler colonialism, rapping:

> Not your token injun, no, no. /
> Fuck I look like homie, Tonto? /
> Rez boy extraordinaire, ain't never been that's so so /
> Long hair and I don't care, pride tatted on my torso

They claim that their identity is integral to who they are and that settler colonists were only able to colonize the distorted, fake caricatures of their Native identity: "And I've always been me, can't change me / You colonized my fugazi."[56]

HOT PLANET opens with Metz and Nyce sitting outside of a campervan in camping chairs in sweltering heat at the mouth of Palo Duro Canyon, the second largest canyon in the United States, located in the Texas Panhandle, just southeast of the city of Amarillo. The canyon is significant in the history of US–Indian relations as it was once home to the Clovis and Folsom peoples several thousand years ago, and more recently, the Apache, Comanche, and Kiowa Nations used its resources. However, in 1874, a battle between the 4th US Cavalry against a camp of Comanches, Kiowas, and Cheyennes who were fighting together against the American settler colonists in the Red River War

(1874–1875), resulted in defeat for the Plains Indians after Colonel Ranald S. Mackenzie and his men slaughtered their ponies, burned all of their teepees and winter stores of food and supplies, and removed them to reservations in Oklahoma.[57] Soon after, the canyon became part of the JA Ranch, founded by Charles Goodnight and John Adair, and in 1934, the canyon was set aside as a state park. Throughout the video, viewers see several landmarks and icons of the Texas Panhandle, such as a Route 66 air freshener hanging in the rearview mirror of the campervan, the duo rapping in the parking lot of the Big Texan Steak House (famous for offering a free 72oz steak to anyone who can eat it and its accompanying sides in an hour), cattle, and miles of flat yellow grassland. Toward the conclusion of the video, the song's ecological and political message about global warming becomes even more evident in the visual elements of the video when the campervan overheats to the point that it explodes in a fireball, knocking the members of SNRK into the canyon. The video ends as the camera zooms out from inside the camera all the way out into space where viewers see the world becoming engulfed in flames.

Drezus is the stage name of Jeremiah Manitopyes, a member of the Plains Cree-Saulteau people. He has overcome a great deal of personal adversity, including a personal history of drug abuse and spending time in jail for drug-related crimes, and now uses the trap and gangsta rap subgenres of hip-hop to tell the story of his life and to fight for social justice on behalf of First Nations and Indigenous groups. He first found some professional success with the hip-hop collective Team Rezofficial in the 2000s, releasing two nationally distributed albums through EMI. The group was invited to perform in a concert that was part of the opening ceremony of the 2010 Vancouver Olympic Games, but Drezus was in jail in Winnipeg on his second distribution charge and thus unable to participate.[58] In a deal to reduce his sentence, he agreed to enter rehab in 2012, where he took part in a cultural course in which he was introduced to aspects of his ancestry, such as Native songs and traditional drumming. In an interview with journalist Reed Jackson for *Vice*, Drezus explains how his song and video WARPATH (2014) were designed to give hope to the men in his community on similar paths to his, saying: "I just wanted to be like, 'Yo be strong. We don't have to be selling dope or stabbing people. We have a bigger fight to take on.'"[59]

WARPATH opens with striking visuals closely linked to Indigenous culture, namely a teepee and a campfire. Clutching a beaded cross necklace, Drezus begins rapping in black light, talking about how he has "risen through the fire in colorful buckskin" to overcome hard times, and how although there is a division between various Indigenous groups and death and genocide has been a long part of his people's history, he still stands, "a singular red man / with a Jupiter-sized heart, forever reppin' my clan." And although he's not advocating for literally "going on the warpath," Drezus proposes in the song's chorus that men in his community lay aside their differences and join him in community advocacy:

> Big Chief in the building, everybody take your place (hooh) /
> Remove your feelings if you wanna ride with me (hooh) /
> We about to go to war right now, no petty ass beef (hooh) /
> And when it all go down, who's gonna ride with me? (Hooh)

Throughout the video, audiences see more visual symbols associated with Indigeneity that are linked in the cultures of settler colonists with going to war with Native groups, such as a large collection of arrowheads, war bonnets, warpaint (including a large white handprint over Drezus' mouth), ceremonial drumming, and running horses. Several children also appear in the video wearing warpaint, representing strong familial links and the importance of passing various aspects of Native cultural heritage to the next generation. WARPATH won the award for Best Music Video at Canada's Indigenous Music Awards in 2015.[60]

So, if young Native Americans are creating these videos, who is watching them, and why? Burgess and Green argue that:

> The dominant discourses around participatory culture (including the very idea of a gap in participation) appear to frame passive engagement as a kind of lack—continuing to affirm and reward those who speak more than those who listen. Some of the excitement and energy around participator culture was motivated by the possibility that those of us who had been limited to the role of the "passive" audience could become producers, and therefore more "active" participants in the media. While the affordances of the technologies have increased the range of producers, and undoubtedly move a significant number of people toward cultural production, continuing to value only those who produce replicates the politics of the previous system.[61]

Not only do Native hip-hop music video producers interface with Black hip-hop culture by producing their own hip-hop videos, but audiences also become involved through their own participation in online forums and social media posts, and merely engaging with the content of these videos by watching them. It is important to consider consumption and audience practices as significant modes of participation; therefore, in a way, listening to and commenting on Indigenous hip-hop music videos gives other Indigenous youth yet another way to find their own voices. And although great value can be found in the ability of young Indigenous people to represent themselves within the dominant media culture, these videos are clearly valuable tools, serving as representative media for others in Indigenous communities in a format to which they can relate and in a forum that is much more open for their participation.

4

Camp, Kitsch, and Cowboys

Queerin' Country Music Videos

Stereotypes are hard to break, and in few places is this more painfully obvious than in the American South. The South is often portrayed as a rural, working-class place where education is undervalued, drawls and twangs are signs of inferior intelligence, and bigotry is either welcomed with open arms or hiding in plain sight. This perception often extends to uninformed or prejudicial opinions about country music. In the late 1970s, Michael Bane wrote in *Country Music Magazine*, "At best, [country music is] the living image of Southern culture; a fusion of the varied and sometimes antagonistic elements of southern life. At its worst, it's awful, a sort of mindless, shake-your-butt- disco music for the smash-the-beer bottle-over-the-waitress'-head set."[1] These stereotypes often hold little to no truth whatsoever: three out of four Southerners live in metropolitan areas, the "Research Triangle" of North Carolina, the "Silicon Prairie" of Dallas-Fort Worth; and other areas, such as Houston, Austin, Atlanta, and South Florida, prove to be academic and corporate epicenters rivaled by few places above or below the Mason-Dixon line. And attitudes about race, gender, and especially sexuality are quickly changing down South and across the entire United States. The LGBTQIA+ community still faces many obstacles and still fights for many equal rights that have not yet been won; however, public support for same-sex marriage has risen from 22% in 2003 to an astounding 71% in 2023, and it has consistently been above 50% since the early 2010s.[2]

Riddled with toxic masculinity, racism, sexism, Christian nationalism, and so on, country music potentially represents the ills of Southern culture (or frankly any culture). Conversely, country music and its stars have also been at the forefront of championing social justice issues and in advocating for society's most progressive changes. Ranging from blatantly homophobic depictions of weak, effeminate men to compelling portrayals of healthy same-sex relationships, country music videos embody this cultural split quite well. This chapter explores the ways in which the slow turn toward acceptance in country music of the LGBTQIA+ community can be viewed in country music videos. It also examines the reception history of videos that fall within this category and discusses the success many of these videos enjoy, despite appearing online only or in niche

Audiovisual Alterity. Michael L. Austin, Oxford University Press. © Oxford University Press 2024.
DOI: 10.1093/oso/9780190277789.003.0005

markets rather than on mainstream outlets such as Country Music Television (CMT). Further, it sheds light on the delicate aesthetic (and career) choices country music stars (whether personally identifying as queer or as an ally) and drag performers make when creating country music videos with queer themes.

History, Homophobia, and Hillbilly Music

In *Rednecks, Queers, and Country Music*, the musicologist and gender studies scholar Nadine Hubbs explains the connection between these enduring stereotypes and country music:

> Long heard as an affront by those targeted with it, the word *hillbilly* marks one as being from the country, originally, from Appalachia, and it bears connotations of ignorance and lack of sophistication. Notably, "hillbilly" was also for thirty years the standard industry label for the music now known as country. The music's name changed to "country and western" in the 1950s recognized hillbilly's derogatory status, but it was not a complete image makeover. Country audiences are still associated with white working-class, provincial, and southern identities, as well as ignorance and in recent decades, bigotry.[3]

Hubbs goes on to discuss ways in which, despite having shed the name "hillbilly," country music continues to drag behind itself a *phantom hillbilly*, a cultural albatross of sorts that represents the negative stigma associated with country music and its storied past. Country is a genre from which people are quick to distance themselves when asked to declare their musical tastes; with a quick, condescending dismissal, many attempt to avoid the curse of the phantom hillbilly by answering, "I'll listen to everything *but* country," and in doing so, they escape the sociological stigma that comes with it.

Detractors of country music conjure up the phantom hillbilly that Hubbs describes by pointing out instances in country music lyrics and images in country music videos that are particularly hateful or otherwise harmful, particularly those associated with racism, sexism and the treatment of women, and hyper-masculine heteronormativity. Likewise, country music has always maintained a tenuous relationship with topics and issues surrounding homosexuality, fluid gender roles, and gay performers. Of course, as long as there have been cowboys and cowgirls, there have been LGBTQIA+ people in these roles, and their lives have long been reflected in country and western music. In an essay titled "Frontier Comrades: Homosexuality in the American West," Jim Wilke writes about how men would sleep together, paired up with their "bunkie," and would engage in "mutual solace," or what Wilke calls "a tender, expressive, and euphemistic terra for sexual relations."[4] And songs that described "phallic size, virility, and sodomy were sung around the campfires.[5]

As early as 1939, Vernon Dalhart's "Lavender Cowboy," a song about an effeminate cowboy troubled about his lack of chest hair, was banned from the radio; the Sweet Violet Boys' "I Love My Fruit" (1939) was so laced with double entendres, it's hard to imagine how the song ever even made it onto the airwaves. Some in country music have found an outlet for LGBTQIA+ topics in parody and comedy songs: In 1973, the band Lavender Country, led by singer/songwriter Patrick Haggerty, released the first gay-themed, self-titled country album, which included songs such as "Back in the Closet Again" and "Cryin' These Cocksucking Tears." Although humor and entertainment played a large role in their music-making process, the driving force behind the band was activism and raising awareness. Journalist Graeme Thomson writes about some of this work:

> The band were active at an organisation called the Counselling Service for Homosexuals, so in return it "passed around the hat", enabling them to buy studio time, press 1,000 copies of their album, and send it out to alternative radio stations and community groups along the Pacific coast. One DJ lost her license for playing Cryin' These Cocksucking Tears.[6]

Haggerty viewed the record as part of an information drive to explain what it meant to be gay in the early 1970s—and to provide reassurance to those in the community who needed it. "It was primarily a record for the lesbian and gay community, especially for people trying to come out," he says. "In the early days of the gay movement, public education was a big deal. I mean, the American Psychological Association still felt gays were mentally sick. All that horseshit. There was so little valid information and the record was good for that. It gave definition to ourselves, rather than accepting the absurd definition handed down by society."[7]

As time went on, songs about gays, lesbians, and drag performers continued to be released by members of the LGBTQIA+ community, and *straight* artists alike, in the form of novelty songs, such as Don Bowman's "Hollywood Clothes" (1964). Borrowing some of the rhythms, chord progressions, and instrumentation from the exotica genre of music popular at that time, "Hollywood Clothes" transports listeners to the foreign locale of Hollywood, California, where they are greeted by an especially campy native: "Hi ho, clothes fans! It's me, the world's best dressed creature!" Listeners are regaled with stories about his sartorial adventures, which include wearing a small suit with a tight jacket that got him confused for a bellhop and a valet.[8]

Other examples of these novelty songs include Rod Hart's "C.B. Savage" (1977), "The Ballad of Ben Gay" (1973) by Ben Gay and the Silly Savages, the Charlie Daniels Band's extremely homophobic "Uneasy Rider '88" (1988), and Richard Thompson's "Woman or a Man" (1982), all of which were dripping with innuendo and crude humor. For many years, it seemed as though camp and humor were the only acceptable ways to address queer issues in country music, most of which was either self-deprecating at best, or more likely, blatantly homophobic. Even outspoken LGBTQ-supporter Willie Nelson released a couple of LGBTQ-themed novelty songs, such as "Ain't Goin' Down on Brokeback Mountain" (2009), the chorus of which is:

> But I ain't goin' down on Brokeback Mountain /
> No, I ain't goin' down on Brokeback Mountain /
> That shit ain't right (That shit ain't right) /
> That shit ain't right (That shit ain't right)

Writing about the role that humor plays in the social construction of gendered and ethnic stereotypes, social scientist R. Kirk Mauldin recounts the various ways young men use homophobic humor as a means of socialization that reinforces heteronormativity and stigmatizes any variance from this norm.[9] Many of the humor categories Mauldin delineates directly correlate to many of these comedy and novelty songs—specifically, "Normative Prohibition" (it is funny because it is naughty), "Stereotypical—Sexual Fixation" (it is funny because it turns someone on too much)," "Stereotypical—Effeminacy" (it is funny because it is girly), "Latent Homosexuality—Who's Gay?" (it is funny because someone is secretly gay), and "Latent Homosexuality—Crossing Over" (it is funny because it might turn you gay)—have clear parallels in these comedy and novelty songs. Many of these examples rely heavily on homophobic tropes and reinforce the stereotypes of ignorance and bigotry of the phantom hillbilly. For example, Lonzo and Oscar address the stereotypes of incestuous rural families in their song "I'm My Own Grandpa" (1948). Even Freddy Weller's "Betty Ann & Shirley Cole" (1973), one of the most superficially innocuous country songs about same-sex couples, played up stereotypes about lesbians in a song about a couple, named in the song's title, who lived the life of spinsters under their families' care and wear their hair short. Going even further, the song employs the "psycho lesbian" trope and even insinuates that the women killed Betty Ann's brother-in-law, Parson Brown, so they could be together, ending with the lyrics:

> Now bad news travels fast especially in a little town /
> But still no one was sure what took the life of Parson Brown /
> Rumor has it his last breath cried out for Betty Ann /

But at the gravesite she and Shirley Cole were holdin' hands /
Oh, could it be there're some things even God don't understand?

While most of these earlier songs did not have videos, per se, country music has been featured on television for almost as long as people have been watching TV. Country and western became quite popular in America after World War II, and by 1956, "almost 100 live local country and western shows aired on more than 80 stations in 30 states. Famous shows such as *Ozark Jubilee*, *Tennessee Ernie Ford Show*, *Stars of the Grand Ole Opry*, and later *Hee Haw* brought the visual elements of country music into homes across the nation, and most of the time, they capitalized on the stereotypes used in the Western-themed films and TV programs that were also popular at that time. Depictions of LGBTQIA+ people on these shows were rare, but often harsh; for example, Roy Clark is infamous for a pejorative sketch on *Hee Haw* in which he played the role of a lisping, effeminate country poet named Claude Strawberry who wore a frilly shirt under his overalls and delivered quatrains about trying to enlist in the military but having to settle instead for a martini when he was rejected by each branch, presumably for being a homosexual. In these early days, the LGBTQIA+ community had no voice on country music television unless straight country stars under the guise of a campy persona spoke for them—with an exaggerated lisp for comedic effect. Even with CMT's premier in 1983, country's answer to MTV, gay country singers did not—and currently still do not—have a mainstream commercial media outlet for music videos that depict the LGBTQIA+ community on its own terms.

The first country music video with a *possible* gay theme is Pirates of the Mississippi's FEED JAKE (1991). Although the executive producer noted the video was "not meant one way or the other," the song does feature seemingly LGBTQIA+ affirming lyrics:

If you get an ear pierced some will call you gay /
If you drive a pickup you must be straight /
What we are and what we ain't /
What we can and what we cain't /
Does it really matter?

In the vignette at the beginning of the video, the protagonist and his "friend" are seen as teenage boys, horsing around and teasing one another about asking out girls they like. On the one hand, I should note that many young gay men date young women when they are young for a number of reasons, some of which have little to do with sexual attraction; on the other hand, this could also be seen as a latent homosexual relationship couched in furtive heterodoxical expressions of platonic male friendship. Some believe the two primary male characters in the video are lovers, that the fashionable protagonist is "cruising" a cowboy at the gas station as they trade a "long hard-to-read look" as the gay-referencing lyrics are sung, and the singer implores his lover to feed his dog, Jake, if he dies, presumably as a victim of the ravaging AIDS epidemic of that time.[10] Perhaps because this video was not overt in its lyrical or visual references to homosexual relationships, this music video was played on CMT and enjoyed wide distribution.

The Pirates of the Mississippi's tacit, heuristic support for—or better yet, ambivalence toward—same-sex relationships was not nearly as controversial as other instances in which country artists were much more outspoken about their support. Although those with a queer reading of this song presumed that the person who would die in the song would be a victim of AIDS, Gulf War I was also occurring around the time this song was released, so many more took the view that it was simply that his friend may die in combat. *Billboard Magazine*'s Nashville columnist Edward Morris even wrote, "I think it would take an English teacher doing a dissertation to come up with a gay story there. (But) the fact that it`s been interpreted that way may signal some sort of advance."[11] When asked about the song's possible meaning, Jennifer Dunn, a member of Ken Stilts Co., the Nashville-based management firm that represented the Pirates of the Mississippi, exclaimed, "That's the first I've heard of that! Has that been in print?" Kimberly Lansing, executive producer at Nashville's Deaton Flanigen Productions, Inc., the company where the video was directed and produced, seemed less surprised when she said, "The video means different things to different people, (but) it was not meant one way or the other . . . The (various) interpretations are not startling to us at all. We're just really pleased with everyone's thoughts and feedback."[12]

Critics may be quick to dismiss any queer readings of mainstream country music as "wishful thinking" or an exercise in finding connections where there are none. Rest assured that the goal of this chapter is not to conjure up *queer* "phantom hillbillies" from the ether that could possibly haunt country music, nor do I seek to drag country music from the closet (or force it into one). Instead, in cases such as FEED JAKE, it is better to scrutinize these videos from an open "hermeneutic window," *à la* Lawrence Kramer. With this metaphor, Kramer argues that analysts can approach music via *textual inclusion* (such as "texts set to music, titles, epigrams, programs, notes to the score, and sometimes even expression markings"), *citational inclusions* (which are links between musical elements and other inter- and extra-musical influences, such as a shared title with a literary work, for example), and through what Kramer a *structural trope*—"a structural procedure, capable of various practical realizations, that also functions as a typical expressive act within a certain cultural/historical framework."[13] He goes on to explain that structural tropes, "the most powerful of hermeneutic windows," are "units of doing rather than units of saying" that "cut across traditional distinctions between form and content. They can evolve from any aspect of communicative exchange: style, rhetoric, representation, and so on."[14] As such, our reading of country music—or any music—is not limited by what is actually there in the music, but rather should be informed by the culture in which we as analysts find ourselves. And notice I did not say "in which the music finds itself." All anthropomorphizing aside, just as Kramer argues that the "texts" that are scrutinized in these readings "do not establish (authorize, fix) a meaning that the music somehow reiterates, but only invite the interpreter to find meaning in the interplay of expressive acts,"[15] queer theorist Alexander Doty argues that "queer readings and positions can [and do] become modified or change over time as people, cultures, and politics change . . . thereby suggesting that queerness does not reside in the text, but rather is produced in and through the ever-changing relations between texts, readers, and the world."[16] In other words, although the meaning of music is an inextricable part of the music itself and its constituent formal and stylistic elements, its meanings are "produced as part of the general circulation of regulated practices and valuations."[17] It is here in the "general circulation of regulated practices and valuations" that we can investigate the queerness of country music, especially when considering the role that the appropriation of camp, kitsch, and other aesthetic elements that exist in the actual media, in the material culture surrounding it, and in the zeitgeist from which it arises might play in the interpretation, reinterpretation, and reception of these videos.

In trying to address uncomfortable, yet culturally relevant topics like homosexuality or heteronormativity, artists sometimes make things worse rather than better, further reinforcing the pejorative stereotypes. For instance, country music superstar Taylor Swift has found herself in hot water on several occasions for her questionably homophobic song lyrics and representations of gay men in her music videos. Released on her self-titled album of 2006, her break-up revenge song "Picture to Burn" featured the lyrics:

> State the obvious, I didn't get my perfect fantasy /
> I realize you love yourself more than you could ever love me /
> So go and tell your friends that I'm obsessive and crazy /
> *That's fine I'll tell mine that you're gay /*
> By the way . . . (emphasis mine)

Many felt as though Swift was insinuating that spreading a lie about someone being gay was acceptable behavior, and worse, that being gay was somehow a bad thing, further perpetuating negative attitudes about the LGBTQIA+ community.

In response to the resulting controversy, the offending line: "That's fine I'll tell mine that you're gay . . ." was changed to "That's fine you won't mind if I say . . ." in the music video. In 2011, Swift released "Mean," a song to hit back at music critics, and marketed the song and video as an anti-bullying campaign of sorts. Many critics were shocked that Swift would go to such lengths; for example, *Entertainment Weekly* incredulously asked, "Is she really equating a professional critic questioning her ability to sing at an awards show to getting bullied because you're different?"[18]

Aside from the seemingly mixed messages Swift was sending with the marketing of this video, the message sent about support for the bullied through the video is also a little unclear. As Swift sings, "You, pickin' on the weaker man" at the end of the first verse of "Mean," a young high school student is sitting in a locker room, wearing a lavender sweater and bow tie, and reading a fashion magazine—a stereotypical gay teenager in almost every way. As one can see in Figure 4.1, several football players stand around him, jostle and taunt him, and try to take away his magazine. During the chorus, the lights in the locker room darken, leaving only a spotlight on the bullying victim, his mouth in sync with Swifts, singing "Someday, I'll be big enough so you can't hit me."

Here, little interpretive license is required to see the visual and aural representation of young homosexual men as effeminate (replacing the "gay" teenager's voice with Swift's female voice) and helpless (as he longingly looks into the distance waiting to be big and strong enough to defend himself).

Figure 4.1 "Gay" bullying victim in Taylor Swift's MEAN (2011). (Screenshot by the author.)

Camp Fires and Camp Aesthetics: How Camp Is Country Music?

Despite the rugged masculinity, down-to-earth sensibilities, and performative "traditional" values adopted by many country stars and personalities, and as the aforementioned comedy songs can attest, country music has long had its wagon hitched to camp aesthetics. Anyone familiar with the work of Dolly Parton, or who has seen the rhinestone-encrusted "Nudie Suits" (named for the Hollywood haberdasher, Nudie Cohn, that made them) worn by Porter Wagoner, Roy Rogers, Dale Evans, Gene Autry (and many others), or who has ever ridden in a Pontiac Bonneville with Texas longhorns strapped to the hood knows that camp aesthetics are in no way limited to marginalized homosexual country singers. In her essay, "Notes on Camp," Susan Sontag provides a sort of stream-of-consciousness-styled assessment of camp as expressed in the middle of the twentieth century wherein she prescribes the qualities of camp and delineates that which does and does not count as camp. Mark Booth helpfully summarizes this list, sorting each aphorism and maxim into one of five categories, claiming that Sontag qualifies things as camp when:

1. They are marginal
2. They are artificial or exaggerated
3. They are *démodé*, that is, out of fashion
4. They emphasize style at the expense of content
5. They are objects of the kind prized by daring and witty hedonists, and by "the Dandies of Mass Culture."[19]

Booth goes on to offer his own definition of camp, that is, "to present oneself as being committed to the marginal with a commitment greater than the marginal merits."[20] He also points out that non-camp things can exhibit aesthetically camp qualities without actually being camp, such as artificiality, theatricality, stylishness, sexual ambiguity, tackiness, and poor taste.

Few genres of popular American music meet these criteria for camp as well as country music. Although country is currently the sixth most popular genre of music in the US and responsible for 8.7% of the nation's total music sales, the "phantom hillbilly" that still stigmatizes it keeps it closer to the margin of American culture than hip-hop, pop, and other more popular genres.[21] The perception that country music often centers around traditional family values, America First ideology, and stereotypical and idiosyncratic "Southern" themes (pickup trucks, cold beer and sweet tea, small rural towns, etc.) contributes to the idea that, with some exceptions, the genre as a whole does not have mass appeal and is thus out of fashion. Further, Merle Haggard's 1969 hit "Okie from

Muskogee" makes it clear that for decades, country music singers and audiences have often seen the genre as the voice of the counter-counterculture, a vehicle for conservative pushback against progressive society in support of more traditional views. But even the performative conservative virtue signaling prevalent in contemporary country music typifies Booth's definition of camp, where being seen as being committed to these ideologies seems to be as much or more important than the ideas themselves. Many elements of country music can also be artificial or exaggerated, from the whitewashing of Southern culture and the rebranding of rural America as a place only for white people, affected accents that singers might adopt for "street cred" (or its rural equivalent), and the virtue signaling of exaggerated patriotism or false mythologies about the "good ol' days" that may have been good for some, but certainly not all, citizens of rural America.

Style-over-content is also a common perception of contemporary country music, again leading to stereotypes about country songs focusing on breakups, hometowns, blue jeans, and trucks. In a longitudinal study of the lyrics from the Top 30 songs played on country music radio from 2014–2019, country music social media influencer and commentator Grady Smith and data analyst Dana Gibbon found that some of these stereotypes were justifiable. The most popular words identified by Smith and Gibbon were filler words, such as "yeah," "girl," and "baby," and most songs center around breaking up or getting over a breakup with a woman in particular as a shockingly small number of the Top 30 songs during this time were by women.[22] Country artists Maddie & Tae even wrote "Girl in A Country Song" in 2015 as a reaction to the apparent lack of variety in topics found in popular country music, critiquing the representation of women in contemporary country as being barefooted, bikini-clad sex objects, who, if they are lucky, get to ride down dirt roads against their will in their boyfriend's truck. YouTuber "Sir Mashalot" took six popular country hits released between February 2012 and February 2014, and created a mashup using elements from each song, proving that, because the verses, choruses, chord progressions, and so on of these songs are so interchangeable, and their lyrics so similar and banal, the formula for a hit country song, at least at that time, seemed to favor particular stylistic characteristics over substantive content.[23]

"All Hat, No Cattle"

"All hat, no cattle" is an idiom used in my home state of Texas and other places in the American South to refer to someone who cannot support their claims with substantive evidence; they "talk the talk," but do not "walk the walk." Unfortunately, music videos often earn producers and recording artists the reputation of being "all hat, no cattle." For instance, Shania Twain's MAN! I FEEL LIKE

A WOMAN (1997) is a well-known example of a music video meant to "flip the script" regarding the representation of women in music videos, and begins by featuring the singer in a top hat, necktie, and overcoat, backed by sexualized and (ever-so-slightly) gender-bent men wearing tight clothing and makeup—an obvious homage to Robert Palmer's ADDICTED TO LOVE (1985); however, despite what they are wearing, they remain decidedly masculine, with the focus still on their muscles and chiseled jawlines and their fingers playing their white, phallic instruments at crotch level. And after several costume changes, each of which reveals a little more skin than the first, Twain ends the video in a short black dress, high leather boots, long black gloves, and a choker necklace. What began as, and arguably remains, an empowering, feminist perspective on gender roles in music videos ends as the star of the video nevertheless transforms into a highly sexualized feminine subject.

"Bro-country" is a term coined by music critic Jody Rosen to describe the recent advent of "music by and of the tatted, gym-toned, party-hearty young American white dude," and some of the most homophobic artists in country music today write or perform music of this genre; for example, Dallas Davidson, co-writer of "Honky Tonk Badonkadonk" and "Country Girl (Shake It For Me) was arrested in July 2014 for his involvement in a bar fight during which he reportedly yelled many racist and homophobic slurs. Jason Aldean's "Dirt Road Anthem" (2010) is all about drunk driving a pickup truck, carousing with girls in wet t-shirts and bikinis, trespassing, smoking, fighting, and thinking about the good ol' days—many of the things that epitomize the phantom hillbilly; since 2022, Aldean and his wife Brittany Aldean have become outspoken critics of the LGBTQIA+ community, especially against issues that affect the trans community.

These negative attitudes are, and have long been, prevalent within the contemporary country music industry. There is also rampant sexism and heterosexism in the contemporary country music scene. The country band Big & Rich, most popular for their song "Save A Horse, Ride A Cowboy" (2004), are outspoken critics of marriage equality, and have equated loving LGBTQIA+ relationships to incest. 2008 CMA and ACM Male Vocalist of the Year Award winner Brad Paisley's song, titled "I'm Still a Guy" (2007) features blatantly heterosexist language. Condemning anything that is not hyper-masculine, he sings:

> Well love makes a man do some things he ain't proud of /
> And in a weak moment I might walk your sissy dog, hold your
>   purse at the mall /
> But remember, I'm still a guy / . . . /
> These days there's dudes getting facials /
> Manicured, waxed and botoxed /

With deep spray-on tans and creamy lotiony hands /
You can't grip a tackle box /
With all of these men lining up to get neutered /
It's hip now to be feminized /
I don't highlight my hair /
I've still got a pair /
Yeah honey, I'm still a guy

As with his equally misguided "Accidental Racist" (2013) in which he performs with rapper L.L. Cool J., Paisley embodies many of the contemporary social troubles with country music. Writing for NPR about Paisley's plight, Dr. Eric Weisbard astutely observes how country artists often fall into the phantom hillbilly's trap despite their best intentions: "The history of 'Accidental Racist' is the history of how white Southern musicians—heatedly, implicitly, at times self-servingly and not always successfully—try to talk about who they are in answer to what others dismissively assume they are."[24]

As Nadine Hubbs so eloquently outlined, even though sexuality and class are strongly connected, the working class was historically much more accepting of LGBTQIA+ people than it is given credit for. Hubbs describes the shift in acceptance of LGBTQIA+ people and culture between the working class and the middle class:

> From its scientific designation circa 1870 through most of the twentieth century, homosexuality was pathologized in the dominant culture, and both homosexuality and acceptance of it were attributed, negatively, to the working class. Shunning and renouncing homosexuality were lauded and associated, virtuously, with the middle class. But in a process that has become increasingly evident since the 1970s, America has seen a shifting of ideological poles in the realm of sexuality and class. Homosexual acceptance has gone from being working class and bad to middle class and good, while homosexual aversion—what we now call homophobia—has gone from being middle class and good to working class and bad. Even across these 180-degree reversals of meaning, however, a signal feature is conserved: the values attaching to the classes.[25]

As we will see in this chapter, this "middle-classing of the queer" has not dissuaded members of the LGBTQIA+ community and drag performers from embracing country music. It is worth mentioning that the "misremembered," whitewashed history of rural life previously mentioned in this chapter can in and of itself be read as camp by those willing to set aside the legacy of the Confederacy, Reconstruction, Jim Crow laws, and continued persecution of racial, sexual, and other minority communities in the rural South. This very generous—and grossly undeserved—reading leads to real harm to subaltern communities, even if not at the hands of the majority of rural Americans. Reading elements of a culture as camp can often diffuse the *perception* of the harm they can cause, making them all the more insidious. For example, some purposefully misremember or whitewash the Civil Rights movement of the 1960s in order to read the Confederate flag painted on the roof of the "General Lee," the orange 1969 Dodge Charger driven by the Duke brothers in the *Dukes of Hazzard*, as a campy, harmless representation of the South rather than a symbol of racial oppression and hatred. The videos and songs discussed above rely heavily on the inherent camp aesthetics of both country and contemporary culture to make the harmful messages and stereotypes within them about marginalized sexualities seem harmless.

On the other hand, this legacy sets the stage for redemptive appropriation and parody through camp by these same marginalized communities. Tracing the etymology of "camp" from the first uses of the term, derived from the French verb *se camper* (to pose), to the epigram of Oscar Wilde's novel, *The Picture of Dorian Gray* (1890), to the pop art scene of the 1960s and the AIDS crisis of the 1980s, critical theorist Andrew Ross notes that there is a certain historicity to camp, writing:

> The camp effect, then, is created not simply by a change in the mode of cultural production (and the contradictions attendant on that change), but rather when the products . . . of a much earlier mode of production, which has lost its power to produce and dominate cultural meanings, become available, in the present, for redefinition according to contemporary codes of taste.[26]

In his book, *No Respect: Intellectuals and Popular Culture*, Ross reiterates camp's reliance on imagined histories and notes that camp is both an appropriative act and a means through which cultural taste can be challenged:

> Camp engages in a redefinition of cultural meaning through a juxtaposition of an outmoded past alongside that which is technologically, stylistically, and sartorially contemporary. Often characterized by the reappropriation of a "throwaway Pop aesthetic", camp works to intermingle the categories of "high" and "low" culture.[27]

Further, the appropriation of camp sensibilities is also seen by some as a mode of survival, especially by those who view Susan Sontag's "Notes on Camp" as de-homosexualizing. As Cynthia Morril writes:

> Central to Sontag's claim is the presumption that camp is a discursive mode offered to heterosexuals as a means for homosexuals to gain acceptance. What

> is entirely excluded from her analysis is the possibility that Camp might be a discursive mode which enables homosexuals to adapt to the conditions of heterosexual homophobia.[28]

But this in no way implies that camp needs to be defended or explained, especially to those who see the adoption of a camp aesthetic as trivial or as playing into stereotypes (rather than against them). As Andres Britton argues, the positive connotations of camp (such as the refusal to pass as straight or claiming one's "otherness") still uphold the "traditional, oppressive formulations" of that otherness; however, there is still value in camp as it "is simply one way in which gay men have recuperated their oppression, and it needs to be criticised as such."[29] As we will see later in this chapter, members of the LGBTQIA+ reappropriate the outmoded cliché and camp elements already present in country music—the cowboy hats and tight jeans, the guitars, the broken hearts, and the wide open spaces (to name a very few)—and add even more camp of their own in order to redemptively appropriate the genre, reach new audiences, and truly represent themselves.

Two-steps Forward

In sharp contrast to most of the songs mentioned thus far in this chapter, there are recent country music videos that successfully challenge heterosexism and/or cis-gendered masculinity, either through parody or comedy, or through serious portrayals of LGBTQIA+ relationships, gender expressions, and drag performance. Although there are currently few of these videos, and though they are mostly viewed through alternative means such as YouTube or iTunes rather than major media outlets such as CMT, they provide a welcoming and affirming discursive context for discussions of sexuality and gender within country music. These music videos demand close readings to adequately examine the depth and breadth of the cultures, subcultures, lifestyles, sexualities, intersectional identities, and self-expressions they represent.

Ned Sublette's humorous "Cowboys Are Frequently Secretly (Fond of Each Other)" (1981) is a country waltz that satirizes a number of the stereotypes associated with both gay culture and cowboys, particularly in relation to Western wear. In the midst of the "Urban Cowboy" fad of the late 1970s and 1980s, gay culture appropriated and adapted many of the hyper-masculine characteristics of rough-riding cowboy figures from popular culture, such as the Marlboro Man, a fictional character featured in Marlboro cigarette marketing campaigns from the 1950s to 1990s; and the Buffalo Bill Cody-esque "plainsman hunter" seen in many Western films, with long hair, horseshoe mustache, and slim-fit denim shirts and blue jeans. This trend, according to Chris Gibson in his essay titled "The Global Cowboy: Rural Masculinities and Sexualities," was:

> an open invitation to camp, and unsurprisingly it became a *de rigueur* model of deportment in the urban gay subcultures of the 1970s and 1980s. Meanwhile leather chaps provided handy accoutrement for overt butch performances and, without crotch and backside pieces by definition, were easily incorporated into fetish and sadomasochistic (S&M) subcultures.[30]

Based on his experiences as a young man in Portales, New Mexico, a ranching town on the *Llano Estacado*, Sublette makes direct references to rugged cowboys and their clothing as a signifier of queerness and camp in the song's chorus:

> Cowboys are frequently secretly fond of each other. /
> Say, what do you think all them saddles and boots was about? /
> And there's many a cowboy who don't understand the way that he feels for his brother. /
> And inside every cowboy there's a lady that'd love to slip out.

Pansy Division, an American "queercore" punk rock band also covered the song, adding new lyrics for the chorus on the same topic, singing:

> Cowboys are frequently secretly fond of each other /
> That's why they wear leather, and Levi's and belts buckled tight /
> There's many a cowboy who don't understand the way that he feels towards his brother; /
> There's many a cowboy who's more like a lady at night

Willie Nelson most famously covered the song in 2006, releasing it on Valentine's Day in conjunction with the film *Brokeback Mountain* in which his version of the folk song "He Was a Friend of Mine" was featured. According to the *Dallas Morning News*, "Cowboys Are Frequently Secretly Fond of Each Other" was the first LGBTQIA+-themed mainstream country song by a major artist. Subsequently, a video for the song was released shortly after the release of the single.

In contrast to the lyrical references to the phantom hillbilly and the mythology that gay cowboys have hard exterior facades but really feel like women inside, viewers of COWBOYS ARE FREQUENTLY SECRETLY FOND OF EACH OTHER (2006) will notice the way the dancers in the video challenge the stereotypes about gender and sexuality that are usually associated with country music through a camp appropriation of hyper-masculine clothing and dancing. With the exception of a couple of drag performers whose presence in the video might refer back to the cowboy in the song's chorus whose internal persona is "a lady that'd love to slip out," the male-coded dancers in the video are seen taking part in two typical Western dance styles. The first is line dancing, which is not usually particularly masculine or feminine; however, the ways in which the dancers hold their cowboy hats, hook their thumbs into their belts, and perform acrobatic kicks give this line dance a decidedly masculine aesthetic. In the scenes which take place inside a bar, viewers can also see male dancers taking part in the Country Western Waltz, a folk dance for partners traditionally in which a cis-male leads a cis-female partner around the dance floor in a circle of other couples. Here, these gender roles are subverted as both partners are men.

Other non-dancing scenes point just as clearly to the queerness of the song and the dancers featured in the video, also relying heavily on camp and queer subversion of other hyper-masculine tropes. For example, one dancer can be seen riding on the back of another as if he were on a horse or mechanical bull. Nods to S&M subculture can be seen in a scene in which someone uses an acoustic guitar as a sort of fraternity paddle, dragging it across the tight jean-covered bottoms of about a dozen men, in a quick shot of a burly man in a leather vest walking past the camera with a bridle in his mouth, and in one of the final scenes of the video when a rope-bound cowboy is dragged through the street by a team of dancers (read: "stallions").

Even more to the point, the choice of clothing for nearly all of the dancers in the video is decidedly masculine: standard blue jeans, cowboy hats, boots, belts with large rodeo buckles, cotton tank tops/A-shirts, Western-style shirts with conventional pearl snaps and cutoff sleeves, or actual working ranch wear (chaps, leather waistcoats, etc.). In contrast, Burt Reynolds, a pop culture exemplar of hyper-masculinity, is the person who is dressed the most stereotypically gay in the entire video, acting as the video's flamboyant director and seen wearing a bright yellow blazer and music-themed Mardi Gras beads. The conceit of the video is that everything that appears on screen is recorded as one take that Reynolds directs, even though it is clearly composed of multiple scenes that were recorded in many takes in multiple locations. The "take" we see as the video begins sees Reynolds using a bullhorn to yell "cut" for a previous take and asking for another one, this time with more testosterone. As the video ends, when Willie Nelson asks him for his opinion about the take, Reynolds minces, occasionally shrugging his shoulders and clutching his Mardi Gras beads as if they were a string of pearls, and replies, "Well, I think we should do one more, because I'd like to see a little more, you know, a little more . . . 'husky,' you know?"

COWBOYS ARE FREQUENTLY SECRETLY FOND OF EACH OTHER was actually created by the Broken Lizard Comedy Troupe (an American group most famous for writing and starring in the films *Super Troopers* and *Club Dread*), and choreographed and directed by Darrin Davis and performed in line-dancing style by thirty dancers at the Round-Up Saloon, a country and western dance club in Dallas' Oak Lawn area, one of the premier country-themed gay bars in the United States.[31] The very existence of gay country bars and the prominence of the Round-Up in the video, in addition to featured clips from a Texas Gay Rodeo Association event, demonstrates the profound impact country music and culture continues to have on parts of the LGBTQIA+ community despite the perception and/or reality of hostile attitudes toward it. The song itself says a lot about heterosexual elitism and gender identity, and the fact that it was covered by a country star with as much cultural collateral as Willie Nelson speaks volumes about the accepting attitudes of many within country music's elite and their willingness to embrace a subculture that shares many of their values, style, and tastes. In a prepared statement, Nelson said, "This song's been in the closet for 20 years. The timing's right for it to come out, I'm just opening the door." The video premiered on Logo, a predominantly gay cable television channel, and was made available on iTunes after the song's debut on the Howard Stern Show; although it did not appear on mainstream broadcast television, COWBOYS ARE FREQUENTLY SECRETLY FOND OF EACH OTHER was played for several years on heavy rotation in gay bars with and without a country theme.

Independent Chicago-based singer-songwriter Steve Grand is an out gay musician, and at the release and viral success of his video for "All-American Boy" in the summer of 2013, he was heralded as the first openly gay country music star. Grand, who also stars in the song's video, falls in love with an apparently straight male friend who has begun to send mixed signals regarding the nature of their friendship. After getting dumped and left on the side of the road by his girlfriend when she starts to catch on, the two young men end up "skinny dipping" and even kiss. The video ends as the straight man reconciles with his girlfriend, leaving Grand heartbroken and longing for a more meaningful relationship. As one of the first few country music videos to visually portray any kind of LGBTQIA+ relationship and affection explicitly, in addition to other equally serious subtexts regarding the impact of "the closet" on young gay people and their relationships, Grand's ALL-AMERICAN BOY (2013) was quite rare indeed and stood at the forefront of changing attitudes in country music.[32] Still, even though the video, which Grand self-funded, has over 8.4 million views on YouTube (as of mid-July 2023), Grand still has no support or contract from a major country label; instead, he launched a Kickstarter campaign in late February of 2014 to fund the recording of his debut album under the auspices of his own record label, G.R.A.N.D Nation, LLC.

In his second video STAY (2013), Grand is seen riding in the back of an old red pickup with a group of friends as they drive to a lakeside party in Chicago, where Grand, his boyfriend, and other couples of mixed- and same-sex couples dance together in the water. The video cuts to more intimate scenes of Grand and his partner in various stages of undress in other locations, namely a bedroom, perhaps a reference to the lyrics, "So when my old man's out of town for a couple days/I think that you should/Stay with me . . ."[33] The gay relationship featured in STAY is depicted as being a much healthier, happier relationship than the surreptitious relationship in ALL-AMERICAN BOY. The video opens with galloping banjo arpeggios as a group of friends ride together to a beach on Lake Michigan in the back of a red pickup truck. The video primarily centers around scenes of the larger group of friends having fun together, swimming in the lake, having a barbecue and a subsequent food fight, throwing water balloons at each other, and an impromptu concert with the addition of a few members of a marching band. In many of the group scenes, Grand and his love interest, played by model Jayson Smith, can be seen dancing together and kissing, not unlike any display of affection one might expect to see in a video made by a heterosexual artist. The carefree theme of the video echoes the song's lyrics, especially the chorus:

> Stay with me all summer /
> we might never have to leave /
> You're my southern king /
> we live it for the daydreams.

Discussing the video, Grand remarks, "Summer is about freedom. I tried to capture that in the video. It's a reawakening, it's about summer love, about being young and free."[34]

At a Crossroads: Intersectional Identities and Country Music Videos

Unfortunately, Steve Grand did not become a household name among all country music fans; in fact, even though many of the songs he initially released were decidedly "country," Grand has distanced himself from the genre, claiming that he never called himself a country singer, and that he considers his music to be pop.[35] Of course, it goes without saying that Grand's relative success as a country singer, or a singer of country-styled rock songs, and the generally warm public reception afforded to him and other contemporary gay country artists who have followed, such as Ty Herndon and Billy Gilman (both of whom were already mainstream artists but who did not come out publicly until 2014), T.J. Osborne, Orville Peck, Brandon Stansell, Cameron Hawthorn, and others, comes at a great personal and professional cost and sacrifices made by country artists who have come before. This is especially true for those country artists who were not conventionally attractive cis-male performers with the relative freedom to dance with or kiss equally attractive, equally masculine, cis-presenting men in their videos, but rather, who embody intersectional identities for whom the country music world has not yet made sufficient room and who have had to encode expressions of their identities in lyrical subtext and visual symbolism. Wilma Burgess, an early queer country music pioneer (although she was only out among colleagues in the country music industry), famous in the 1960s for songs such as "Misty Blue" and "Baby," insisted that even though she did not want to "play straight," the love interests in her songs would still be gender-neutral or ambiguous.[36] Burgess would later leave the music industry altogether and open "The Hitching Post," an early lesbian bar in Nashville. Through the 1980s and 1990s, country artists who identified as lesbians, such as Melissa Etheridge, k.d. lang, and the Indigo Girls, were "passed off as 'neo-hippies' and were not recognized seriously as contributors to the country music scene."[37] Take Chely Wright's experience for example: She made her Grand Ole Opry debut in 1989, but after coming out as the first mainstream contemporary country artist to be openly gay on the cover of *People Magazine* in 2010, she suffered many setbacks in her career, including no further invitations to perform at the Grand Ole Opry, the loss of a large chunk of her fan base, and a damaged relationship with her mother. She was not invited back to the Opry until the summer of 2019.[38] More recently, artists such as Brandi Carlile, Holly Miranda, Jill Sobule, Katie Pruitt, Jamie Wyatt, and others have launched careers with varying degrees of professional success and acceptance of their sexuality. But unfortunately, perhaps with the exception of Carlile, lesbian performers in the world of country music still suffer from a serious lack of recognition and visibility, although recent music videos featuring lesbian relationships have helped. Katie Pruitt's LOVING HER (2019) addresses the struggle many people in the American South feel when trying to reconcile conservative beliefs and religious traditions in which we have grown up and living an authentic life, or often, as was Pruitt's case which inspired this song, the struggle loved ones face when someone they love comes out.[39] Pruitt sings:

> If loving her's a sin I don't wanna go to Heaven /
> No, there's nothing else up there I could need /
> And if I'm sinning every day, guess I'll sin all seven /
> If I can still have her by the end of the week.

Views from Nashville Pride comprise most scenes of LOVING HER, with members of the LGBTQIA+ community, advocates, and supporters marching or riding on floats in a parade, performing in drag, playing in a fountain, and dancing and celebrating at the pride festival. The remaining scenes of the video feature Pruitt singing and playing her guitar in a backyard while her love interest sits in a hammock behind her; the video ends as Pruitt joins her there.

In SUNROOF (2021), lesbian singer-songwriter Brook Eden purchases a classic Ford Mustang and takes her girlfriend on a road trip to the beach in it. They spend the day visiting a park to sit together on swings, shopping at a beach store and having drinks at a beach bar, and riding bicycles together. Throughout the video, Eden and her partner occasionally exchange romantic glances, hold hands, and kiss each other the way one might expect to see in any country video featuring a heterosexual couple in love.

Five years after Grand's debut with ALL-AMERICAN BOY, another genre-defying openly gay artist well and truly rocked the global music industry, especially the country music world, as it was finally forced to seriously reckon with burning questions related to the representational politics of country music: What makes a song "country"? Who gets to decide? And who even gets to make country music? In late 2018, Lil Nas X (the stage name of Montero Lamar Hill) first released "Old Town Road" independently, but the single was re-released by Columbia Records in March 2019 after the song became popular on TikTok as the background track used in the popular "Yeehaw Challenge" on the social media platform. In April 2019, a remix featuring legendary country singer Billy Ray Cyrus was released. The song peaked at No. 1 on the *Billboard* Hot 100 and held that position for a record-breaking nineteen consecutive weeks. The song also reached No. 19 on the *Billboard* Hot Country Songs chart in March 2019, but by the end of the month, the magazine quietly removed the song from inclusion. In a statement to *Rolling Stone Magazine* about the decision, *Billboard* claims that the inclusion of the song on the country charts was a mistake, primarily because of its compositional style: "While 'Old Town Road' incorporates references to country and cowboy imagery, it does not embrace enough elements of today's country music to chart in its current version."[40] To this day, it is still unclear to which elements *Billboard* is referring. Lil Nas X classifies the song as "country trap," a subgenre of country rap that incorporates elements of trap music, itself a subgenre of hip-hop music developed in Atlanta and other urban areas of the American South that features sparse synthesized snare drums, tuned kick drums, and complex hi-hat patterns.[41] However, the backing track does retain country elements. Despite the fact that the banjo sample that appears in the song's backing track is from industrial rock band Nine Inch Nails' song "34 Ghosts IV" (2008), the instrument is closely associated with country music and other white folk music traditions, even though its roots in West and Central Africa and the history of how it was brought to the Americas by slaves is often whitewashed and overlooked. Historically, when the banjo's legacy is not ignored, it has been part of gross mischaracterizations of African Americans; for instance, "banjo mania" swept the United States in the mid-1800s as both Union and Confederate soldiers were introduced to the instrument through minstrel shows during the Civil War. Even long after the connections between the instrument and blackface minstrelsy became less prominent, the "phantom hillbilly" still haunted the instrument due to its connection to country, bluegrass, jazz, ragtime, folk, and other "low-class" musical genres. Further, the inclusion of Cyrus, one of the most famous country singers from the 1990s, and the fact that both he and Lil Nas X sing with a distinctive country "twang" (for example, the word "can't" is pronounced "cain't" by both men), serve as additional proof that the song fits at least as well in the country genre as it does in hip-hop.

The removal of "Old Town Road" from the Hot Country Songs chart was especially surprising considering the fact that country-rap songs had previously charted, such as "I Play Chicken with the Train," by Cowboy Troy, ft. Big & Rich (2005), which was the first country-rap song to chart, and Jason Aldean's single "Dirt Road Anthem" (2011), which reached No. 1 on the Hot Country Songs chart. Plus, country-rap songs had previously earned recognition from *Billboard*, such as "Cruise" by Georgia Florida Line, which won Billboard's award for top country song of 2014, and country rappers Colton Ford, Bubba Sparxxx, and Redneck Souljers all had songs that appeared on *Billboard*'s country charts. Some writers baselessly claimed that the fact that the song first became popular on TikTok made it easy to ignore because it lacked sufficient depth or could be dismissed as kitsch. One such was *Billboard* staffer Bianca Gracie, who argued: "In Lil Nas X's case, I think he caught lightning in a bottle with 'Old Town Road,' and is at risk of getting lost in the next wave of rappers who are ready to enjoy a quick hit. As much as the song is fun, it's still a bit gimmicky."[42] The country music industry advocate and provocateur Kyle "Trigger" Coroneos made a similar unsubstantiated argument, dismissing the song as nothing more than an internet meme and falsely claiming that Lil Nas X never claimed it was even part of the genre or that he even is a country artist. Coroneos argued further that the song does not belong on the country charts because Lil Nas X has no ties to "the greater Nashville music campus in any capacity."[43] Of course, this argument further marginalizes already marginalized groups, particularly Black and/or gay country artists, who have historically been excluded by the Nashville elite. Coroneos even evokes the "phantom hillbilly," claiming that the decision to include the song on the charts in the first place was based on a "bigoted stereotype bred from the fact that horses and cowboy hats are referenced in the lyrics . . . the song is basically a 1:53 joke," expressing serious concern about how "Old Town Road" is pushing "actual songs, country or otherwise" down the charts and challenges records held by those he would consider to be "real" country musicians.[44]

These clear inconsistencies led many on social media to suspect that *Billboard's* removal of "Old Town Road" from the charts had more to do with Lil Nas X's race, as he was a young Black man who grew up outside of Atlanta, than it did with industry pressure and concern about the song's "country" elements. And when he came out publicly as gay on June 30, 2019, his intersectional identity as a gay Black man further complicated the identity politics surrounding "Old Town Road." As the public found out about Lil Nas X's sexuality and began to wonder whether or not the song had a homosexual subtext, he tweeted "old town road is literally about horses."[45] The perception that country music is primarily for white audiences is just as misguided as the presumption that it is for straight audiences. In her book, *Black Country Music: Listening for Revolutions*, the scholar of African American culture and Gender and Queer Theory Francesca T. Royster discusses the long legacy of Black country musicians and their impact on the genre, and addresses the whitewashing of country music's history that has led Black fans of country music into a "closet" of sorts, a queer "phantom hillbilly:" "For some of us, loving country music—or even just having an intellectual curiosity about it—is the *other* 'love that dares not speak its name,' to evoke that old-fashioned description of queer, closeted life" (emphasis in original).[46]

The OLD TOWN ROAD video, which features the remix of the song and won a Grammy for Best Music Video of 2019, was released in May 2019 and subverts stereotypes about the place of both Blackness and queerness in country music. The longer "Official Movie" cut of the video opens in much the same way an old Western film from the 1960s or 1970s would begin, with the song's title emblazoned across the screen in a stylized "Western" font commonly associated with wanted posters. With an A♭ minor chord strummed on a guitar to mimic the galloping of horses playing non-diegetically in the background, three men are racing down a dirt road on horseback chasing another two men on horses further ahead as a subtitle reveals that they are all traveling on "Old Town Road" in the year 1889. Soon, the identity of one of the riders is revealed; at the sound of a bullwhip cracking, we are introduced to Lil Nas X, who is holding a bag of money. After the sheriff (played by comedian Chris Rock) gives up pursuit, the two fugitives stop at a pioneer home, and as he dismounts (with another whipcrack), we find out that the second horseman is Billy Ray Cyrus. As Cyrus suggests that they could rest at that location for a while, the residents of the home sneak around the corner with a shotgun as Lil Nas X says, "I don't know, man . . . the last time I was here they weren't too welcoming to outsiders," a clear jab at the Nashville insiders who called for the removal of the song from the country charts. Cyrus responds, "Eh, you're with me this time. Everything's gonna be alright," further evidence that his inclusion in the remix and the video are intended to lend the project country credentials, while simultaneously suggesting that young Black (and/or gay) men are not yet allowed in the world of country music without a qualified chaperone to vouch for them. As the homeowner starts shooting at Lil Nas X, he runs and dives into a mine shaft, crawling toward a light at the other end of the tunnel.[47] As he gets about halfway through, he suddenly gets sucked toward the light, falling quite violently out of the sky and landing at the feet of a young Black boy playing with a basketball in his yard on Old Town Road—in 2019.

When the song begins, we hear Billy Ray Cyrus sing "I'm gonna take my horse to the old town road / I'm gonna ride 'til I can't no more," and we see various members of the neighborhood (all of whom are Black), working on their car, looking out of their front door, skipping rope and riding on a scooter in front of their house, watering their lawn, having a cookout, and so on. They all stop what they are doing and stare in amazement as Lil Nas X rides down the road on horseback, dressed as he was back in the nineteenth century. Although such a sight may not be particularly common, especially in dense, urban areas, and seeing a Black man riding down a neighborhood street might come as a shock, there is a tradition in the American South of that very thing. Members of the Black Creole community have sustained a centuries-old tradition of horse riding, and in recent years, Creole trail rides have become increasingly popular throughout Louisiana, East Texas, and the Deep South, which include trail rides in more rural areas and at urban parks.

As he sings "can't nobody tell me nothing," Lil Nas X stops in front of a house where two men are sitting on their porch, dismounts his horse, and begins to dance; one of the men on the porch proceeds to record a video of the spectacle playing out in front of them. In front of the house's fence, a young woman seems to interpret Lil Nas X's dancing as competition, and she replies in kind with the Whip, Nae Nae, and other hip-hop dance moves, ending with the horse-riding dance move made popular in Psy's GANGNAM STYLE (2012), a reference both to Lil Nas X's horse riding and the popularity of "Old Town Road" as a meme on TikTok where many participants in the "YeeHaw Challenge" would also perform similar horse-riding motions.

In the next scene, we see Lil Nas X preparing to race an automobile in a street race on his horse, as a young man passes in front of both race participants waving a checkered flag. Lil Nas X wins the race as he reaches the end of the block before the car, and a man sitting on a tractor waves another checkered flag. In a cut scene, the car's driver pays Lil Nas X the money he is owed for winning the race (presumably as a bet), while the woman dancing in the previous scene dances while standing with one foot on top of the fence and the other on the horse's saddle.

Taking his winnings to the "Super Mall," Lil Nas X emerges from the store having replaced his more authentic, brown Western duds for a more updated, and arguably more feminine, look: "rhinestone cowboy"-inspired jacket and pants with white fringe, intricate embroidered flowers, horses, and horseshoes; a bolo tie and black cowboy hat, silver rings on several fingers, and studded belt with silver belt buckle, and silver-tipped black cowboy boots. At that moment, Billy Ray Cyrus pulls up driving a red Maserati convertible, wearing an outfit equally flamboyant to Lil Nas X's (white cowboy hat, hot pink jacket with white stars and fringe, and white sunglasses), and dangling the bag of money they stole back in 1889 over the side of the car.

In the final scene of OLD TOWN ROAD, Lil Nas X and Cyrus (who is now carrying a white electric guitar) throw open the swinging double doors of the Town Hall as if they were saloon doors, to find a crowd of older white people playing bingo, all of whom silently turn toward the door in unison to see who walked in (playing into the trope common in Western films when a stranger walks into a saloon), with the exception of a single woman, oblivious to the visitor's arrival, who holds up a red paddle and shouts "Bingo!" Nodding to each other, Lil Nas X and Cyrus decide to take the stage at the front of the hall and perform the rest of the song. As you can see in Figure 4.2, Cyrus is playing his white guitar, Lil Nas X holding a Shure Super 55 microphone (commonly associated with Elvis Presley, the Grand Ole Opry, and other historic touchstones of country music), and a band is playing mandolin, banjo, and washboard.

When the chorus returns, the bingo tables have been moved, leaving room for the bingo players to line dance, a nod to Cyrus's "Achy Breaky Heart" (1992) and the line dancing craze it inspired in the 1990s.

Despite his assertion that the song is "literally about horses," Lil Nas X does perform—and subvert—many tropes of cowboy masculinity throughout the

Figure 4.2 Lil Nas X and Billy Ray Cyrus in OLD TOWN ROAD (2019). (Screenshot by the author.)

video. As previously mentioned, his exchanging of very stereotypical, masculine "cowboy" clothes for something much more flamboyant and floral, can easily be read as a rejection of societal expectations and a "coming out of the closet" of sorts wearing more comfortable, updated expressions of individuality. Both the visual costume change and references in the lyrics to "Cowboy hat from Gucci / Wrangler on my booty" drip with camp. Lil Nas X was also able to "come out" as a performer at the end of the video by being himself on stage, winning over a crowd of people who were of a different generation and race who initially did not seem to welcome him.

"A Drag Queen is a Cowboy's Best Friend": Country Music Videos and Drag Performance

In March 2023, Tennessee became the first American state to ban drag shows in public places after several months of moral panic by political and religious conservatives who feared that minors might see them perform. Governor Bill Lee signed Tennessee Senate Bill 3, citing homophobic conspiracy theories to claim that drag shows are too sexual and explicit for children and that drag queens and their supporters are "grooming" kids. This drag panic has spread to other countries, such as the United Kingdom and Canada, where protestors have objected to popular "Drag Queen Storytime" events in which drag queens read books about tolerance and respecting other people's differences to children at libraries and museums; in the United States, these protests have even emboldened far-right protesters to send death threats to participating queens and to bring semi-automatic weapons to threaten and intimidate participants and attendees of these events. While Tennessee's anti-drag bill was the first to be signed into law, at least 14 other states have introduced similar bills. Using language to prohibit public "performances" by "male or female impersonators," LGBTQIA+ community members and advocates fear that the language in these bills is intentionally vague and can both chill free speech and lead to the criminalization of the expression of transgender identities. As was the case for much of the twentieth century, when cross-dressing laws in the United States made drag performance, cross-dressing, and more fluid expressions of gender illegal, drag performers and the trans community now find themselves fighting again for the right to exist in public.

Whether the radical opponents of drag like it or not, drag is everywhere; however, some argue that this was not always the case. According to anthropologist and camp theorist Esther Newton, drag queens and female impersonators are by-and-large city folk, writing:

> Like all "city slickers," [female impersonators] refer contemptuously to rural areas and small towns as "the sticks," and to rural people as "hicks" . . . These exotic flowers may have their roots in "the sticks," but they bloom in cities. Their urbanism is more profound than simply a desire for "bright lights." Organized nightlife is found in cities, and impersonators need the anonymity of cities to exist. But, more than this, impersonators see themselves as "unnatural," and in our culture, the city can accommodate every unnatural thing. It is the country that represents to us "nature" and ultimately, what is real. Impersonators said they felt uncomfortable in the country.[48]

But this assessment was drawn from Newton's fieldwork in the late 1960s and early 1970s, and despite the "phantom hillbilly" homophobe alluded to by Newton's interlocutors, much has changed since then. There has long been a special place for country music deep in the heart of many southern drag performers, and likewise, there now seems to be a special place in country music for drag queens and kings. Dolly Parton and Tammy Wynette have been rhinestone-encrusted, hyper-feminine, big-breasted inspirations for many drag performers; Wynonna Judd and Pam Tillis have served as judges for *RuPaul's Drag Race*, a reality show highlighting the arts of drag and lip-synced musical performance.

Within the past several decades, there have been a few country songs featuring cross-dressing men and drag performers, including Bobby Bare's "Tequilla Sheila" (1980), about a man who wears his Mexican lover's red dress to escape the *federales.* The Trailer Park Rangers' "Drag Queen" (1996) is a Western Swing-style song about a drag maneater from Southeast Asia, while Dale Watson's "Truckin' Queen (I Got My Nightgown On)" (2006), is a truck-driving country song based on a true story about a truck driver in Oklahoma City that would dress up in women's clothing and make obscene calls on his CB. Although these are clearly designed to be comedy songs, the representations of drag performers and/or those who may be genderqueer or gender non-conforming in these songs are still rather disrespectful and harmful to these communities.

There are, however, more recently released exceptions that are starting to buck this trend; Blackburn, Nance & King's "Daddy Is a Drag Queen" (2011) is about a ten-year-old child whose father wears high heels to his school play. The chorus of the song recounts:

> Daddy is a drag and that's alright by me /
> That's the way it's always been in our family /
> Oh yes, my Daddy is a drag and I don't really care /
> If he wants to go to town in women's underwear.

Although the song still relies heavily on stereotypes that have historically been used to criticize and belittle drag queens, the humor in this song lies in its subversion of expectations, trading the turmoil and embarrassment one might expect the protagonist of the song to feel for acceptance and healthy family relationships. Miranda Lambert's "All Kinds of Kinds" (2011) features lyrics about cross-dressing with much less humor or the camp such topics formerly required:

> Thomas was a congressman /
> with closets full of skeletons /
> and dresses that he wore on Friday nights.

In an interview with *Spin Magazine*, she remarks on her surprise regarding the song's warm reception:

> Yeah, it's pretty crazy that country radio embraced cross-dressing and played it on the radio. It's fricking [sic] awesome, actually . . . I had just sort of come to this realization that it was all about being who you are, no matter what you are about, where you come from, what color you are, or if you're gay or straight, or whatever it is. I was just getting to that point in my life where I was starting to accept people for who they are, and myself.[49]

As drag personalities become more popular on YouTube, TikTok, and other social media platforms, and growing audiences watch drag-themed programs such as *RuPaul's Drag Race* and *Queen of the Universe* on television and streaming services, the market for music videos featuring drag performers also grows.

Drag performers have appeared in music videos since at least the 1980s, including RELAX by Frankie Goes to Hollywood (1984) and RuPaul's iconic cameo in the B-52s' LOVE SHACK (1989). In 1994, several drag queens impersonated Gloria Estefan in the EVERLASTING LOVE video as she was too far along in her pregnancy to perform in the video herself. In the 1990s and early 2000s, drag queens who appeared in music videos were often seen in the background as participants in sexual deviance or drug-fueled parties, such as Rihanna's video S&M (2010). More recent videos feature drag queens in a wide range of scenarios, such as terrorists that destroy a wedding dress boutique with medieval weapons and sabres in Kacey Musgraves' SIMPLE TIMES (2021), as fashion models and drag ball performers in Icona Pop's ALL NIGHT (2013) and Kat Graham's ALL YOUR LOVE (2016), and as members of a rag-tag geriatric biker gang in Miley Cyrus's YOUNGER NOW (2017).

Nonetheless, there are music videos—even country music videos—that focus more directly, and in a much healthier way, on drag performers. A DRAG QUEEN

IS A COWBOY'S BEST FRIEND (2013), written and produced by gay pop star Boy George and performed by the Supreme Fabulettes, a London-based drag performance trio, is a British tribute to the American cowboy. What the music video lacks in authenticity, it makes up for in camp. Dressed as cowgirls in some scenes (with audacious cowskin duds, long fringed gloves, giant star-spangled sombreros, and plastic cap guns) and as short-skirted saloon girls in others, the Fabulettes sing:

> Oh, Holy Moses! /
> He's a lover, he's an angel, he's my friend /
> I'd tuck, pluck, and lie just to keep this dream alive /
> A drag queen is a cowboy's best friend.

They decry the cowboy's wife, her hair, and her nasty shoes, and claim that he needs "a girl with poise and social grace / with hips and lips and everything in place," suggesting they would be a suitable replacement. The video also features famous gay porn star Johnny Hazzard, and other men in various stages of undress. The video eschews the phantom hillbilly by virtue of its extreme camp and the burlesque nature of the performance. The hyper-masculine gay porn actors who serve as the "real cowboys" accept the drag queens categorically as objects of their affection; the drag performers are ludicrous cowgirls but convincingly realistic saloon girls, cementing their position as objects of desire, and the regular townspeople carouse with the Fabulettes in the saloon, happily accepting them as they are. Even with the backing of a star as famous as Boy George, this video, too, is relegated to the Internet for distribution, and A DRAG QUEEN IS A COWBOY'S BEST FRIEND is clearly a camp, tongue-in-cheek novelty song.

MAMA DON'T MAKE ME PUT ON THE DRESS AGAIN (2017) is another camp tribute to both drag performance and country music but one with a slightly more serious tone. Trixie Mattel (the stage name of Brian Michael Firkus), most famous for her appearances on *RuPaul's Drag Rac*e and as the third winner of *RuPaul's Drag Race All Stars*, is perhaps one of the most well-known drag performers working today.[50] Mattel also enjoys a relatively successful career as a country and folk singer. Although her genre has recently shifted more toward electro-folk, her first two studio albums, *Two Birds* (2017) and *One Stone* (2018) have both charted on the *Billboard* Folk Albums chart. "Mama Don't Make Me Put on the Dress Again" (2017) is a song Mattel wrote just after a breakup and during a time in her life when she was expected to get into drag for at least five shows each week while physically and emotionally exhausted. In an interview with staff writers at *Merry-Go-Round Magazine*, Mattel explains:

> "Mama Don't Make Me Put on the Dress Again" is a song about when you want to pursue all your dreams, and you put all your time and work and heart into it, but you worry about, "Am I living my dreams or am I wasting my life?"[51]

Mattel explores this question in the chorus of the song, singing:

> Well, I'm coming home alone for the hundredth time or so /
> It gets harder on my hard-earned money's dime /
> To the bottle in my basket, will it answer if I ask it: /
> Doing right or am I doing time?

Mattel recalls that she did not even want to make a video but was reminded by a colleague about the need for one in order to sell albums. She recalls:

> I'm glad I did because I enjoyed making it . . . The video came out exactly as I wanted. A puppet show being put on for adult cowboys as a metaphor for a drag queen in a gay bar, it's very real and arduous and tiring.[52]

This metaphor is clear in the video from the very beginning. It opens with an anxious Mattel, dressed in pink and wearing an exorbitant amount of makeup, an extraneous number of eyelashes, and a particularly large blonde wig (all part of Mattel's signature look), who is selling popcorn to an audience of eager cowboys pushing each other and clamoring for her attention. Eventually, comedy legend Leslie Jordan impatiently walks onto the stage wearing a campy pink Western-style vest with fringe, bejeweled cowboy hat and bolo tie, and white boots. He whistles to quiet the crowd (an action accentuated by the sound of a scratching record) and spits invisible chewing tobacco into an imaginary spittoon (indicated through the use of more sound effects). After scolding the crowd, Jordan introduces the upcoming puppet show, at which time Firkus (Mattel out of drag) appears on the side of the stage wearing traditionally masculine clothes: a dark brown cowboy hat, brown plaid pearl snap shirt, and dark jeans, and playing an acoustic guitar to perform the song. The "boy" version of Firkus appears elsewhere in the video as a singing boy scout against a fake mountain backdrop and performing in black and white film singing against a backdrop representing the Grand Ole Opry stage, and later with a distinctively Western backdrop featuring Monument Valley, Arizona. Occasionally, we also see Firkus sitting at a table as a disinterested audience member and not performing. The puppet show itself features Mattel in drag and Firkus in Western wear; the audience of cowboys watches while the Mattel puppet spins around the stage, exposes her bottom, and twerks, and the Firkus puppet dances and plays the guitar. Meanwhile,

Leslie Jordan dances exuberantly just off stage right with a much taller and younger man.

In an interview with musicologist Shana Goldin-Perschbacher, Firkus explains how humor and the camp aesthetics of drag, as clearly displayed in MAMA DON'T MAKE ME PUT ON THE DRESS AGAIN and several of his other music videos, provide a way for him to discuss with his audience topics ordinarily seen as taboo in country music, explaining that with drag:

> You're taking something that's traditional and conservative, and you're taking maybe the most treasonous gender act there is, cross-dressing, and you're marrying the two. If you can marry it with a sense of humor, you're not getting political. You just accidentally are importantly political. You're not preaching, you're just existing as a violation of natural law... To me, I can get up there, and the sense of humor that I do, the comedy that I do, with this actual developed musical gift, it really doesn't leave a lot of room for anybody in the audience to criticize it, because it has a large sense of, "I know this is a joke because I'm dressed like a joke."[53]

Firkus goes on to explain that the humor and camp that drag affords serves as a sort of "permission slip" that allows him to discuss topics as controversial as school shootings, as humor makes these difficult conversations easier for audiences to digest.[54]

FOR YOU (2018) by Brandon Stansell plays out like a modern romantic comedy; in it, camp and humor are used as tools to broach the more serious topics of healthy body image and self-acceptance. The central character of the video is Eureka (O'Hara), the stage name of trans drag performer and Eastern Tennessee native Eureka D. Huggard, who rose to fame as a participant on Seasons 9 and 10 of *RuPaul's Drag Race* and Season 6 of *RuPaul's Drag Race All Stars*. She is also a co-host on HBO's *We're Here*, a program in which Eureka and other famous drag performers from the *Drag Race* franchise (Bob the Drag Queen and Shangela) travel to rural parts of America to stage drag shows as a way to bring more visibility and acceptance for LGBTQIA+ community members and allies in far-flung parts of the country. Eureka is also an advocate for body positivity, and in an interview with a local newspaper, she discussed this important work:

> My platform really focuses on body positivity and I want it to be more than just plus-sized individuals but just people loving and accepting their bodies for whatever shape they are — whether they think they're too small, too big, awkwardly shaped . . . If you carry yourself a certain way, people will see you that way.[55]

Although it relies on destructive heteronormative tropes to do so, the narrative of FOR YOU reflects this advocacy work. The story begins as Eureka and Stansell arrive at a party, but because Eureka is dressed like an unattractive "nerd," wearing black glasses with white tape on the bridge, scrunchies of two different colors holding her ginger hair in pigtails, ill-fitting plaid shirt with sweat stains, jean skirt, backpack, and so on, the other party attendees do not seem to welcome them. Eureka spots an attractive man across the room and undoes the top button of her shirt to reveal a little more skin in an attempt to get his attention. When he does look over, she draws an invisible heart over her torso, acting giddy to indicate her attraction to him. In response, he points and laughs at her with his friends. Heartbroken, Eureka runs outside onto the balcony to cry, and Stansell follows to comfort her with a listening ear and a plate of tortilla chips to eat.

At this point in the video, Stansell removes Eureka's glasses, magically transforming her appearance from an undesirable nerd to a glamorous drag queen with hot pink hair, comically long eyelashes, and a form-fitting dress. This is an example of the "beautiful without your glasses" or "beautiful all along" trope used in a wide variety of media, for example, films such as *The Princess Diaries* (2001), in which the proverbial "ugly duckling" instantly becomes a swan when a woman's glasses are removed as they are the only thing keeping the world from recognizing her true beauty. In her new bombshell form, Eureka leaves Stansell to catch up with the man who had originally rejected her but who now approves of her appearance. While flirting with him on the couch, she notices Stansell still sitting outside, dejected because he had feelings for Eureka. With a palm to the face, Eureka pushes away her superficial suitor and returns to the balcony with a plate of potato chips to return the favor and cheer up Stansell. Not only was Eureka always beautiful, but Stansell, the more suitable choice for a love interest, was right under her nose all along. In cut scenes throughout the video, we also see Eureka's torso through a hole surrounded by large sequins while crepe paper streamers move behind her. Here she is wearing an especially camp top featuring shirtless, homoerotic cowboys, drawn in a vintage Tom of Finland-inspired, 1960s male beefcake style.[56]

"Friends in Low Places:" The Role of Music Videos at Country Gay Bars

As with any genre of music with queer fans, country music helps members of LGBTQIA+ subgroups and cultures find community. It perhaps goes without saying, then, that country-themed queer spaces, namely bars and clubs, are sites of community building for queer country music fans. These spaces also serve as places where queer country fans learn about new music and share favorites with others. These spaces are also important as they are often places where queer country music fans build community by viewing music videos together, especially videos with LGBTQIA+ themes.

Live and recorded music performances, and music videos have been a staple in queer spaces for about as long as artists have been making them. While depictions of gay bars in popular culture primarily focus on lounge singers in gay piano bars or dance clubs with loud, throbbing pop and electronic dance music, light shows, and video screens, the musical culture of gay country bars is distinct while still serving many of the same roles in regard to community building and serving as a safe place for self-expression. In the late twentieth century country gay bars served as lifelines for country music fans in the queer community when negative attitudes made meeting together much more dangerous. For example, The Round-Up Saloon and Dance Hall, mentioned earlier in this chapter as the site where COWBOYS ARE FREQUENTLY SECRETLY FOND OF EACH OTHER was filmed and which opened in the Oak Lawn area of Dallas, Texas (affectionately known as the "Gayborhood") in July of 1980, was often raided by police in its early days. However, as the club's co-owner Alan Pierce recalls the community persisted and banded together:

> same-sex dancing was illegal, so they had coping mechanisms when the police came in in those days during dance time: they would just turn off the music and everyone would sit down on the dance-floor until the police left.[57]

The Round-Up was even destroyed by arson in 1989 when a fire was started next door at the AIDS Resource Center to cover up a burglary. As of 2023, while attitudes have shifted dramatically, The Round-Up Saloon remains open and serves as a refuge for the LGBTQIA+ community in the Dallas-Fort Worth area. The Round-Up has also become a place where members of the queer Latinx community also feel welcome, as the venue now has nights dedicated to playing Tejano, Cumbia, and other regional Mexican music with stylistic and/or cultural similarities to country music, featuring Latinx drag performances, and hosting annual birthday party celebrations for the late Tejano star Selena Quintanilla.

Country queer bars provide a space where the community can be themselves and find others like them, often providing them room to explore both their sexuality and various expressions of gender. In his discussion of connections between the bear subculture within the gay community and country-themed gay bars in the 1990s, Lars Rains describes how gay men would often subversively appropriate mainstream country music in karaoke performances. He writes:

> country songs, generally speaking, are easier to sing because of their straightforward rhythmic structure, their narrow range, and their reliance on repetition.

> The most popular song by far among gay male country music fans is Tammy Wynette's "Stand by Your Man," with its ironic opening line, "Sometimes it's hard to be a woman." This playful approach to gender may actually be a response to some of the misogyny inherent in both country music and certain gay male circles.[58]

Here, Rains is in no way insinuating that all country music fans who frequent country-themed gay bars prefer to enact feminine performances of songs by female artists, nor do they feel a need to hide their affinity for more masculine singers or their music. To the contrary, Rains admits:

> The juxtaposition of desire and identification with country artists is by no means limited to my own experience. I have several friends who drool all over the television set whenever a music video by the all-bear group Confederate Railroad appears on the screen. The band members portray themselves as a close-knit group of drinking buddies who ride Harley-Davidson motorcycles and who back each other up in barroom brawls. Normally excluded from such non-conformist groups, my lustful friends yearn for the type of male bonding displayed by these and other country "outlaws."[59]

And as more stars in the country world come out, a growing number of country fans will be ready for country songs and music videos that reflect the lives and experiences of the LGBTQIA+ community.

The musical culture of gay country bars is clearly distinct, and music videos are a big part of that culture. Many bars play music videos and some host music video-themed parties, focusing on particular decades or singers. Although many country bars cannot afford to *exclusively* play country music, and hope to attract as many patrons as possible to remain financially viable, The Round-Up prides itself on being able to play country music seven nights a week, starting with slower and older country songs and ramping up the tempo as the night progresses; as stated in the club's published music philosophy, "if you request a slow, belly-rubbing love song at 11:30pm on Friday or Saturday, the deejay will likely say 'sorry.'"[60] As is the case with The Round-Up Saloon and New York City's Flaming Saddles Saloon, country music videos play on flat-screen TVs throughout country bars, providing fans with an opportunity to see the music videos that accompany the music to which they are dancing. Videos of a particularly campy Western or Southern nature will also be played in these bars; for example, often before playing Reba McEntire's video THE NIGHT THE LIGHTS WENT OUT IN GEORGIA (1991), country bars will first play an iconic scene from the 1980s sitcom *Designing Women* (CBS, 1986–1993), in which Julia Sugarbaker (played by Dixie Carter) dresses down a beauty pageant contestant that insults her sister, Suzanne, as bar patrons recite the monolog together with the video (a practice that gave rise to the first ever spoken-word lip-sync performance on the 2022 all-winners season of *RuPaul's Drag Race All Stars*). Music videos also play a role in the philanthropic life of some country bars; The Round-Up Saloon, for example, created several music videos (of varying degrees of quality) in which bar employees and supporters would lip-sync to various country songs, such as Dierks Bentley's "Am I the Only One" (2012) and Dolly Parton's "A Lil' Ole Bitty Pissant Country Place" from *The Best Little Whorehouse in Texas* (1982) to support efforts to raise money for REBA, The Round-Up Employees Benevolent Association, a 501(c)(3) organization that supports the local LGBTQIA+ community.

New Frontiers in Country Music Videos

Are attitudes shifting within country music? Once gay marriage became legal across the entire United States in 2015 as a result of the Supreme Court's decision in favor of same-sex unions in Obergefell v. Hodges, and as public attitude toward LGBTQIA+ relationships and alternative forms of gender expression or gender performance continues to improve, so too will attitudes about the place of the LGBTQIA+ community in country music. And things are already beginning to improve slowly but surely. Even though they have not yet performed a song in support of LGBTQIA+ people and relationships, several megastars such as Carrie Underwood, Martina McBride, and Toby Keith have come out in support of marriage equality, and it is well-known that many songwriters (such as Shane McAnally) and many industry insiders in Nashville are members of the LGBTQIA+ community. Some high-profile country singers have included short references to LGBTQIA+ relationships in their songs and quick glimpses of them in videos, or have written music especially for other media that features these relationships or gender expressions. Garth Brooks found himself embroiled in controversy over his song "We Shall Be Free" (1992)—a song that became an anthem for the LGBTQIA+ community in the early 1990s—especially because of the line "Cause we shall be free / When we're free to love anyone we choose." Brooks won a GLAAD Media Award that year, and he performed the song at "Equality Rocks," a gay rights rally in Washington, DC in 2000. Dolly Parton received an Oscar nomination for "Travellin' Thru" (2006), a song she wrote and sang for the film *Transamerica*, and Willie Nelson and Emmylou Harris wrote songs for *Brokeback Mountain* (1996). "Love Who You Love" (2009), performed by Rascal Flatts is also thought to be a song in support of marriage equality, and Court Yard Hounds, a country duo comprising Emily Robison and Martie Maguire of the Dixie Chicks, wrote "Ain't No Son" (2010) in response to a documentary about boys who are kicked out of their homes by their fathers for being gay. Even more recently, Kelly Clarkson's video for "Tie It Up" (2013) features images from the weddings of straight couples and a few fleeting images of gay and lesbian couples. Kacey Musgraves performed her song "Follow Your Arrow" at the Grammy Awards ceremony in 2014, encouraging listeners to "Make lots of noise / kiss lots of boys / or kiss lots of girls / if that's what you're into." Also in 2014, Haggerty's *Lavender Country* was re-released by the independent label Paradise of Bachelors, earning the critical acclaim that it long deserved. When asked about the renewed interest in his music and the record producers who expressed interest in his decades-old project, Haggerty said:

> These people were not not gay. They were straight white men who worked in the music industry. There's not a whole raft of bigots running into that career, musicians make really poor bigots! . . . It's really a nice thing, and these straight white men are making it possible for everybody's ear to open up. Lavender Country jumped out of the gay ghetto because these straight men in North Carolina with their brave new label allowed it into the mainstream. What they're doing is giving a whole bunch of straight people permission to go and listen. We've been doing a lot of shows to general, not gay-specific, audiences, and when people have permission they go nuts![61]

Further, stalwarts of the country music industry have now become staunch allies of the LGBTQIA+ community. When the Tennessee state legislature attempted to pass a discriminatory "bathroom bill" targeting transgender citizens and visitors of the state, CMT and its parent company Viacom released a statement remarking how the move was "inconsistent with our values," while Sarah Trahern, chief executive officer of the Country Music Association said, "CMA is not a lobbying organization, but we are working closely with the City of Nashville to offer all of our visitors and residents an inclusive environment where they feel welcome."[62] Despite such strong support from some organizations, country record labels were noticeably silent at the time. However, in April of 2021, Sony Music, Warner Music, and Curb Records joined a long list of corporations, local business leaders in Nashville, medical professionals, and other advocates to oppose anti-trans legislation as it made its way through the Tennessee legislature.[63] Country music welcomed the LGBTQIA+ with more or less open arms in a particularly symbolic way as Miley Cyrus filled the pews in Nashville's historic Ryman Auditorium for "Stand By You," a recorded Pride month concert special for NBC's streaming service Peacock in 2021.[64] In March 2023, just after Tennessee lawmakers passed legislation targeting drag performances and transgender youth in that state, Grammy-winning artists, such as Sheryl Crow, Brittany Howard, Jason Isbell, Maren Morris, and Hayley Williams, performed alongside trans and queer singer-songwriters and drag performers in a benefit concert called "Love Rising."[65] Black Opry, an organization founded to support Black artists, fans and industry professionals in country and roots music, hosted a similar event, "We Will Always Be," the following day.[66] The following month, Kelsea Ballerini opened the CMT Awards with her song, "If You Go Down (I'm Goin' Down Too) (2022)," flanked by drag queens from the *RuPaul's Drag Race* franchise, a move that won her both praise and consternation from country music fans.[67]

Despite this progress, queer representation in country music is still an issue. Hunter Kelly, host of Apple Music Country's biweekly "Proud Radio," a podcast that focuses on LGBTQ+ performers and allies in country music, describes the current situation:

> Something I hear often is that people have stepped away from country music because the lack of LGBTQIA+ representation and diversity in general was getting to a point where it felt like this is a place that is not welcoming . . . Doing this show really woke me up to wonder why I've been OK with not seeing myself represented on country radio, at the award shows, for so long . . . I've never even thought to ask it. Now that I am asking it and advocating for these artists because they're worthy, it does make me question the status quo and think about, OK, what are we leaving behind for the next generation.[68]

As Nashville and the rest of the country music establishment becomes increasingly comfortable with white, cis-gendered queer artists, trans and other intersectional queer voices still struggle to be heard and work toward the acknowledgement and support they deserve. Amythyst Kiah, member of Our Native Daughters; rural Alberta's D'orjay The Singing Shaman; Crys Matthews, from southeast North Carolina; and Grammy-nominated Brittany Howard are a few of the growing number of Black queer artists who are making their mark on country music. Trans country pioneer Rae Spoon continues to push boundaries, clearing a path for other emerging trans artists, such as Ryan Cassata, Eli Conley, Lafemmebear, Brody Ray, Joe Stevens, and Shawna Virago. And queer country artists are still challenging the Nashville establishment, even in urban centers where one might not initially expect to find emerging country music scenes; for example, in Brooklyn, the Gay Ole Opry and Queer Country Quarterly, events hosted by the Branded Saloon, have been supporting country artists within the LGBTQIA+ community now for over a decade. Although there is still lots of work to do—and many in the LGTBQIA+ community and drag community are still sorely under-represented and misrepresented—as support for this community continues to grow, more country music videos that feature its members are sure to follow.

5

Iconic and Iconoclastic Representations of New Religious Movements in Music Videos

Religion and religious themes have long been a staple in music videos. However, even though representations of religion in music videos have been critiqued and studied since the 1980s, thus far (and with rare exception), academic research on music videos and religion seems to myopically concentrate on Judeo-Christian symbolism at the expense of religious minorities. In the early days of MTV, sacrilegious music videos were often played on heavy rotation, replete with glowing-eyed chorister zombies (as in Bonnie Tyler's TOTAL ECLIPSE OF THE HEART, 1983), burning crosses and sexualized Jesus figures (Madonna's LIKE A PRAYER, 1989) and motorcycles flying through stained glass windows to interrupt a gothic wedding (Billy Idol's WHITE WEDDING, 1982), but most of the controversy surrounding the representation of religion in music videos since the 1980s usually only centers around Christian images and symbols. As music videos matured, other images of other religions were featured in music videos, sometimes without controversy (such as the depiction of non-specific Hindu deities in R.E.M.'s LOSING MY RELIGION, 1991) or with instant accusations of blasphemy (as with the disintegration of an Allah pendant in Katy Perry's DARK HORSE, 2013).

Several of the most prominent controversies that centered around MTV, especially in its early days, arose from the ways in which audiences saw themselves and others represented on screen. Critics of the format often went so far as to read into the videos meanings that may or may not correlate with the intentions of recording artists and video directors; for example, music videos that were played on heavy rotation on MTV's first decade featured rockers whose actions, appearance, and lyrics certainly fanned the flames of the "Satanic Panic" of the 1980s and became the primary malefactors against which paranoid politicians and "concerned" parents waged war. Crusaders in this fight against the evils of MTV, including prominent televangelists and the Parents Music Resource Center (a socially conservative political action committee founded in 1985), listened intently to recordings played in reverse in hopes of saving their children

Audiovisual Alterity. Michael L. Austin, Oxford University Press. © Oxford University Press 2024.
DOI: 10.1093/oso/9780190277789.003.0006

from messages from the devil,[1] and they often pointed to sacrilegious imagery and actions found within videos as a primary cause of teenage suicide and delinquency. And this "Satanic Panic" is still alive and well today, even if MTV is no longer the primary purveyor of music videos: Lil Nas X's MONTERO (CALL ME BY YOUR NAME) (2021) has caused a substantial amount of hand-wringing among some fringe politicians, parents, and clergy.

Because of the dominant place Christianity holds both in secular and sacred music videos, I begin this chapter tracing the history of Contemporary Christian Music (CCM) as the dominant religious alternative to contemporary popular music and the development of music videos for this genre. I then explore many of the ways American religious minorities, particularly Scientologists and members of the Church of Jesus Christ of Latter-day Saints (whose members are formerly known as Mormons),[2] are represented by current members, former members, and critics through the use, appropriation, or parody of iconography, music, and reenactments of various religious rites and traditions of these faith groups within music videos. The music videos discussed in this chapter often highlight various theological principles or doctrines of a particular sect which may be unfamiliar to readers. Due to the secrecy in which the religion is practiced, and more often due to hearsay and popular rumors about these groups, I have also provided a very rough overview of some of the basic tenets and teachings of each religion covered here. Please note that although I do have some formal academic religious training, I am by no means a theologian, so I owe a debt of gratitude both to religious scholars and to current and former members of these religious communities who have published their hermeneutic and epistemological analyses, theological critiques, and personal beliefs about these religious groups through formal avenues and various forms of social media as a means to understand the literal and symbolic meaning of the music videos analyzed here.

"Why Should the Devil Have All the Good Music?": The Roots of Religious Music Videos

It should come as no surprise that music videos have been created to support or reinforce particular religious views or that some music videos are designed by adherents of various religious traditions for proselytizing purposes in an attempt to appeal to a wider audience of prospective converts. At least since the invention of Johannes Gutenberg's printing press and the subsequent printing of the *Bible*, the *Mainz Psalter*, and Martin Luther's *95 Theses*, religious groups have certainly taken advantage of the opportunities afforded by mass media. Whether they were Protestant propagandists utilizing the printing press to popularize revolutionary religious ideas, or Catholic church officials seeking to counter the Reformation, religious leaders were eager to exploit this new medium—the printed page—to get their message into the hands of the literate public. In the early-1800s, Bible and tract societies mass produced flyers and other publications to spread their Gospel message.[3] The same holds true for newer media forms: only two months after the first non-experimental, regular radio broadcasts began at KDKA in Pittsburgh, the station began to air church services from the city's Calvary Episcopal Church on January 2, 1921, demonstrating radio's huge market potential for religious groups. In fact, by 1925, of the 600 stations in operation, sixty-three were owned by churches.[4] By the beginning of World War II, 25% of revenue for the Mutual Broadcasting System came from religious broadcasters.[5] The early days of Christian radio programming was relatively controversy-free, and any consternation centered around whether or not live broadcasts of sermons would cause parishioners to skip worship services and eschew mediocre sermons at their local church in order to tune in from home to hear some of the leading preachers of the day. For at least the last fifty years, some of this programming has been designed to appeal to youth in particular. While early Christian radio featured music as part of church services or special programs, most Christian radio stations today feature music created specifically for radio play and enjoyment outside of traditional corporate worship settings.[6] The Southern Baptist Convention launched a thirty-minute teen talk and music radio show called *Powerline* in Fort Worth, Texas in 1969, during which a DJ would answer submitted letters and comment on contemporary issues and their relation to the church's teachings during breaks between Top 40 hits. By 1971, six hundred radio stations across the US broadcast the program.[7]

In addition to preaching and teaching programs, talk and call-in programs, and conservative political opinion that dominate the contemporary religious radio landscape, music has long been a part of the Christian radio format. CCM, Christian rock, rap, and country, and gospel music feature heavily on American Family Radio (AFR), Air1, and K-LOVE. CCM emerged from the "Jesus Movement," a counter-countercultural movement in the late 1960s and early 1970s on the US West Coast, marked by "a search for authenticity, the rejection of liberal rationality, a middle-class counterrevolution against 1960s 'permissiveness,' and a search for community."[8] However, new converts retained the hippie aesthetics and musical practices of their former lives, creating what they called "Jesus Music," mimicking the popular folk-rock style of the era (which itself was borne from the folk revival of the 1940s–1960s). But these songs consisted mainly of a single, repeated chorus and were infused with markedly Christian messages focused around a personal, affectionate relationship with God. During the late 1960s, there was already a heavy rotation of music on secular radio stations that mentioned Jesus, such as "Put Your Hand in the Hand of the Man from Galilee" (1970) by Anne Murray, "Spirit in the Sky" (1969) by Norman

Greenbaum, and covers of "Jesus is Just Alright" by the Byrds (1969) and the Doobie Brothers (1972), and musicals with religious themes, such as Andrew Lloyd Webber's *Jesus Christ Superstar* (1971) and Stephen Schwartz's *Godspell* (1971) were hits. This new style of Christian music was "free-flowing, participatory, and impassioned, supplanting the stage-focused, tightly arranged evangelistic songs of radio-era crusade music. This was not their daddy's churches [*sic*]—neither the sedate and classical style of the mainline nor the respectable if energetic Graham-era crusade clones."[9]

The popularity of Jesus Music gave rise to another form of popular Christian music: "Message Music," which was focused more on individual performance than participatory group singing. Early artists such as Andre Crouch, Keith Green, and Larry Norman paved the way for CCM, which soon became a multimillion dollar industry with its own charting mechanisms (such as *Billboard*'s Christian Albums and Hot Christian Adult Contemporary charts), a Christian equivalent to the Grammys (the Gospel Music Association's "Dove Awards"), trade magazines, and a host of record labels that cater to Christian tastes for a very wide range of styles and genres. Although adult contemporary/rock music has consistently been the mainstream genre of CCM, other CCM artists made (sometimes cringeworthy) forays into rap (such as Carmen and dc Talk), third-wave ska (such as the O.C. Supertones, Five Iron Frenzy, BUCK, and The Insyderz), and R&B (such as Mary Mary and BeBe and Cece Winans). Amy Grant, Switchfoot, Sixpence None the Richer, and a number of other "crossover" artists have enjoyed successful careers both within the CCM and secular music industries.

Following the lead of religious radio programing, televangelism began in earnest in the 1950s as televisions became more popular in American homes. Many radio evangelists successfully transitioned to the newer medium, and Christian television programming enjoyed a relatively high level of respectability throughout the 1960s and 1970s, helping some televangelists, such as Billy Graham, reach a degree of stardom and professional success that had heretofore never been seen. Others, such as Oral Roberts, Jimmy Swaggart, Jim Bakker, and Kenneth Copeland, became famous (and infamous) for using television to spread a "prosperity gospel," that is, a conflation of capitalism, work ethic, and faith in which practitioners believe God rewards believers with physical health and monetary wealth in exchange for faithful donations to a particular ministry. Christian television networks, such as the Trinity Broadcasting Network (TBN) and Daystar Television Network continue to churn out wide-ranging programs for cable television, and through syndication on network television, programs such as the "Hour of Power" (hosted by the late Robert H. Schuller until his retirement, followed by his son, Bobby Schuller) and "The 700 Club" (hosted by the late Pat Robertson) still reach millions of homes in nearly every media market in the US.

Christian television featured music from its earliest iterations. In the late 1960s, Oral Roberts switched the format of his syndicated TV broadcasts, which featured scenes from his popular tent revivals to a quarterly prime time televised ministry special with a studio-based, variety show format that consciously and purposefully blended religious content and entertainment. The show regularly featured his son Richard singing with the World Action Singers (formerly called the Oral Roberts Collegians, from Oral Roberts University in Tulsa, Oklahoma) and other well-known performers from the secular world such as Pat Boone, Roy Rogers, Shari Lewis, and Johnny Cash.[10] These programs successfully served both as an evangelical ministry outlet and a recruiting tool for his new eponymous university. Other similar programming included *Day of Discovery* (1968–2018) which featured vocal ensembles singing on-location at Cypress Gardens, a botanical garden and tourist theme park in Winter Haven, Florida.

The newfound success of the CCM industry and televangelism in the 1980s and 1990s coincided with the apex of music videos on MTV and other cable television channels. In 1982, Sparrow Records, one of the world's most prominent Christian record labels, began to create music videos for CCM artists. Seeing the potential of music videos for the future of CCM, the label eliminated four to five potential new album releases that year in order to free up the budget for videos for artists such as Phil Keagy, Michael & Stormy Omartain, and others.[11] In the same year, in addition to selling Betamax and VHS tapes of concerts at Christian bookstores, Word Records, another leading Christian label, also launched More than Music, one of the first television series to primarily feature CCM.[12]

But as with CCM itself, CCM music videos appealed to a very small subset of the market; however, over the years, there have been a few exceptions: In 1983, MTV played CONSTANTLY CHANGING (1982) and IT'S MAD (1982), two videos by Swedish Christian band Jerusalem, marking the first time Christian music was played on the channel. According to a *Billboard Magazine* article about the occurrence, an MTV spokesperson said that they agreed to the arrangement "on the quality of the video first, the music second. We didn't know it was a Christian rock group, and that is irrelevant to our uses."[13]

DeGarmo & Key were the first CCM group to have their music in regular rotation on MTV. Their video SIX, SIX, SIX (1983), coincidentally from their sixth album, *Communication*, was featured on MTV in the mid-1980s; somewhat ironically, though, the video was removed in reaction to US Senate hearings at the time that decried sex and violence in music, due to the fact that it featured a scene in which the Antichrist is being set on fire.[14] The metal group Deliverance was the first Christian band of that genre to be played regularly on MTV, and the video for their song "Weapons of Our Warfare" (1990) was featured among the top three songs on the weekly show *Headbanger's Ball* (MTV, 1987–1995) for twelve weeks in a row, and in 1999, Lars Ulrich (drummer for Metallica) named WEAPONS OF OUR WARFARE (1990) one of his top ten metal videos of all time.[15] The Gospel Music Association, the primary trade organization for CCM and other popular Christian music genres, has been awarding their prestigious "Dove Awards" for short form and long form Christian music videos since 1987. There has been more of an appetite for Black gospel music on secular networks such as Black Entertainment Television (BET), where *Bobby Jones Gospel (Hour)* (1980–2016) was the station's longest-running program.

Unlike secular music videos, which rose to prominence in dance clubs even before they were accessible on cable television, there were few, if any public places that featured Christian music videos beyond church youth group meetings, rallies, and summer camps. In March 1993, a service called Z Music Television was made available to cable operators by Gaylord Entertainment Company (which, at the time, also owned Country Music Television, or CMT, and the Nashville Network). In order to appeal to more distributors, though, advertising for the channel later in the 1990s dropped any mention of the channel's Christian content, opting to highlight the fact that its content was "objection-free (NO sex, NO violence, NO customer complaints)," claiming "Z attracts the widest, cross-cultural, cross-generational audience of cable viewers—from teens and young adults to parents and maturing baby boomers!"[16] Graham Barnard, Z Music's manager of programming claims:

> This is the only network where you can hear music like this—you won't hear it everywhere because of a lot of editorial decisions. But the music is still in step with what you would hear on VH1, and in the case of Generation Z [the network's alternative Christian rock program], on MTV. But you will notice something is missing, images that are not wholesome—we leave out the violence, raw sex appeal and disrespect for authority.[17]

While videos featuring CCM generally seemed to be a welcome means by which to reach contemporary youth and bring them the Good News, there were those who feared that videos presented dangers in and of themselves. Explaining how even CCM music videos might be problematic for impressionable viewers, Seventh-day Adventist theologian and Biblical literature scholar Ed Christian writes that music videos

> demand more attention than the songs alone, they glorify the performers beyond their musicianship, they often introduce themes of sex or violence not present in the songs themselves, and because they are often lip-synched, they seem insincere. The primary exception is some videos of concerts. Even Christian music videos move the focus from the song to the performer,

degrading the spiritual message. If the purpose of CCM is to turn the hearts of listeners to God, as claimed, we do well to notice that Christian music videos turn the attention to the performer.[18]

Christian goes on to warn that when CCM videos are produced, non-Christian scriptwriters and directors take over and use their "unsanctified imaginations" to dilute the message of the original song in order to make the video more entertaining.[19] I should note that while this position may have been held by some more conservative factions of American Evangelicalism, it was not widely held, especially not after the 1990s.

Although the vast majority of contemporary Christian radio and television programming is produced for Evangelical Christian audiences by networks that cater to Catholic Christians (CatholicTV Network and Catholic Faith Network on television and the Eternal Word Network for radio), and the CCM or Christian folk music featured on many of these programs was allowable due to liturgical reforms made during the Second Vatican Council (also known as Vatican II, 1962–1965), which paved the way for a more contemporary style of music in Catholic worship. In the General Instruction of the Roman Missal (*Institutio Generalis Missalis Romani*, or IGMR), a governing document concerning the way in which the Mass of the Roman Rite was to be conducted after Vatican II, the following direction is provided:

> Great importance should . . . be attached to the use of singing in the celebration of the Mass, *with due consideration for the culture of the people* and abilities of each liturgical assembly. Although it is not always necessary (e.g. in weekday Masses) to sing all the texts that are of themselves meant to be sung, every care should be taken that singing by the ministers and the people is not absent in celebrations that occur on Sundays and on holy days of obligation (emphasis mine).[20]

Further, the Council decreed in the *Sacrosanctum Consilium* (or "The Constitution on the Sacred Liturgy") of 1963 that Catholic music should be made more accessible to the general public:

> Composers, filled with the Christian spirit, should feel that their vocation is to cultivate sacred music and increase its store of treasures.
>
> Let them produce compositions which have the qualities proper to genuine sacred music, not confining themselves to works which can be sung only by large choirs, but providing also for the needs of small choirs and for the active participation of the entire assembly of the faithful.

> The texts intended to be sung must always be in conformity with Catholic doctrine; indeed they should be drawn chiefly from holy scripture and from liturgical sources.

As a result, a folk-rock aesthetic has permeated Catholic music since the 1960s and is featured regularly in Catholic radio and television broadcasts.

Notably under-represented or altogether missing from mainstream religious broadcasting are non-Christian religions and Christian sects that lie somewhat outside of mainline Protestant or Evangelical denominations. There are, however, a few exceptions: the Church of Jesus Christ of Latter-day Saints and Seventh-day Adventists have their own media networks (BYU Radio and Three Angels Broadcasting Network, respectively), and others present at least some religious content for Muslim (such as PeaceTV, Muslim Network TV, and Bridges TV) and Jewish (for example, Jewish Life Television, Jewish Broadcasting Service, and The Jewish Channel) communities.

Parable or Parasite?

Since the birth of the Contemporary Christian Music industry, singers, songwriters, record executives, and media moguls claimed there was a missiological value in CCM, believing that it contained parables, metaphors, and other important messages that would teach the lost valuable lessons about the rewards of a Christian life and the inherent risks of a sinful one. Some who study CCM, such as media scholar Eric Gormly, view this value in the co-optation and appropriation of secular music styles, claiming that such an approach "softens" the market for Evangelical messages, and "adds legitimacy to their positions and beliefs by injecting them into public discourse and into the general culture as a result."[21] In an interview for *The Week*, Kevin Max, singer-songwriter and former member of Christian band DC Talk, discussed the newer, more prominent trend in CCM to focus on worship music that appeals to Christian congregations, rather than performative, artist-driven songs that actually had a chance to reach possible converts with Top 40 tastes:

> We were reaching out. We were trying to communicate to the non-believer as much as we were communicating to the believer. Today, when I listen to Christian radio and see the festivals and see what's happening in the church, I don't see a whole lot of that interactivity. Where I'm at right now, it's almost like the doors have shut on the experimenting with lyrics and images and ideas to get people interactive.[22]

Statistics corroborate Max's claim, indicating that the audience for Christian music is a small group of Christians, not the global or national music market. According to the 2021 Year-End Report on the Music Industry, published annually by MRC Data (formerly Nielsen Music and SoundScan), music in the "Christian/Gospel" genre outperformed the "Children," "Jazz," and "Classical" genres, but still only accounts for 1.8% of the total volume for all music sales, 2.1% of total album sales, 1.7% of physical album sales, 3.1% of digital album sales, 3.4% of digital song sales, 1.8% of on-demand audio streams, and 1.8% of on-demand video streams.[23] Radio listenership of Religion/Christian programming is likewise very small, with only 7.1% of eighteen to twenty-four-year-olds tuning in for a measurable amount of time at least once a week recorded in Fall 2021. Only between 16–19% of adults aged twenty-five to fifty-four listen to the genre via radio each week, while 22.2% of adults in the fifty-five to sixty-four category and 19% of listeners over the age of sixty-five listen to the format for any amount of time on a weekly basis.[24] Of course, thousands of listeners—Christian or otherwise—find relevance, joy, and comfort in CCM, and do actually find value in the teachings embedded in the music's lyrics.

Still, by some accounts (even among its biggest purveyors), CCM is primarily a media artifact that favors substance over style. According to Billy Ray Hearn, founder of Sparrow Records, "Contemporary Christian Music has nothing to do with the musical style. It has only to do with the lyrics."[25] In fact, from the outset, CCM purposefully broke ties with proceeding forms of popular Christian music, such as gospel, that had a distinctive sound and style in its own right and because of the socio-cultural milieu from whence it came. John Styll, former editor of *CCM Magazine* (arguably CCM's preeminent trade magazine) explains why "Jesus Music," and subsequently CCM, was not considered to be "gospel music":

> I wouldn't say it was deliberate in the sense of wanting to distance it [Jesus Music] from anything, but "gospel" meant black or southern. What went out of the Jesus movement had never been called gospel music. We have just called the music [and all that surrounds it] Contemporary Christian Music . . . By the way, the term "CCM" had never been used until we started using it out in California."[26]

The fact that its lyrics are its only defining stylistic feature, religious media scholar William D. Romanowski describes CCM as "a parasite on secular industrial and artistic achievements, sanitized versions of various secular styles."[27] In this way, CCM (and its accompanying paratexts, such as music videos), function as what Frederic Jameson calls "pastiche," which "like parody, the imitation of a peculiar or unique, idiosyncratic style, the wearing of a linguistic mask, speech in a dead language. But it is a neutral practice of such mimicry, without any of parody's ulterior motives, amputated of the satiric impulse, devoid of laughter."[28] In other words, it is the unironic mimicry of popular styles and genres that voids (or at least renders impotent) CCM's critique or criticism of the secular world and its music through its cultural production.

For others, there is cultural meaning inherent in the style, and the fusion of secular styles to religious texts redeems that meaning for a higher purpose as a form of redemptive appropriation:

> [T]here are musical and visual gestures embedded within the practice of worship music that are unintelligible without understanding the ways in which they already function in more "mainstream" rock and pop performances. These gestures are "baptized" into Christian praise and worship music, but their meaning is inextricably bound up with the musical vocabulary and modes of fan engagement that are always-already synchretically linked to other music subcultures.[29]

Christian music publishing titan, Bob MacKenzie further explains how the Christian music industry viewed various pop genres as hosts to carry its message to a wider audience:

> People that were artists identified with a specific stylistic culture: rock, folk, black, rhythm and blues, etc. . . . We started moving out into the enormous stylistic possibilities that we found in the pop world. And what happened is that it just opened the market broadly. And, because people had all these diverse interests, each found a hearing. Once somebody got the idea, "Oh we can use the current, commercial music culture to communicate our faith," then the barn door was open. Then everything was fair game.[30]

It is important to understand that even though CCM labels may sometimes claim that the musical styles that they appropriate appear to them, at least on a surface level, to be vapid, empty shells, devoid of meaning and that Christian artists can repurpose it for God's glory and to give those styles *real* meaning, that is not at all the case, and I do not get the impression that CCM's practitioners believe such a thing. In fact, I think they clearly see the value and meaning already associated with popular styles and genres make them all the more appealing, understanding that secular tastes in music can serve as a touchpoint with both Christian culture and Christian commercialism. In fact, when I was a teenager in the late 1990s, the youth minister at my Southern Baptist church would often distribute church literature which included advertisements for CCM records. These advertisements would include comparison charts linking secular styles and artists to similar Christian artists; "If you like ____, you'll love ____" seemed to make a direct link between the cultural value that teenagers held for secular music and artists and the CCM music products they offered as an alternative.

"We Must Have Knocked a Thousand Times": Parody Music Videos for Latter-day Saints

In his 1942 study of the Church of Jesus Christ of Latter-day Saints, Wallace Stegner wrote that "it is almost impossible to write fiction about the Mormons, for the reasons that Mormon institutions and Mormon society are so peculiar that they call for constant explanation."[31] It is for this reason that I feel as though a brief introduction to the Church of Jesus Christ is in order to understand the parody music videos created by current and former church members and missionaries, replete with specialized language and abbreviations, idiosyncratic scriptural and subcultural references, and insider humor.

The Church of Jesus Christ was founded in the United States in the early nineteenth century, making it one of a few major world religions that are native to the New World. According to church doctrine and teachings, the Christian Church entered into a state of apostasy, called the Great Apostasy, wherein the teachings of Jesus and his disciples were corrupted, and unauthorized changes were made to the organization of the church and to the priesthood ordinances, that is, the sacred acts wherein the power and authority to baptize and confirm new church members, to bestow the "gifts of the Holy Ghost," to name and bless children, to administer other sacraments and dedicate graves, and so on, is conferred onto other Brethren—all of whom are men.[32] The Church of Jesus Christ of Latter-day Saints is thus named because in "latter days," or the Modern Era, Latter-day Saints believe that the true church of Jesus Christ was restored through new apostles and prophets—or saints. The first of these Latter-day Saints is Joseph Smith, who, according to church teaching, through a vision received a visit in 1820 on a hill outside of Palmyra, New York from "two Personages," understood to be "Heavenly Father" (which is the name given to the god of this world by Latter-day Saints because of their unique system of theism through which all worthy men in the Church become gods of other planets) and Jesus Christ.[33] It was during this visit that Joseph Smith was told that he should join no other church or denomination because of this apostasy. Beginning on September 21, 1823, Joseph Smith had subsequent visions wherein he was visited by an angel named Moroni who revealed that golden plates were buried on a hill called Cumorah (in Manchester, New York). On these plates was written an account of an ancient, "lost" tribe of Israel that traveled by boat to live in the Americas from 2200 BCE to 421 CE whom Jesus supposedly visited shortly before his final ascension into heaven after his death and resurrection. Aided by "seer stones" placed in a hat, Smith translated these stories from the "reformed Egyptian" in which they are said to be written into Early Modern English, similar to the style of the authorized 1611 version of the King James Bible. Smith and his associate Oliver Cowdery were subsequently visited by John the Baptist who anointed them as priests giving them the authority to baptize other followers. A great number of other Biblical characters and figures from the *Book of Mormon* are said to have also visited Smith to further establish church doctrine (outlined in the Church's *Doctrine and Covenants*), and to rightfully restore Christ's church as the "only true and living church upon the face of the earth."[34] Many of these doctrines include practices that are considered unorthodox, and even un-Christian, to other Mainline and Evangelical Christians, such as baptism on behalf of dead relatives and celebrities, eternal marriages sealed in secret ceremonies in Mormon temples (which are open only to Mormons in good standing with the Church), and "plural marriage" (or polygamy) which was outlawed publicly by the Church in 1890, but still practiced today by fringe, fundamentalist offshoots of the denomination in defiance of US law.

Joseph Smith organized the first meeting of his new church on April 6, 1830 in Fayette Township, New York, and as it rapidly gained converts, the new sect spread to parts of Illinois, Ohio, and Missouri. These early Mormons faced great persecution at the hands of some of their "Gentile" neighbors (that is, Christians who were *not* members of the Church of Jesus Christ of Latter-day Saints), mainly due to their unorthodox beliefs and religious practices, and concentrated political power when they voted as a bloc. This anti-Mormon violence resulted in the murder of Smith by a mob in Carthage, Illinois, and included several other armed insurrections and mass poisonings. As refugee pioneers, the Mormons were led by Smith's successor, Brigham Young, from Nauvoo, Illinois to Utah, reaching the site of present-day Salt Lake City, Utah in July of 1847 where a temple was built. This city and its temple serve as the world headquarters for the Church.[35]

From these humble beginnings, the Church of Jesus Christ of Latter-day Saints has grown one of the fastest-growing religions with over 17,000,000 members worldwide. Its scriptures are currently published in 188 languages, it maintains four universities/colleges and 300 temples (including the most well-known one on Temple Square in Salt Lake City). Of particular interest is the fact that although day-to-day evangelism is a duty of all Latter-day Saints, the Church currently directs over 62,500 full-time missionaries.[36] Single males aged eighteen to twenty-five (the age limit was lowered from nineteen to eighteen in 2012) who hold the office of Elder in the Melchizedek Priesthood are strongly encouraged to undertake a two-year proselytizing mission. Single women (aged eighteen to twenty-five) can also serve missions, but only for eighteen months, and married retired couples can serve from six to thirty-six months. This mission is seen by some Latter-day Saints as a milestone that marks the beginning of adulthood as young men (and some women) postpone college or careers to go on their mission. In fact, according to a 2012 report in the *Salt Lake Tribune*, "approximately 30 percent of all 19-year-old men in the United States serve, while between 80 percent to 90 percent of those from active church families go. At BYU, for example, there are virtually no 19-year-old men."[37] According to the same report, around 80% of all Latter-day Saints missionaries were young, single men. The remaining 20% percent were young single women (13%) and retired couples (7%). And although all Latter-day Saints are encouraged to incorporate evangelism into their everyday lives, it is remarkable that one of the fastest-growing religions in the United States, and arguably the world, can credit its spectacular growth largely to the missionary work of single young men (and women) leaving home for the first time. They are commissioned by their local stake president in a ceremonial laying on of hands before they embark on their mission.[38]

But being away from their mothers and fathers does not at all mean that the lives of the Church's missionaries are without structure. They first undertake a short period of training at one of the Church's fifteen worldwide Missionary Training Centers (or MTCs) where they learn to use the published proselytizing materials with which they are equipped for their mission, study scriptures, and when necessary, they stay a little longer to learn a new language if they are called to a mission site where one is required. While at these training centers, missionaries are also supplied with a copy of the *Missionary Handbook*, affectionately called the "White Bible" by some missionaries, in which the rather strict rules of missional dress and deportment are outlined. Under the guidance and watchful eye of the Mission President (a high priest in the Church who supervises all of the missionaries within a specific geographic area, called a mission), missionaries join another young church member of the same gender (called a companion) to knock on doors and proselytize for the Church, do community service, and various other church-related activities.

As was required before their mission calling, missionaries must adhere to a strict code of conduct that includes regularly attending church meetings, prayer and scripture study, abstinence from dating and any sexual activity (including masturbation), tithing, and adherence to the *Word of Wisdom*, that is, part of the *Doctrine and Covenants* that prohibits Latter-day Saints from smoking or drinking alcohol, coffee, tea, or other "hot drinks," and demands a general consciousness of healthy eating and living. Missionaries are encouraged to refrain from using "slang and inappropriately casual language, even in your apartment with your companion or in letters to your family," and schedules are a rigorous agenda of early-rising, memorizing, and proselytizing before bed time at 10:30 pm.[39] According to the *Missionary Handbook*, a missionary's sartorial choices are few: although the rules are a little flexible depending upon local customs and climate, men must wear conservatively-colored traditional business suits, white shirts, colored (yet conservative) ties, polished dress shoes, and socks that match the missionary's slacks. Women must "maintain a high standard of modesty," wearing clothing that "is neither too tight or too loose, is not transparent or revealing in any way . . . does not draw attention to any part of the body, is not casual, wrinkled, sloppy, or faddish."[40] Guidelines on outfits, shoes, accessories, hair, and makeup are equally restrictive, and all highlight the Church's desire for a woman not to highlight her own appearance. If anyone finds themself with questions regarding what is or is not appropriate, the part of the Church's website dedicated to missionaries has a "Dress and Appearance" section to help a missionary determine whether or not their newly-permitted sunglasses are too flashy, for example (prohibitions against sunglasses were lifted in 2016).[41]

Among other restrictions regarding who a missionary is allowed to spend time with, how much alone time he or she is permitted to have, how much contact and through what means a missionary can have with his or her parents, whose car missionaries are and are not allowed to ride in, and so on, there are also guidelines regarding entertainment. Until recently, missionaries were prohibited from watching television, watching movies, listening to the radio, and reading books and magazines that are not pre-approved during their mission.[42] They are only permitted to use the Internet under a small number of very specific circumstances, such as emailing their family (permitted only once a week on the day dedicated to preparation for the week ahead), using social media to proselytize, or to introduce new converts to family genealogy research tools. Cameras were previously only allowed as long they are not used while proselytizing, a missionary is careful not to look like a tourist while using the camera, and that too much money is not spent on equipment and supplies. New guidelines instituted in 2014 relaxed many of these restrictions:

> All use of electronic devices and media, including cell phones and computers, should be in harmony with gospel principles and should not detract in any way from the spirit and calling of your mission. Avoid anything that is vulgar, immoral, violent, or pornographic in any way. Refrain from using your cell phone during your service assignment hours.[43]

In October 2017, the Church announced that in order to be more strategic, it would introduce the use of smartphones on missions to help missionaries pinpoint people who are interested in religion.[44] Missionaries are allowed to watch only videos or DVDs that have been approved by their mission president.

The Church's *Missionary Handbook* goes into greater detail to specify the criteria of acceptable music:

> Listen only to music that is consistent with the sacred spirit of your calling. Music should invite the Spirit, help you focus on the work, and direct your thoughts and feelings to the Savior. Do not listen to music that pulls your thoughts away from your work, merely entertains, has romantic lyrics or overtones, or dulls your spiritual sensitivity by its tempo, beat, loudness, lyrics, or intensity. Listening to music must never interfere with your personal preparation or proselyting. If you have any questions about music, discuss them with your mission president.[45]

The *Missionary Handbook* also admonishes missionaries, "Do not use headphones; they isolate you from your companion."[46] A newer publication released in 2015, called the *Young Church-Service Missionary Guiding Principles Handbook*, goes into even further detail about the musical elements against which missionaries should guard their ears and hearts: "Do not listen to music that *encourages immorality, glorifies violence, uses offensive language*, or dulls your spiritual sensitivity through its beat, instrumentation, volume, lyrics, or intensity."[47] Although generalizing and paternalistic, these prohibitions against "questionable" songs are much more preferable to the Church's complete prohibition against any song from a particular genre as had historically been the case, especially when they had been forbidden for racist reasons. There have long been restrictions limiting the music to which young church members can listen, especially while on their mission. These date back to at least the early 1900s, and in addition to moral considerations much of the concern was tinged with racial anxiety. For example, church leaders warned against syncopated "coon songs" in the 1900s, and there were concerns that listening to rock-and-roll music in the 1950s would "reduce whites [Church of Jesus Christ members] 'to the level' of blacks."[48] Jazz was altogether prohibited in the early twentieth century; in an article published in *The Improvement Era*, the Church's official magazine of the time, an article warned against jazz music's "questionable" origins, because it "came from the Jungle. It belongs to the savage who cannot produce or appreciate the beauty in music as we of the cultivated and enlightened races are supposed to be capable of doing . . . Why insist upon music that has been copied from savage tribes."[49] The same magazine published a similar article decrying the crooner's style:

> From every standpoint it is a most reprehensible prostitution of art. It violates every ideal and tradition of real singing, and makes its appeal purely because

> of the sensual and too-often vulgar accentuation of sex, so frequently and flagrantly contained in the popular songs of the day.[50]

And some of the first anti-rock rhetoric comes from apostle Ezra Taft Benson (who would later become 13th President and Prophet of the Church), some of which is quoted in the *Missionary Handbook* and other training material (mentioned previously) and also recycles the racist dog-whistles used to condemn jazz music:

> Now what of the entertainment that is available to our young people today? Are you being undermined right in your home through your TV, radio, slick magazines, rock records? Much of the rock music is purposely designed to push immorality, narcotics, revolution, atheism, and nihilism, through language that often has a double meaning and with which many parents are not familiar. Parents who are informed can warn their children of the demoralizing, loud, raucous beat of rock music, which deadens the senses and dulls the sensibilities—the jungle rhythm which inflames the savagery within.[51]

The Church was definitely not alone in its condemnation of popular music, and the concern of jazz, rock, metal, and many other genres of pop music were not the purview of only the religious. But the criteria outlined in missionary training literature and in official church teaching excludes most any form of popular music from the listening diet of Latter-day Saints missionaries, leaving only classical music, recordings of the Mormon Tabernacle Choir (called "the MoTab" by missionaries, but now officially known simply as the Tabernacle Choir), and a few other exceptions (made on a case-by-case basis by the mission president). The Tabernacle Choir even produced a special album specifically designed for Latter-day Saints missionaries, released in 2014, that features hymns selected for their missiological import, such as "A Poor Wayfaring Man of Grief" and "Called to Serve," and several songs performed by famous young Latter-day Saints; returned missionaries (called "RMs"); and *American Idol*, Season 7 runner-up, David Archuleta (himself a former church member and missionary).[52]

While the Church generally, and understandably, frowns upon music that carries the potential to turn the focus of missionaries from their duties, it appears as if "lightening up" about music's acceptability is as much a Latter-day Saints tradition as is being scrupulous about music's power to lead youth astray. In his discussion about the encroaching pervasiveness of popular music into the social life of church members, musicologist and BYU professor Michael Hicks writes:

> After more than a century of polemics, the futility of proscribing popular dance and musical styles became clear: each generation found its own tastes

> superior to those of its young. Not unlike many denominational leaders, Mormon leaders almost always came to accept the music and dances once forbidden by their elders . . . As musical contexts changed, musical meanings blurred. Only the profane messages of popular lyrics were consistently fought. But even lyrics proved to be problematic; one generally found adults revealing and interpreting the textual meanings supposedly discernible only to the young.[53]

Considering the strong link between popular music and youth culture, it is somewhat understandable that missionaries often seek alternatives to the prescribed classical or choral music to which they are permitted to listen.[54] There is such a thing as Latter-day Saints-themed popular music that grew up parallel to the Contemporary Christian Music of more mainstream Protestant denominations discussed earlier in this chapter. Most notably, the Osmonds, an American family musical group that was widely associated with the Church, got its start singing barbershop music, later switching to bubblegum and R&B-styled pop and rock-and-roll. After years of success in the mainstream music industry, the Osmonds released *The Plan* in 1973 on the MGM Records label. This record gets its name from the Church's "Plan of Salvation," or "Plan of Happiness," which is the name given to a set of church doctrine that spells out the Church's soteriological beliefs. And despite being a concept album about the Latter-day Saints' faith, it appealed to general audiences, reaching No. 58 on the *Billboard* Top LPs charts, while singles from the album "Goin' Home" and "Let Me In" both reached No. 36 on the *Billboard* Hot 100. Despite the relative popularity of CCM in the United States, especially since the 1980s, rarely if ever has explicitly Church-themed popular music reached such a wide audience: only very few standout groups with some degree of notoriety perform church-inspired (or at least adjacently religious) popular music, such as David Archuleta (mentioned previously) and pseudo-classical, Grammy-nominated violinist Jenny Oaks Baker. There are, however, dedicated Latter-day Saints musical groups that specialize in popular music of various genres that are not themselves popular outside of church circles, such as the Nashville Tribute Band (a Latter-day Saints country music group), Hilary Weeks, Afterglow, and NlightN. Again, writing about music in the life of church members, Michael Hicks observes:

> This then may be the essential conundrum for the Saints and their music as they push forward toward the Millennium: how to reconcile their thirst for progress with their fear of contamination. While the Saints once wondered how they could sing the Lord's song in a strange land, they now wonder if they can sing a strange song in Zion.[55]

Perhaps the best way to be in the world without embracing the ills of the world is through comic parody. Among the many ways that various religious groups redeem their own reputation through music videos is through the use of parody. The etymology of the term "parody" already suggests a musical quality, wherein the Latin root *parodia* is derived from the Ancient Greek *parōidía* (παρῳδία), itself a combination of *pará* (παρά, with several meanings, including "beside," "beyond," and "against") and *ōidé* (ᾠδή, meaning song or poem).[56] Literary theorist Linda Hutcheon's *A Theory of Parody: The Teachings of Twentieth-century Art Forms* provides a number of contextual frameworks within which we can understand the various functions of parody and its various forms. She outlines the structure of parody, indicating that two levels of understanding exist simultaneously: "a primary, surface, or foreground; and a secondary, implied, or background one . . . The final meaning of . . . parody rests on the recognition of superimposition of these two levels."[57] Here, Hutcheon implies a constant negotiation of meanings between the original text and the new paratext (read: "replacement text" or "critique"). It should be noted, though, that "many parodies today do not ridicule the background texts but use them as standards by which to place the contemporary under scrutiny."[58] Still, comparisons, referentiality, and contradictions (even if only playful, rather than malicious) are required for parody, since "postmodernist parody is a value problematizing, denaturalizing form of acknowledging the history (and through irony, the politics) of representations."[59] Through parody, then, the politics of representation rise to the surface of art and other forms of cultural production for observation and scrutiny.

And there is now a large (and growing) body of comedic parody music videos on YouTube, created by Latter-day Saints, most of whom are presumed to be current or former missionaries, that highlight the missionary lifestyle in these videos. Writing about the intersection of humor and media for Latter-day Saints, particularly film, religious studies scholar Elisha McIntyre notes that "the way that religious people and their beliefs are handled comically can reveal much about how that group understands itself although in the case of the LDS church, this understanding can become limited in depth and accessibility when the humour relies on in-jokes and hence becomes restricted to those who have the stereotypical Utahn [*sic*] Mormon experience . . . ."[60] Filled with this type of insider references and self-deprecating humor, these YouTube parody videos appeal not only to those in the church community, but also to any outsider with a cursory interest and appreciation for Latter-day Saints culture.

On April 6, 2016, HELLO (MORMON MISSIONARY PARODY) (2016), a parody music video based on English singer-songwriter Adele's "Hello," was published by the group Joseph & Smith, named for the video's creators Marcus Joseph and Korey Smith but conveniently also a play on the name of the founder of the Church. According to the video's description, Joseph and Smith were both students at BYU at the time this video was produced. The song is performed in the video by Parker Cressman and Conner Hein, both of whom had previously served on a two-year mission but were not missionaries at the time the video was produced.[61] The video recounts the visits made by Elder Berry and Elder Pete to various homes during their door-to-door proselytizing work. In the song's first chorus, they sing:

> Hello from the other side /
> We must have knocked a thousand times /
> To tell you about everything our church does /
> But when we knock you never seem to be home /
> Hello from the outside /
> At least we can say that we tried /
> To ask you if you'd like to meet with us next week /
> And it don't matter if you don't wanna see us again anymore.

In the song's verses, Joseph & Smith have the missionaries joke about being different for eschewing tea (in keeping with the "Word of Wisdom"), about wanting to schedule home visits to lead potential converts in programmed discussions about church doctrine and lore, about the three hours Latter-day Saints usually spend at church on Sundays, about rumors of polygamy, and so on. The elders in the video wear the iconic Latter-day Saints missionary uniform and name tags, ride bicycles, mow someone's lawn as a form of community service, and lead in a teaching visit near the end of the video when a woman finally invites the missionaries inside to discuss the *Book of Mormon* over a slice of pie.

The video's humor lies both in its appeal to non-members who may have been visited by a pair of eager missionaries, possibly hiding, pretending to be home, or simply not answering the door, and to the missionaries who stood on the outside looking in. Adele's original version debuted at No. 1 on the *Billboard* Hot 100 and remained there for ten consecutive weeks, even becoming the first song to sell over one million digital copies in one week; the original song's video also broke records, including the record for views on its first twenty-four-hours on Vevo, the shortest time to reach one billion views on YouTube (eighty-eight days at the time), and received seven nominations for an MTV Video Music Award, including "Best Female Video" and "Video of the Year." Though not nearly as popular as the original, Joseph and Smith's version garnered over 500,000 views on YouTube within the first two days of publishing it on the video-sharing website.[62]

Less humorous and much more troubling is VIRTUE MAKES YOU BEAUTIFUL (2013), a parody video based on "What Makes You Beautiful," by British boy band One Direction. In what seems at face value to be quite a noble gesture, several young men's groups from various Latter-day Saints churches made YouTube cover videos in which they lip sync to One Direction's original version of the song, created to send a message to the girls and young women of their church that they are beautiful and appreciated.[63] According to an article published by *Deseret News*, a daily newspaper owned by the Church, a group of young men from the Lone Peak Sandy Stake (a group of Latter-day Saints congregations in the suburbs of Salt Lake City), led by Kellie Jeppson and Tammy Ogden, planned on creating the video for the stake's Young Women's Standards Night. According to Section 10.8.5 of *Handbook 2: Administering the Church*, "Standards Events" are annual events that include "special programs that emphasize moral values and eternal goals. They encourage young women to live the standards in *For the Strength of the Youth*, which will bring them closer to the Savior."[64] Alex Boye, a singer-songwriter born to Nigerian parents in London and a rising pop star outside of church circles, became involved in the video when Jepson called Boye's wife, Julie, to borrow a sound system after theirs had malfunctioned. Boye recounts, "Julie said, 'Hey, do you mind taking this sound system down to Alta High School where they are shooting a music video? . . . Oh, by the way, they want you to do some choreography for the kids.'"[65] Throughout the video, the young men, dressed in their Sunday best, dance on a football field, pointing and singing to the camera, extolling the virtues of modesty and asserting that young women do not need to wear short skirts or revealing tops to have value. Although this is a great message on its surface, the rest of the song insinuates that young women who do not adhere to their very specific ideals regarding modesty are not beautiful and have no integrity or self-respect. For example, the chorus includes the following lyrics:

> Baby you light up the world like nobody else /
> By the way that you speak and respect yourself /
> Girls with integrity are hard to find these days / . . . /
> If you only saw what I can see /
> You'd understand why I need your modesty / . . . /
> You gotta know, virtue is so beautiful /
> That's what makes you beautiful.

"Water Doesn't Always Turn to Wine": Ex-Mormon Representations

Not all music videos that feature positive portrayals of the Church of Jesus Christ of Latter-day Saints, its beliefs, or its practices. In 2014, Tyler Glenn, frontman for the Neon Trees and later star of the Broadway musical *Kinky Boots* (2018–2019), came out as gay. A former church member disenchanted by the Church's exclusion and mistreatment of him and others in the LGBTQIA+ community, Glenn released his debut solo album, *Excommunication*, in 2016. The album's title has two meanings:

> Sometimes I'm talking to God, but a lot of times I'm talking to my ex throughout the record. The title Excommunication is a play on words, if you look at it that way... religious excommunication, as well as communicating with my ex.[66]

Around the same time he broke up with his boyfriend, Glenn had lost the church in which he had grown up, which was already famously hostile to the LGBTQIA+ community, having recently issued newer, even more draconian policies that excluded the children of same-sex couples from being baptized until they were adults and forcing them to renounce same-sex relationships, even including their own parents' relationship.

The video for one of the album's singles, TRASH (2016), features several representations of the Church. The song begins with several diatonically planing synth triads before a much grungier, heavy synth-pop track that includes the ticking hi-hat of a step sequencer, a dark, distorted bass line, and interjections from what almost sounds like a synthetic choir of voices. The video's visuals begin with Glenn sitting on a hallway floor next to elevator doors drinking wine directly from a bottle. Drinking wine, or alcohol of any kind, is strictly forbidden by the Church; in fact, due to the fact that residents of Missouri tried to poison Church members in 1839 by tainting their communion wine, the Church celebrates this sacrament using water (Glenn even refers to this practice with the lyric in this song: "Water never turns to wine"). Visibly angry throughout the video, Glenn stands up and sings as he walks down a hallway that looks much like the hallways of a local Latter-day Saints meetinghouse, passing several famous church-related paintings hung on the walls. He first passes "Joseph in Liberty Jail" by Liz Lemon Swindle, in which the Church of Jesus Christ founder, Joseph Smith, is on his knees with his face uplifted toward heaven. In the video, though, Smith's face is painted black and white to look like a skeleton. Turning toward a portrait of Joseph Smith by Alvin L. Gittins further down the hallway (shown in Figure 5.1), whose face again has been painted like a skeleton, Glenn sings the lyrics "Yeah, you remind me that seven sins are deadly / you used to baptize me when I wasn't ready." He then passes yet another famous Latter-day Saints painting, "Moroni Appears to Joseph Smith in His Room)" by Tom Lovell; both faces in this work are also painted like skeletons.

Viewers then witness Glenn travel back down the hallway and into an elevator lit with lavender lighting (lavender being a long-standing symbol for the LGBTQIA+ community in general and gay men in particular) singing "one

Figure 5.1 Tyler Glenn singing near a defaced version of Alvin L. Gittins' "The Prophet Joseph Smith" (1959) in TRASH (2016). (Screenshot by the author.)

man's trash is another man's treasure," referring to the ways in which the Church discards its members who are in same-sex relationships or who feel same-sex attractions. The elevator is elaborately decorated with gold molding and intricate millwork on dark blue surfaces, reminiscent of the inside of a Latter-day Saints Temple, buildings that are usually closed to the general public and even to some church members. Inside, Glenn performs secret handshakes with himself, called "Tokens of the Priesthood," which are taught to devout church members once they have earned the right to enter the Temple for their Endowment ceremony, and which they swear on threat of death never to reveal. When the chorus returns, Glenn uses red lipstick to draw a giant "X" across his own face; he can also be seen on the cover of the *Excommunication* album with a similar mark. In a video interview for Radio.com, Glenn explains that the red "X" is a reclamation of the "scarlet letter" that he claims is placed on gay church members "because you're misunderstood or because to them you're a heretic."[67]

Ex-Mormons, who sometimes call themselves "ex-mos," have also shared musical videos on YouTube and TikTok, finding support and community on the social media platforms. Originally a blog created by millennial ex-Mormons Samantha Shelley and Tanner Gilliland to support others in their generation who have left the Church or who are still members but who are starting to question their beliefs, "Zelph on the Shelf" is now a YouTube channel with content shared widely across many other social media outlets. The channel's name is a parody of the "Elf on a Shelf" toy popular with many young American children at Christmas time; Zelph is a chieftain-warrior in Latter-day Saints theology from the Lamanite tribe, one of several lost Hebrew tribes that church members believe traveled from the Middle East to the Americas by boat in 600 BCE. While the content on their YouTube channel is primarily composed of vlogs, Gilliland has created several satirical comedy rap videos about major figures in the Church of Jesus Christ of Latter-day Saints. In JOSEPH SMITH RAP—AIN'T NO MAN KNOW MY HISTORY (2016), Gilliland appears dressed as Joseph Smith in a clearing in some woods, presumably representing the hill outside of Rochester, New York where Smith is believed to have found golden plates upon which was written the foundational teachings of the Church.[68] Gilliland recounts Smith's discovery of the plates, contemporary public perception of his discovery, and Smith's unconventional method of placing "seer stones" into a hat in order to translate the plates, rapping:

> Folks are realizing that I'm lying when I'm scryrin /
> Cause my game-rigging gold digging they ain't buyin /
> So in a hat I look to invent a rad book /
> A secret combination of some stories that I took.

Gilliland also refers to the early Church of Jesus Christ of Latter-day Saints' controversial practice of polygamy: "I got bitches left and right, I call each of them my wife / We'll be rough stones rolling in the hay tonight."

Similarly, Gilliland adopts the persona of Brigham Young, the second president of the Church and successor of Joseph Smith who led church members fleeing persecution to the Salt Lake City Valley in the 1840s. BRIGHAM YOUNG RAP (2018) is similarly acerbic, referring to Joseph Smith as "Joe Sleazy," Young's thirty-five wives (and the fact that many of them were children), the Church's belief that Black people are "the seed of Cain" and their dark skin is a punishment from God (a belief abandoned by the Church in 1978), and the Church's doctrine about "Kolob," a star or planet in space on which Jesus is said to live.[69]

On TikTok, user Big Crick (big.crick.music) shares songs he writes that are critical of his former religion in a series of videos called "Exmo Hymnal," parodies based on beloved Latter-day Saint hymns and children's songs. In a parody of "I Love to See the Temple," Big Crick describes the excitement of a young church member going to the Temple for the first time, only to realize, "Oh shit, I'm in a cult," having been taught secret handshakes and made to wear a new "baker robe" (referring to the Masonic-style apron worn during temple ceremonies).[70] In his parody of "Hark, the Herald Angels Sing," Big Crick sings about the Church's belief, as recorded in Section 20 of *The Doctrine and Covenants*, that Jesus was born on April 6, 1 BCE (coincidentally, the Church of Jesus Christ of Latter-day Saints was also officially organized on April 6, 1830).[71] As with many musical TikTok videos, these parodies are rather informal, shot in portrait mode and featuring Big Crick playing his guitar wearing a backward cap and casual clothes.

"We Stand Tall": Scientology Music Videos

As with the Church of Jesus Christ of Latter-day Saints, the Church of Scientology is a modern religious movement with roots in the United States, and similar to the public perception of the Church of Jesus Christ, the organization, beliefs, and practices of Scientology are viewed by many outsiders to be rather mysterious, scandalous, and controversial, perhaps even more so, due to the famously aggressive and litigious ways in which the Church has historically responded to its critics. Vilified as a scam or religious pyramid scheme (at best), or worse a brainwashing cult, the Church has been the subject of serious media scrutiny and exposés for decades and has thus far withstood investigations by the FBI, IRS, and the FDA.

Published on a section of the Church of Scientology's website, titled "What is Scientology," the Church describes itself:

> Developed by L. Ron Hubbard, Scientology is a religion that offers a precise path leading to a complete and certain understanding of one's true spiritual nature and one's relationship to self, family, groups, Mankind, all life forms, the material universe, the spiritual universe and the Supreme Being. Scientology addresses the spirit—not the body or mind—and believes that Man is far more than a product of his environment, or his genes. Scientology comprises a body of knowledge which extends from certain fundamental truths. Prime among these are:
>
> *Man is an immortal spiritual being.*
> *His experience extends well beyond a single lifetime.*
> *His capabilities are unlimited, even if not presently realized.*[72]

Perhaps no one embodies these unlimited capabilities, however realized or unrealized, more to church members than the Church's founder, Lafayette Ronald (L. Ron) Hubbard (1911–1986). Hubbard was a larger-than-life character whose own biography is greatly mythologized. Born in Nebraska, Hubbard's family moved to Montana while he was still a very young boy. A video biography showcasing Hubbard's early life published on the Church of Scientology's website makes a number of unsubstantiated (and sometimes even demonstrably false) claims about his early life, including:

> "... he rode barely broken range broncs at the age of three and a half"
>
> "At the age of six, he earned a place in Blackfeet lore [referring to Hubbard's claim to have studied with a Blackfoot shaman].
>
> "Just days beyond his thirteenth birthday, he became the youngest Eagle Scout in American history."
>
> "[In his extensive tour of Asia as a teenager] ... he gained access to forbidden Buddhist lamaseries in China's western hills, and there witnessed wonders beyond any known scientific explanation."
>
> "Beginning in June of 1932, he organized the first of several expeditions to remote and primitive lands. Initially a 5,000-mile voyage into the Caribbean, where he mingled with a people predating Columbus by at least ten centuries."
>
> "[In] Puerto Rico ... he not only completed the island's first complete mineralogical surveys, but also studied yet another ancient culture deep within the hinterland."[73]

However false, dubious, and/or xenophobic and Orientalizing these claims about Hubbard's early life may be, the fact that he was an extraordinary storyteller is undeniable. Hubbard became a prolific writer of pulp fantasy and science fiction in the 1930s, first publishing his work in *The Hatchet*, the student newspaper at George Washington University where he was briefly a student, and later in *Thrilling Adventures*, *Astounding*, *Unknown*, and other pulp magazines. He would abandon science fiction writing for decades, only to return in 1982 with the publication of *Battlefield Earth* (1982) and the *Mission Earth* series (1985–1987). He is now counted with Isaac Asimov and Arthur C. Clarke as one of the most influential pulp fiction writers of the twentieth century.

Hubbard laid out many of the Church's early tenets in his book *Dianetics: The Modern Science of Mental Health*, first published in 1950. Initially billed as a "revolutionary new science of the human mind" rather than a religion, Hubbard's *Dianetics* was a pseudoscientific study of the connection between the mind and ailments of the body. According to Hubbard, unpleasant mental images or memories of traumatic events, called "engrams," are stored in the subconscious "reactive mind." Through a process of guided meditation and confession, called "auditing," an "auditor" leads the person receiving auditing, called a "preclear," through sets of questions in order to "locate areas of spiritual distress, find out things about themselves and improve their condition" by bringing these memories from the unconscious to the conscious "analytical mind."[74] Because he believed these "engrams" had measurable mass and energy, Hubbard was convinced he could detect them with scientific equipment. In the early 1950s, Hubbard introduced the use of electropsychometers, or *E-meters*, into the auditing process. Described by the Church as "a religious artifact used as a spiritual guide in auditing," an E-meter reads fluctuations in the electrical charges on the surface of the user's skin (called electrodermal activity, or EDA).[75] As mental images of past trauma are moved to a person's mind during an auditing session, Scientologists believe that they are actually moving mass and energy to another part of the body, and E-meters supposedly can detect this shift in energy. Through the auditing process, engrams are erased, unblocking a person's spiritual, or "somatic" mind, allegedly freeing them from a wide range of ailments Hubbard considered to be psychosomatic, such as allergies, asthma, headaches, sexual deviation, and so on, and ultimately rendering the person as "clear."

Unsurprisingly in a time in which popular psychology really began to pique public interest, books such as Norman Vincent Peal's *The Power of Positive Thinking* (1952) and Hubbard's *Dianetics* were huge commercial successes of the early 1950s. Over 500 Dianetics clubs were started across the United States, and thousands of copies of the book were sold as it climbed the best-seller charts.[76] Throughout the 1950s, these clubs became a loosely organized movement with an increasing number of religious elements, and in 1952, the Hubbard Association of Scientologists and the *Journal of Scientology* were founded. In 1954, the first official church of Scientology was founded in Los Angeles, followed by the development of a national headquarters in Washington, DC in 1955.

More religious elements were introduced to the foundational beliefs laid out in *Dianetics* and Scientology grew to become a full-fledged religion. Through the "ARC Triangle," or affinity (love), reality, and communication, Scientologists can increase their understanding of the ways in which the universe works. Through further auditing (called "training" and later "processing"), Scientologists progress through various levels of awareness, first to become an "Operating Thetan," or a "clear" person free of engrams, and ultimately reaching infinite survival for eternity; this step-by-step, hierarchical process is called the "Bridge to Total Freedom."

The more controversial beliefs of Scientologists can be found in what L. Ron Hubbard called "space operas," named after the action- and romance-packed melodramatic science fiction genre of the same name. Although these beliefs are not immediately available to new converts, access to these stories are granted to church members at higher levels of the "Bridge to Total Freedom." Similar to creation myths found in other religions, space operas recount the origins of Earth and its inhabitants; however, according to Hubbard, the story begins around 75 million years ago when Xenu, the leader of a "Galactic Confederacy" of extraterrestrial civilizations, sent billions of thetans (or souls/beings) to Earth (known as Teegeeack) in a ship resembling a 1950s-style DC-8 aircraft to alleviate overcrowding within their galaxy. Once on Earth, the thetans were killed when hydrogen bombs were detonated inside volcanoes, separating the thetans from their bodies. According to church teachings, many of these thetans were brainwashed and were left on Earth. Now known as "body thetans," they roam the Earth and attach themselves to human psyches, causing or contributing to many of humanity's problems. Through auditing, a person can free themselves of these thetans and the problems they cause.[77] These controversial beliefs have become key tools that critics of Scientology use in their attempts to discredit the religion, and elements of these stories figure prominently in parodies designed to mock Scientology, even in music and music videos.

Music plays a surprisingly important role in Scientology, even if its use within this religion is not as closely connected to devotion and worship as it is in others. And while it may surprise some that L. Ron Hubbard was an amateur musician of sorts, it should come as no surprise that the Church of Scientology boasts about his purported musical accomplishments. The Church of Scientology's official biographical information about Hubbard frames him not only as a talented performer and composer, but also as an accomplished acoustician, musicologist, and theorist. Hubbard authored essays in which he analyzes "Country Western, traditional Oriental (*sic*), and even Rock music (which [the Church argues] he correctly observed was growing increasingly primitive)."[78] Although no analytical technique or analysis is provided, Hubbard claims to have analyzed several thousand popular recordings while at sea in 1974 and concludes:

> Studying the more popular groups, listening to their "singing," listening to their arrangements, instrumentation and drum shifts of emphasis to sticks and by other signs it became fairly visible, at least to me, that the sophisticated world was rolling back into the past and reaching for its tribal roots. The savage breast was stirred by rhythms mostly because they had very little in the way of instruments. But it seems the savage breast is with us again.[79]

The Church also claims Hubbard discovered—and solved—the issue of frequency masking, through the use of what he called "the laws of proportionate sound." Hubbard writes:

> It has been known but only as a theory without application that two cannons, fired at each other at the same instant could cancel each other's sound waves and result in silence. I doubt any scientist ever tried it out. However, the truth is that sound waves *can* cancel sound waves. And this is the basic fact behind proportionate sound.[80]

As it turns out, frequency masking is a well-known physical and psychoacoustic phenomenon in which one sound is rendered partially inaudible by the presence of another simultaneous sound. It has been widely studied by physicists, psychologists, and acousticians since at least the mid-nineteenth century, long before Hubbard's birth. Perhaps most absurd of all, there is even a widely circulated account from among Hubbard's close followers in which Hubbard claims to have invented music many incarnations ago near the beginning of time when he was "Arp Cola," a primordial thetan.[81]

In August 1967, the Church of Scientology established The Sea Organization, or "Sea Org." Although most scholars believe that Sea Org was developed out of paranoia about nuclear war and as a way for Hubbard and other church leaders to escape the scrutiny of several bureaucratic arms of the United States government, namely the Internal Revenue Service and the Food and Drug Administration, the Church itself describes it as an organized non-organization that only Scientologists can understand:

> Although there is no such "organization" as the Sea Organization, the term Sea Org has a colloquial usage which implies that there is. There are general recruitment posters and literature for "The Sea Org" which implies that people will be employed by the Sea Org when in reality they will join, making the billion year commitment, at some church that is staffed by Sea Org members and become employees of that church corporation. . . . The Sea Org exists as a spiritual commitment that is factually beyond the full understanding of the Service or any other but a trained and audited Scientologist.[82]

The church initially purchased three ships, the *Apollo* (the fleet's flagship), the *Athena*, and the *Diana* in the late 1960s. By the early 1970s, Hubbard and other leaders were traveling aboard these ships, and the highest levels of Scientology auditing and training were taking place aboard the *Apollo*. Here in 1973, Hubbard formed the "Apollo Stars," a jazz-rock band composed of church members and members of the ship's crew. From 1973 to 1975, the Apollo Stars would present goodwill performances at various ports and were seen as "public relations exercises—important at the time when Scientology and Hubbard's flotilla were struggling to find port—or were simply not welcome."[83] In 1974, the band released an album that was not particularly well-received, titled *Power of Source*, that was produced and recorded by Source Music, a Scientology-affiliated record label. Almost exclusively an instrumental album, it included both original songs that were not, at first glance, particularly religious in nature and bizarre arrangements of George Gershwin's "Summertime" and the American folk song "When Johnny Comes Marching Home."

The Church of Scientology claims that Hubbard's next album, *Space Jazz* (1982), was "the first to fully utilize the capabilities of the Fairlight Computer Musical Instrument." The anonymous author of the Church's biography of Hubbard claims that he was one of the first to really understand the potential of this "wholly unexplored device," moving beyond the "gimmick" of using natural sounds in music (citing the Beatles' *Sergeant Pepper's Lonely Hearts Club Band* as an example of an album employing such a gimmick).[84] Although these claims about the album are demonstrably false, *Space Jazz* is likely the first concept album created by a fiction author to serve as a soundtrack for a book. Produced by Hubbard to accompany his novel, *Battlefield Earth: A Saga of the Year 3000* (1982), *Space Jazz* does include extensive use of the Fairlight CMI, and performers on the album, such as Chick Corea, Nicky Hopkins, and Stanley Clarke, were world-renowned jazz and/or rock musicians and Scientologists.

Unlike the Church of Jesus Christ of Latter-day Saints, Scientology has been billed as a religion for the elite of Hollywood, a sort of "Church of the Stars," likely due to the fact that a number of people who are (or once were) A-list celebrities, such as Kirstie Alley, John Travolta, and Tom Cruise, are counted among the Church's members. In fact, one of Scientology's key methods of proselytizing is through celebrity endorsement. Beginning with the launch of "Project Celebrity" in 1955, Hubbard sought to recruit leading popular figures to become members—and spokespeople—for Scientology. In a 1976 Scientology policy letter, L. Ron Hubbard writes that "rapid dissemination [of Scientology's message] can be attained by the rehabilitation of celebrities who are just beyond or just approaching their prime. This includes any person well-known to the public and well liked but who has passed his or her prime, or any rising figure."[85] He goes on to further define celebrities as anyone who is important in their field, an "opinion leader"—or their entourage, business associates, family, or friends—within the arts, sports, management, and government.[86] Such was the appeal of celebrities to L. Ron Hubbard and their usefulness to the broader mission of Scientology that he began to establish a number of "Celebrity Centres" to cater specifically to the spiritual needs of the Church's most popular members. The first of these centers was the Celebrity Centre International in Los Angeles, founded in 1969 and housed inside the landmark Château Élysée building; there are now ten Celebrity Centres in cities across the United States and Europe, including New York, Nashville, and Paris. Thus, it is not surprising that Hubbard would start to rely on famous church members and their relative star power to legitimize the Church and its message in all media, including its musical output.

Hubbard's next album, *The Road to Freedom* (1986), is the first to publicly and overtly share Scientology's religious values, and was released after Hubbard's death that year by Golden Era Productions, the media arm of the Church of Scientology. According to the Church:

> The album offers ten L. Ron Hubbard compositions to convey essential Scientology truths for what he described as "wide public acquaintance with what Scientology is all about." If the result does not immediately match preconceived ideas of devotional music, it is because Scientology does not require

> blind devotion. Its truths are self-evident and not a matter of faith. *The Road to Freedom*, then, does not preach; it informs.[87]

As with *Space Jazz*, *The Road to Freedom* included famous Scientologists from the entertainment world, including jazz legend Chick Corea, musical theater stars Julia Migenes and David Pomeranz, 70s teen heartthrob Leif Garrett, and actors Karen Black and John Travolta. Although the Church falsely claims that the album reached "Gold" status—it was not officially certified by the RIAA—it was widely circulated by church members eager to advance the Church's message and public image at a time in the mid-to-late 1980s when the Church was reaching wider audiences with TV commercials for Hubbard's *Dianetics* book, marketed on daytime television as "the Owners (sic) Manual for the Human Mind," and the Church was under growing scrutiny as the public and various national governments continued to question its status as a legitimate religion or a cult. And as CCM and its albums became a dominant force in Christian missiology during this time, perhaps it stands to reason that Scientology would benefit from releasing its own devotional music, which like CCM included catchy hooks and singable, repetitive choruses, both as a means to reach potential converts and to further legitimize its status as a church. Golden Era Productions released one additional album of music dedicated primarily to Scientology's teachings in 2001, called *The Joy of Creating*, which included famous musicians such as Chick Corea, Isaac Hayes, and Edgar Winter.

Since the 1990s, the Church of Scientology has tapped into another trend in popular music—music videos—and has created videos designed either to promote the Church's mission and vision to the general public, or that serve some specific purpose within the organization. Perhaps the earliest, and best known, example of this type of video is WE STAND TALL (1990).[88] However, rather than being a video designed to spread the message of Scientology to the general public, WE STAND TALL was produced for internal consumption by church members, and as such, information about its creation and usage remains a mystery. The song's message about standing tall in the face of adversity and persecution and celebrating the Church's success is clear, and it comes as no surprise that such a video would be warranted at the time. L. Ron Hubbard died on January 24, 1986, leaving a power vacuum at the Church's highest levels for nearly a year before David Miscavige became chairman of the board of the Religious Technology Center in 1987. The Church had been suing the IRS since it was stripped of its tax-exempt status and its headquarters was raided by the FBI in 1977. Many of these lawsuits had come to a head in the late 1980s; in fact, during the summer of 1989, the Church of Scientology even hired private investigators to investigate the personal lives of senior IRS officials.[89] Further, media coverage of the Church at the time painted practitioners as cult members at a time when public paranoia about the occult in the United States and other western countries was surging due to the Jonestown Massacre and the Manson Family Murders of the late 1970s, the broader "Satanic panic" of the 1980s, and a growing sense of anxiety about any new religious movements.

WE STAND TALL clearly appropriates both the look and sound of popular CCM and music videos of the early 1990s, and although the general public may not have been the video's primary audience, it is easy to presume that creating media that matches that produced by other mainstream American religions would lend the Church of Scientology at least some of the credibility and reliability that it had thus far struggled to obtain. According to former Sea Org executive and former church member, Mark Fisher, the song was written by Rick Cruzen (musician, composer, and sound engineer at Golden Era Productions), with contributions to the arrangement and chorus by Peter Schless (former Scientologist and Grammy-nominated composer of Jeffrey Osborne's hit "On the Wings of Love"), and sung by David Pomeranz, who also performed on the *Road to Freedom* (1986) album.[90]

WE STAND TALL opens with several night time scenes, underscored at first by a synth pad and later by piano, guitar, bass, and drums, as people walk the streets of a city, seemingly without direction. As Pomeranz begins singing, the word "Scientology" appears in glowing neon light against a pitch-black background, and we get a close glimpse of a square-jawed, conventionally handsome white man in his mid-to-late thirties, dressed in a light suit and red necktie, giving us reason to believe it was he who was wandering the streets looking for direction. As he looks up, the Scientology sign illuminates his face.[91] We then see a golden eight-pointed cross, one of the principal symbols of the Church of Scientology, against the same black background.[92]

As the camera zooms into the center of the cross, the scene fades to a gathering of Scientologists raising lit candles at a convention, while Pomeranz sings about standing tall and striking down "walls of darkness." The lyrics continue in a pre-chorus, "We decided to take a stand / to defend the rights of men," while, switching to a wide shot of the crowd, the camera pans to the sky where a stylized "S" is created with bright searchlights. As the chorus begins, viewers see footage from the Religious Freedom Crusade in Portland, Oregon in 1985, a twenty-seven-day protest demonstration against the jury verdict the Church had received in which it was charged $39 million in punitive damages for fraud.

During the second verse, the video features church members entering a Hubbard Dianetics Foundation building and participating in auditing wherein practitioners are shown sitting in small groups of three while one of the members of each group seems to be recounting positive memories with their eyes closed to the others sitting around them. When the chorus returns, we see scenes of famous Scientologists involved in professional sports and popular culture: Charles

Lakes, the first African American gymnast to compete for the United States in the Olympics (1988); Roberto Guerrero, a Colombian American race card driver who drove Dianetics branded cars when the Church of Scientology briefly sponsored motorsports; and actor John Travolta; followed by clips of the Church's work through its global branches in South Africa in Japan, and a large black tie event in the United States.

The song features a post-chorus, or secondary chorus, in which a large choir repeatedly sings "Hey la li la / Hey la li we stand tall." Seemingly based on popular videos for charity singles of the 1980s, such as DO THEY KNOW IT'S CHRISTMAS (Band Aid, 1984), and we are the world (USA for Africa, 1985), this section of WE STAND TALL centers around a mass choir called the Scientology Singers and presumably composed entirely of church members. In scenes featuring the choir, high ranking church executives can be seen in the first couple of rows, including David Miscavige (the current leader of the Church), Shelly Miscavige (who, as of this writing, has not been seen in public since August 2007, and whom many former Scientologists are concerned is being hidden, held against her will, and abused by the Church), Heber Jentzsch (former president of the Church of Scientology International), and Michael Rinder (former executive director of the Church's Office of Special Affairs). As most of the participants in the video are likely not professional performers, viewers might notice that, with few exceptions, the enthusiasm the singers may have for the message of the song is not effectively portrayed in their seemingly insincere, affected facial expressions or stilted head movements.

The chorus returns with clips of other Scientology events from the late 1980s, such as the presentation of awards to major donors, the release of the Mark Super VII Quantum E-meter (an upgrade from the previous E-meter), a ribbon cutting ceremony and cannon salute at Saint Hill Manor (Hubbard's former home and Scientology property in West Sussex, England), and the christening ceremony of the Sea Org's ship *Freewinds* in 1988. After a key change, the chorus and post-chorus are repeated a final time by the choir (beginning at around 4:11), accompanied by hand claps and ad libs from Pomeranz. Here viewers see various black and white film clips in which the Church's founder, L. Ron Hubbard, is presenting lectures explaining *Dianetics* and the various levels of what will become known as the "Bridge to Total Freedom," demonstrating how an E-meter works, and sitting at his desk signing papers. The video ends with a final exclamation of "We stand tall" over an Aeolian cadence (♭VI, ♭VII, I) and color footage of Hubbard riding in a parade in the United Kingdom.

In 2010, the Church of Scientology released a video of a live performance of "We Stand Tall," featuring a decidedly updated R&B version of the song.[93] The recorded performance took place at the Church's 2010 New Year celebration at the Shrine Auditorium in Los Angeles, California, and features a female vocalist and backup singers, a guitarist, a large gospel choir, and dancers. As in the original WE STAND TALL video, clips of L. Ron Hubbard can be seen displayed on large screens in the venue. WE STAND TALL was the first of several music videos that have been released by the Church for recruiting and public relations purposes or leaked to the public by former church members. For example, in conjunction with American rapper Chill E.B., the Copenhagen branch of the International Association of Scientologists (or IAS) released DAUNTLESS, DEFIANT, RESOLUTE in 2011. In 2012, the United Kingdom branch of the IAS released IT'S YOU—IT'S ME, featuring famous musicians such as David Pomeranz and Chick Corea, and a number of minor celebrities and their family members, such as Beck's father and stepmother.

WE STAND TALL may be one of a very few music videos created by a minority religious group that has specifically been singled out for parody. On March 29, 2015, "Going Clear," a damning documentary about alleged abuse and fraud within the Church of Scientology, directed by Alex Gibney, premiered on the television network HBO and included WE STAND TALL. In response, the American late-night sketch comedy show *Saturday Night Live* (NBC, 1975–current) created a parody music video based on WE STAND TALL; titled ALWAYS BELIEVE, the skit was an anthem celebrating the fake religion of Neurotology.[94] Many scenes in SNL's lampoon were shot-for-shot recreations of the WE STAND TALL video. Adopting a grainy, VHS video aesthetic to match the version of WE STAND TALL from the documentary, SNL's version begins with scenes of a man wandering on a street at night and discovering a neon sign (although the sign in this video says "Neurotology"), a shot zooming into a golden sixteen-pointed cross, a scene in the "Diametrics Foundation" (a spoof of Scientology's Dianetics Foundation), and an enthusiastic mass choir wearing clothing and hairstyles typical of the early 1990s (Figure 5.2).

Although the lyrics to WE STAND TALL might seem to outsiders to be rather innocuous and essentially free from controversial doctrine or religious ideology,

Figure 5.2 Mass choir scenes from WE STAND TALL (1990) and the SNL parody ALWAYS BELIEVE (2015). (Screenshots by the author.)

the lyrics of SNL's parody focus on what Scientology's critics consider to be vapid and intentionally opaque "New Age" elements of the religion and on its most controversial beliefs and practices:

Reach out your hand and follow me /
I have the code, the code to the key /
The key to the secret, the secret of space /
It's Neurotology

Religion and science intertwined /
Aliens live inside of our minds /
Billion-year contract we have signed /
It all makes sense to me.

ALWAYS BELIEVE features similar (but fewer) clips of the leader of Neurotology, and in them, the Hubbard-esque character is treated with much less respect: he is seen giving a military salute, trying on a metal helmet designed for mind reading (a parody of Scientology's E-meters), and proudly drawing a childish halo-crowned alien with the word "God" written across it on an easel (a nod to thetans as featured in Scientology's doctrine, referred to as a singular alien, "Meepthorp," in the parody video). Although Hubbard did not die of "pink eye" as ALWAYS BELIEVE insinuates, he did suffer from conjunctivitis when serving in the military.

Perhaps the most scurrilous element of ALWAYS BELIEVE that does *not* appear in WE STAND TALL are the occasional "call outs" indicating members appearing in the video's choir who have been disappeared, abused, not allowed to see their families, "sued to death," or constantly surveilled; have left the Church to become outspoken critics; or are abusive leaders in the organization. These call outs refer to claims made in the documentary and by others who have left the Church of Scientology; similar call outs are used when the video appears in "Going Clear," indicating when various members appearing in WE STAND TALL left the Church.

Several of the Church's youth-oriented music videos can be found online, performed by "Kids on Stage for a Better World," a youth performing group active from 1992 to 2012 and based at Scientology's Celebrity Centre International in Los Angeles. According to the group's website, it was established by producer Jean Dale Glass as a way to "allow willing children to be able make a direct, tangible contribution to the creation of a better world through their inherent talents and tremendous enthusiasm."[95] In addition to producing a number of annual public performances and a short-lived video series on the teachings of Scientology aimed at older children and teenagers, this group also produced a number of music videos extolling the virtues of Scientology's message or spreading other, more generic, generally positive messages. One of the earliest of these videos is

STARTS WITH ME (1993), and as with CCM music videos, this video appropriates a number of elements from popular secular music videos in an attempt to appeal to young audiences.[96] STARTS WITH ME opens with a scene of bored children are sitting in study hall, throwing paper at one another, writing notes, yawning, sleeping on an open book, and so on to the sound of a ticking clock as their matronly teacher peers over her glasses and scolds anyone who makes too much noise. The "Stern or Acerbic Teacher" is a common trope in music videos of the 1980s, such as Twisted Sister's I WANNA ROCK (1984) and Mötley Crüe's SMOKIN' IN THE BOYS ROOM (1985). As was often the case with religious media that borrowed from popular culture, including CCM, creators of this media did not often have their finger on the pulse of youth culture and incorporated trendy elements into their songs and videos long after they had become popular and not long before they were no longer cool. Here, references from ten-year-old music videos make STARTS WITH ME seem dated, even at the time of its release in the mid-1990s, and it gives the impression of both being out of touch and pandering to young people.

Not long into the video, a Eurodance/Hip House track suddenly begins to play diegetically, disturbing the class and causing all the visible characters, including the teacher, to look around for the music's source. Suddenly, one of the students begins to sing: "Starts with me / starts with you;" a boy next to her continues: "gotta get busy / follow through." Another group of children walk down the hallway singing the same song, and all of the children in study hall file into the hallway to join them, clapping and marching to the beat of the song. As the video progresses, different students join in taking their turn to sing the song's verse or chorus. The teacher from the first scene is no longer mad, and instead, she watches proudly through the window in the classroom door and dances to the music as the students leave her care.

Like a number of songs from this time period, a rap break occurs near the two-minute mark. Here a pair of young male teenagers rap in a school hallway near a block of lockers. In addition to seeing the large crowd of students, viewers see cutscenes that include boys performing trick jumps on rollerblades and a student dribbling a yellow ball as if it were a basketball. The chorus returns as teenage girls who have sung previously in the video repeat "It starts with me / it starts with you." The video ends abruptly with the lyrics "Are you ready to start?" and all of the students, having returned to the classroom, throwing confetti into the air.

The Urgent Need for Religious Satire and Parody in Music Videos

In contemporary Western society, religion is still a taboo topic to discuss in polite company and remains one of only a few areas in which broad public critique is actively discouraged. Although freedom to practice a religion—or not—is ensconced in law (as in the First Amendment of US Constitution, which expressly forbids establishment of religion or the prohibition of its free exercise), Christian hegemony has normalized Christian values in our society to the point that many are unable to distinguish Christian beliefs and practices from common morality, basic human decency, and patriotism, even in cases where those differences may be quite apparent. Now more than ever, any close examination or critique of the privileged platform Christian dogma is given in our political or cultural institutions is falsely characterized as anti-Western or unpatriotic, and attempts to seek recognition or equal treatment by minority religions or secular groups are often branded as Christian oppression or persecution. We can still feel the effects of 1980s-style "Satanic Panic" today in conspiracy theories peddled online by groups such as QAnon, and we still see the same pearl-clutching and condemnation of irreverent representations found in contemporary music videos as we witnessed in the 1980s and 1990s.

As we have seen in this chapter, parody and satire have long been tools used by artists to provide both commentary and criticism in the fight against the hegemony of the dominant religion and as a way for the religious to adopt prevailing trends within culture to represent themselves (to varying degrees of success). This tradition is likely as old as Christianity itself and its counter-cultural critique stretches across history from the lewd drawings found in the margins of manuscripts copied by disgruntled monks, through the bawdy songs of medieval jesters about misbehaving priests and nuns, the paintings of Hieronymus Bosch and the plays of Molière, to the television sketches of the *Monty Python* comedy troupe. Although some representations of the sacrilegious in today's music videos are rather benign, such as the top hat with devil horns worn by Sam Smith in UNHOLY (2022), others are much more overt, subversive, and intentionally controversial, such as Lil Nas X's trip to hell on a stripper pole to give Satan himself an erotic lap dance in MONTERO (CALL ME BY YOUR NAME) (2021). And as we have already seen in Chapter 4, because the artists in these examples identify as queer, they find themselves brutally condemned by right-wing religious leaders and Christians who fight against LGBTQIA+ equality, labeling them as "perverts" and "groomers"—a clearly false and repugnant accusation lobbied against the entire community, not just those in the public eye. It is therefore not much of a stretch to read these music videos as an indictment of the ever-creeping influence of the more puritanical and dangerous Evangelical Christian nationalism that currently seeks to dominate our politics and culture, rather than a critique of the broader Christian faith and its tenets for whom these right-wing groups absolutely do not speak. At this time in our history, it is still rather untenable for victims of this kind of religious abuse to directly and effectively speak out against this treatment as their testimony often gets intentionally twisted and maliciously conflated into a critique of all Christians everywhere. So now more than ever, religious parody and satire serve as an effective way to provoke reactions through which these abusive Christian groups reveal themselves for who they really are. They also continue to be means through which marginalized religious groups represent themselves and their beliefs and through which former members of these groups can process religious trauma and find community and healing in a like-minded community.

6

How to Make a Prison Music Video If You've Never Been to Prison

The prison population is one of the most often overlooked groups of "others" in the United States and other Western countries. There is a wide range of contested and contradicting narratives in Western media regarding incarceration and life behind bars; those who have been to prison seldom *want* to go back to such a horrifying place. Others who only know of prison from media representations find jail to be an intriguing (and sometimes even fun, sexy, and/or queer) place about which they fantasize. This chapter deals with the romanticization and fetishization of prison life and representations of the incarcerated in music videos from both a "mainstream" and a prisoner's point of view. Although there is a small, but growing, body of discourse concerning the prisoner as *subaltern*, it should be noted that the term was coined by critical theorist Antonio Gramsci while he himself was incarcerated in Italy by Mussolini's Fascist government.[1]

On paper, prison seems to be a reasonable, necessary element of our society—a "correctional facility" designed both as a civil form of punishment for those who commit more serious crimes, and a place to rehabilitate criminals, prevent recidivism, and provide psychological, emotional, and spiritual guidance, treatment for drug and alcohol addictions, and workforce training for life on the outside. In reality, though, prison has transformed far beyond a "necessary evil" into a multi-million-dollar privatized industry whose profits rise proportionally with the number of inmates it confines, all while disproportionately incarcerating racial minorities.

Throughout this book are myriad examples of the music video as spectacle and the ways in which marginalized subaltern communities have been made part of that spectacle. Michel Foucault reminds us that while punishment was once a spectacle, showcased in the stocks, the gallows and the guillotine, the power of prison comes from its secret. He writes:

> Punishment, then, will tend to become the most hidden part of the penal process. This has several consequences: it leaves the domain of more or less everyday perception and enters that of abstract consciousness; its effectiveness is seen as resulting from its inevitability, not from its visible intensity; it is the certainty of being punished and not the horrifying spectacle of public

Audiovisual Alterity. Michael L. Austin, Oxford University Press. © Oxford University Press 2024.
DOI: 10.1093/oso/9780190277789.003.0007

> punishment that must discourage crime; the exemplary mechanics of punishment changes its mechanisms. As a result, justice no longer takes public responsibility for the violence that is bound up with its practice.[2]

Representation takes the form of a commodity through "spectacle," and in Western culture, incarceration has long been a spectacle. Whether locking people in stocks, hanging them at the scaffold, burning them at the stake, watching them on court TV, or listening to a true crime podcast about them, there has always been a public fascination with crime and punishment. And few things are more spectacular than music videos—many of which are infamous mélanges of drama, burlesque, the avant-garde, innovative technology, trendsetting, extravagant fashion, and of course, dazzling music. Critical theorist Lawrence Law writes:

> We live in a Spectacular Society. That is, our whole life is surrounded by an immense accumulation of Spectacles. Things that were once directly lived are now lived by proxy . . . Once an experience is taken out of the real world into the spectacular world it becomes a commodity. As a commodity the spectacular is developed to the detriment of the real. It becomes a substitute for experience.[3]

Perhaps there is some truth in this notion of the commodification of the spectacle, a perception that might have led *Observer Magazine* columnist Barbara Ellen to call music videos "throwaway art . . . the Kleenexes of popular culture."[4] As a commodity, the politics of representing signifiers of alterity leads to the reinforcement of stereotypes, essentialism, exploitation, and fetishism; the "other" is fetishized, objectified, and then consumed along with the music video. As we have seen throughout this book, music videos already draw our consuming gaze to the differently raced, differently gendered, differently sexualized, or otherwise different subject. And this applies just as well to the incarcerated.

And while we hide prisoners away from society to protect ourselves from the way society treats them, the mental images of prison held in our "abstract consciousness" are fueled by film, television, and other media, replacing the stark realities of prison life with spectacular images that romanticize, fetishize, or otherwise glorify prison as a site not only of punishment and pain but also of playfulness, power, promiscuity, and pleasure. Whenever the average Westerner thinks of crime and punishment, incarceration is likely the first form of punishment that springs to mind; however, very few of us have experienced life behind bars or really know what that life entails, and most of what we *think* we know comes from popular media. As criminologist Ian Marsh explains:

> There are obvious dangers with this reliance on media portrayals. The media coverage will almost inevitably highlight the more extreme aspects of prison life, such as riots or deaths in prison—the events they see as newsworthy. However as well as emphasising punishment, prisons can be portrayed as easy going and even privileged places. Indeed these two contrasting aspects of the media representation of prisons—as easy going "holiday camps," as the popular press regularly put it, or as dangerous and violent places (akin to American "boot camps").[5]

Even seemingly objective reporting by news outlets about prisoners, their treatment, and the state of the facilities in which they are held can sometimes be filled with sensational hyperbole. Likewise, atrocities can be under-reported, helping the public to continue to turn a blind eye to the injustices occurring behind prison walls. These willful and uncritical misrepresentations support later "epistemologies of ignorance," or political systems of knowledge that valorize willful and structural ignorance and misinformation, and ignore injustices and systemic inequality through which hegemonic power is preserved.[6]

Unfortunately, the messages we receive from the media about prisoners are missing critical information and context, are wildly exaggerated, are riddled with stereotypes, and rely heavily on gruesome and distasteful tropes that shape prisoners into monsters that deserve the brutal treatment we presume they are receiving behind bars. Many of the tropes employed in prison-themed media have mythic origins, seemingly springing from those who have spent time "on the inside," although often providing little to no proof or context proving that this is the case. For example, communication scholars Franklin B. Krohn and Frances L. Suazo explain the *possible* origin of sagging pants as seen worn in many hip-hop music videos:

> Frequently, rappers set the stage for their music videos in a jail, where they present what apparently many people in jail undergo, superficially of course, because the circumstances of the prison system are practically unknown to the average viewer. Rapper attire includes the wearing of droopy pants, which supposedly started in jail where inmates are not allowed to wear belts for security reasons.[7]

In an article for *Bitch Magazine*, writers Anna Clark and Omar Lee describe how myths and misinformation manifest in the representations of women in prison in film:

> These tales of vulnerable young things navigating a harsh prison are largely vehicles for money shot–style images that are the films' raison d'être: a roomful

> of women being hosed down by their sadistic warden as punishment (1971's *Big Doll House*) . . . or a young reform-school inmate gang-raped with a plunger by her roommates (1974's *Born Innocent*).[8]

While women in prison are often viewed as sex objects and helpless victims, depictions of men in prison vary largely by race. White male prisoners in film and TV are either wrongly accused middle-class men who find themselves in prison, white collar criminals, drug kingpins, or white supremacists, and racial minorities are painted with a much broader brush as violent criminals who often also happen to be gang members both inside and outside of prison. Myths and disproportionate media portrayals of rampant prison rape in male prisons elicit homophobic jokes about "being too pretty for prison" and warnings to be careful "not to drop the soap" when in communal showers, and as a result, they make light of the serious issue of sexual assault among inmates.[9]

The carceral state is well-represented in decades of music videos, and jail and prison serve many more roles in these videos than simply providing a *mise-en-scène*. In a number of music videos, prison is a place in which BDSM fetishes can be discovered and realized; in others, it is a metaphor for inner personal struggles or moral failings. In some videos, jail cells are used to (re)create imaginary histories or warn of possible dystopian futures. Music videos can serve as tools for the carceral state itself, warning would-be criminals about the punishment that awaits them or as propaganda to help maintain the public's trust in the justice system and law enforcement. Notably, many of these videos and the songs they feature only include literal or metaphorical references to jail or prison in their lyrics, and beyond the occasional non-diegetic sound effect of cell doors closing, keys jingling, or locks being locked, there are surprisingly few other sonic representations of prison.

Prison as a Playground

A number of music videos are set behind bars, and often these bars are designed as much for swinging around as they are for being locked behind. One of the earliest (and perhaps one of the most well-known) examples of jail as a musical playground is the musical film and proto-music video *Jailhouse Rock* (1957), in which Elvis Presley plays the part of Vince Everett, a blue-collar worker who accidentally kills a man in a bar fight. He is subsequently sent to the state penitentiary, where he learns to sing and play guitar with the help of his cellmate, Hunk. After proving his worth as a musician in a prison talent show, Vince becomes a rock and roll star upon his release from prison and performs "Jailhouse Rock" on television. Although Vince himself is treated poorly during his time in prison, having been tied up and flogged for accidentally punching an officer during a prison riot, this famous TV-appearance-within-a-film portrays prison as softly and playfully as Leonard Bernstein's *West Side Story* portrays gang violence, which is perhaps as raw and real as congenial 1950s audiences could handle. Choreographed by Alex Romero, this dance scene was designed to showcase Elvis' signature hip shake and included a cadre of smiling, dancing inmates, a couple of loveable police officers keeping time with their billysticks, enthusiastic saxophone and trombone playing, and a pair of comically out-of-place inmates who don't dance as well as the others and at one point share a playful kick in the rear. Even the police brutality is lighthearted—when the inmates are caught sneaking back to their cells, the officer taps the first in line on the head with his baton, sending him into a graceful spin and a choreographed stupor as he is helped offscreen by another inmate.

The song itself is a playful representation of life in prison. During the verses, the song's protagonist is locked in the tonic key, and despite the sliding guitar riffs and the knocking of the snare drum, each verse is chained within a sequence of E♭ chords. At these points in JAILHOUSE ROCK (1957), the prisoners' dance moves are similarly hindered; while the background dancers move relatively slowly and low to the ground in the opening phrases, even Elvis himself seems to be held in place with his wrists locked closely to his waist. Just before the chorus, Elvis is released, finally able to spread into his signature hip shake, slide down the pole, and continue into the chorus. In his analysis of the piece, music theorist-composer Christopher Doll appropriately calls this chorus a "breakout chorus," wherein the song's writers, Jerry Leiber and Mike Stoller release the sixteen-bar blues chorus from its tonic jail cell. He writes, "Such a chorus contrasts with its preceding verse (or preceding transition or prechorus, in some cases) by conveying an increase in intensity with respect to various parameters, including loudness, lyrical content, pitch level (both melodic and harmonic), rhythmic and textural activity, and timbral noise."[10] It seems as though the key that unlocks the chorus from its harmonic chains is Elvis's invitation: "let's rock." The lyrics "Number 47 said to Number 3, / 'You're the cutest jailbird I ever did see. / I sure would be delighted with your company. / Come on and do the Jailhouse Rock with me'" is a not-so-subtle, yet playful reference to homosexual attraction and/or prison sex.

British boyband One Direction paid homage to Elvis and *Jailhouse Rock* in the music video for their single "Kiss You" (2012). The concept of the video draws even more attention to the simulacrum of jail as the video is shot as a behind-the-scenes look at the boys playfully recreating the iconic scene from "Jailhouse Rock" and other films from the 1950s and 1960s in a film studio, under Mole cranes and studio lights, and in front of false backdrops. In the *Jailhouse Rock*-themed scenes in KISS YOU (2012), the members of One Direction are

Figure 6.1 *Jailhouse Rock*-themed scene in One Direction's KISS YOU (2012). (Screenshot by the author.)

superimposed within the composite image on screen; as shown in Figure 6.1, they playfully step in front of each other downstage, fighting for the audience's attention, pointing and singing, and fixing their hair.

In the background, they dance in cells and bang on the cell bars with steel mess plates on which prison food would be served. Later, all iterations of One Direction line up in rows to perform playful choreography together. As with JAILHOUSE ROCK, KISS YOU frames prison as a fun place for dancing with your buddies, not for civil punishment and rehabilitation.

Blink 182's FEELING THIS (2009) is set in a prison-cum-prep school. In an on-set interview with journalist Corey Moss for *MTV News*, singer/bassist Mark Hoppus explained the concept:

> The idea is that it's a very institutionalized school . . . It's kind of a combination of prep school and reform school, and it's very repressed and kids are being held down. There is a lot of authority and a lot of strict regiment, and the kids lash out and take over the school and destroy the place.[11]

As the students rebel, the prison quickly becomes a playground. As they gain their freedom, they strip down to their underwear and deface their uniforms, do acrobatic flips down the cell-lined corridors, scatter toilet paper everywhere, pour milk over each other in the mess hall, and dance at a rock concert in the prison yard while giant inflatable pigs (an overt reference to the police) wave in the breeze just beyond the prison's razor-wire-topped chain link fence. In a similar vein, S.O.B. (2015) by Nathaniel Rateliff & The Night Sweats features what essentially amounts to a fun concert within the walls of a prison. Staged as a clear reference to the end credits scene of the film *The Blues Brothers* (1980), the band performs the upbeat song as prisoners stomp their feet and clap to the music, eventually dancing on the mess hall tables and crowding around the band to dance.

In SWEET ESCAPE (2007) ft. Akon, Gwen Stefani makes escaping prison look especially glamorous and fun. Locked in luxurious, gold-plated prison cells, Stefani and the Harajuku Girls while away the hours dancing, writing letters, exercising with golden weights and medicine balls, and yawning on their beds, all while wearing very fashionable black-and-white striped prison uniforms.[12] Fortunately, a Dogue de Bordeaux brings Stefani the key to her cell in its mouth, and she and the Harajuku Girls are able to escape. After two hours and a costume change, we see Stefani in the penthouse of a tall, golden apartment building. She removes the long hairpin holding her bun in place to reveal a long rope of braided hair that she throws out of the window, Rapunzel-style, in hopes of being rescued. Two Harajuku Girls arrive on motorbikes and climb the side of the building using the hair, and once they reach the penthouse, they cut off the hair and dance playfully to celebrate. They help Stefani change clothes, and after a quick stop at a 7-11 convenience store, they rush her to a golden SUV driven by Akon. After a police chase, which Stefani inexplicably finds funny, we find out in a plot twist that the entire escape scenario was a fun, playful dream and Stefani remains in her golden prison cell. The song itself is also playful and upbeat, despite the fact that the lyrics constitute an apology in which Stefani expresses remorse to her partner for her behavior and vows to be a better wife.

Sex and the Slammer: Fetishizing Prison and Prisoners in Music Videos

The tradition of glorifying the mystique and sex appeal of prison has been quite prevalent in many television programs, films, and music videos, especially since the 1970s. While there are films and dedicated pornography genres dedicated to the male prison experience, the more ubiquitous form of sexualized prison film is women in prison (WiP) films. WiP is a subgenre of exploitation films that feature imprisoned women who experience some form of sexual violence at the hands of guards (both male and female) or other prisoners. These women are often portrayed as innocent when they enter prison, only to lose that innocence once inside. These films include elements of voyeurism (e.g., group showers and strip searches) and other sexual taboos and fetishes (such as lesbianism, BDSM, prostitution, sexual slavery, rape, etc.). These films could also feature racial or political undertones, such as those featuring interracial sexual encounters or Nazi prison camps. There's even a list on the Internet Movie Database (IMDb), created by user "Iankalion," titled "Best of Woman in Prison Movies." A quick scroll down the page and the promotional images that accompany the entry for each film highlights the blatant sexual undertones (or overtones) of most of the films on this list, such as No. 7: *Wanda, the Wicked Warden* (1977); No. 8: *Ilsa, Harem Keeper of the Oil Sheiks* (1976); No. 14: *The Gestapo's Last Orgy* (1977), and No. 44: *Bikini Chain Gang* (2005).[13]

Television shows that are set in prison, such as HBO's *Oz* (1997–2003) and Netflix's *Orange is the New Black* (*OITNB*) (2014–), are often known for their sexual content. Because it aired on premium cable television, the writers of *Oz* were able to feature frontal male nudity, overt homosexual intimacy, and male-on-male rape, seemingly using the show's shock value as an affective way to hook viewers. *OITNB* has been celebrated for its frank depiction of sexual relationships in prison, particularly among same-gendered partners and partners in unequal power structures (i.e., between prisoners and prison guards/personnel). Prison rape, or the threat of it, is also a regularly used trope in both film and television, and is sometimes expressed as a joke—such as warning a man in prison not to drop the soap while showering (*Family Guy*, Season 10, Episode 8), or warning someone about what happens behind bars to "pretty boys" like them (*Law and Order SVU*, Season 11, Episode 9, "Perverted"). However, the issue of prison rape is obviously no laughing matter: according to the US Bureau of Justice Statistics, nearly 80,000 people are sexually abused by correctional officers or other inmates in US prisons.[14]

Music videos recycle these tropes related to the sexualization and fetishization of prison and prisoners with varying degrees of obscenity and explicitness. One of the more subtly sexual prison-themed music videos is singer-songwriter LeAnn Rimes' NOTHIN' BETTER TO DO (2007). Shot in the Old Tennessee State Penitentiary, the same location as the film *The Green Mile* (2000), the video is set in the 1930s in a women's correctional facility in which Rimes' character, Annie Jewel, is being held. At the beginning of the video, Rimes is not dressed in a particularly provocative way, and both her clothing and the finger wave hairstyle she is wearing are very appropriate for the period in which the video is set. However, as the second verse begins, we see a newspaper headline reading "Juvenile No More." Soon after, and lit by a number of lamps pointed in her direction, Rimes appears in her underwear, raising the leg closest to the camera onto a chair so she can remove her nylon stockings. A male police officer holds a camera: at first it seems as if he is taking her mugshot, but instead, it appears this is a *boudoir* photo shoot, as Rimes poses as a Depression Era pin-up girl, glancing over her shoulder toward the camera and offering a coy smile. She and the other inmates dance and sing in the following scenes while clad in short gray prison dresses, tall boots, and dark red lipstick, which, although they are not the epitome of modesty, are certainly not as risqué as what Rimes wore in her photo shoot.

British rock band Kasabian released a UK version of their video L.S.F. (LOST SOULS FOREVER) (2004), which is also set in a women's prison: the fictitious

HM Prison Balmoral. The song became popular after the band performed it at Glastonbury, becoming "an underground anthem, articulating a mood of fear and paranoia surrounding terrorism and the Iraq war" that was very much in the air in the early 2000s.[15] The video's grungy aesthetic matches both the alternative style of the song and the prison setting. In L.S.F., as with other videos previously mentioned, we see the band performing for an audience of prisoners in a common area. The band finishes a song and lead singer Tom Meighan begins to announce their next song when a woman flirtatiously yells out, "Excuse me, can I have your organ," a cheeky double entendre referring both to his sex organ and the harmonica he is holding. This audience of women inmates is framed as being sex-starved and eager to see men: one of them loses control and jumps on stage to kiss a band member. Several audience members exchange sultry glances with band members and writhe in their seats to the music. The harmonica is passed around surreptitiously behind the backs of audience members and slipped into a bucket of dirty water that another inmate is using to scrub the floor. At the end of the video, it is revealed that the band used the harmonica to smuggle in a key which a small group of inmates uses to escape.

The female prisoner is even more overtly sexualized in Romanian Eurodance singer Alexandra Stan's MR. SAXOBEAT (2010), as she and two other female subjects in the video play the dual roles of prisoners and *femmes fatales*. Stan and the two other women, all of whom are wearing skin-tight black leather clothing, are "perp walked" into a busy police station for questioning and booking by a detective and a few police officers. "Perp walking" is a form of public shaming and humiliation in which police parade handcuffed suspects (and not necessarily convicted criminals) into police stations, courthouses, and so on. During the interrogation, Stan seemingly flirts with a handsome detective, dragging her finger under his chin, pouting her lips, and touching the badge he wears on a chain around his neck. When she and her colleagues refuse to provide any information, they are locked into jail cells. From her cell, Stan flirts with the officer charged with guarding her and her accomplices, dancing seductively on the bars of the cell and singing:

> Hey, sexy boy, set me free /
> Don't be so shy, play with me /
> My dirty boy, can't you see /
> That you belong next to me?

The guard succumbs to temptation and makes his way over to Stan's cell, where she reaches through the bars and pushes on his chest to turn him around so that he faces away from her. While Stan gives the guard a seductive shoulder rub with one hand, she uses the other to take from him his guns and the keys to their cell.

The women unlock the cell door, hold the guard at gunpoint, and force him into their cell, locking him inside. Having used their sexual wiles to escape detention, they sneak into a dressing room to exchange their street clothes for sexy police uniforms. The video ends as they storm an office full of detectives, and after binding and gagging them with tape, they casually walk out the front doors of the station to freedom.

Gender play and conspicuously sexual content play even larger roles in representing the incarcerated in "queerer" videos, which exhibit more explicit homoerotic and BDSM elements and (over-)emphasize queer stereotypes (both masculine and feminine). Lady Gaga's TELEPHONE (2010) is a nine-and-a-half-minute sequel to her video PAPARAZZI (2009), wherein she poisons her abusive boyfriend and confesses to the murder in court. The video is Lady Gaga and music video co-writer and director Jonas Åkerlund's tribute both to WiP films and to filmmaker Quentin Tarantino, and represents prison as a sapphic paradise. Gaga reports to sever her time at the "Prison for B#?/7&es" on February 11, 2010, and while wearing a blindfold and black and white-striped, high-fashion mini skirt with winged shoulders she is escorted past a long row of jail cells, flanked by a couple of butch female guards. As they pass cells packed with other women wearing collars, leather bras, and other iconic dominatrix fashion pieces, Gaga is catcalled and ogled by many of these women. Upon reaching her cell, she is stripped virtually naked and thrown onto her bed. One guard remarks, "I told you, she didn't have a dick," to which the other replies, "Too bad," both referencing a vicious 2009 tabloid rumor that suggested Gaga might be transgender or intersex and signifying the sexual intentions they have for Gaga during her stay in the prison. Later in the prison yard, which is filled with a number of muscular, butch women, drag queens, and trans women, Gaga arrives wrapped in large chains and wearing a black dress, tall white boots, and a pair of sunglasses made of lit cigarettes. Almost immediately upon her arrival, she grabs a leather-clad woman on a picnic table from the crowd and passionately kisses her.

Later that same day, Gaga is shown in a cell with several other women, this time wearing a studded leather jacket, bikini, and boots, and using empty beer cans as hair rollers. After a fight breaks out between two of the inmates, she takes a phone call from Beyoncé on a pay phone in the jail cell, at which point Gaga finally begins singing the song (at around 2:54). Throughout the song, she dances with other inmates in the cell block (who are all now wearing leather bikinis similar to Gaga's), and at various points, Gaga can be seen in her cell wearing only police tape, another symbol of the carceral state rendered "sexy."

Mid-song, a prison guard alerts Gaga that it is her lucky day and that she's been bailed out of jail. She walks out of the jail wearing a long black skirt, with long black sleeves and white bodice, and a very large black and white hat. This outfit is much more conservative than anything she's worn previously in the video, essentially "flipping the script" of traditional WiP films: rather than arriving innocent and leaving corrupted, Gaga arrives at the prison dressed for the sexual fantasies waiting inside and leaves dressed almost like a nun. Upon her release, Gaga is picked up by Beyoncé in a pickup with the name "Pussy Wagon" emblazoned across the tailgate in large pink letters; this pickup was also featured in the film *Kill Bill* (2003).

In the second half of the video outside of the jail, Lady Gaga and Beyoncé travel to a diner where Beyoncé adds poison to her scumbag boyfriend's drink, and Lady Gaga makes a sandwich (while dancing in an intricate origami-esque telephone hat) and a poisonous breakfast for Beyoncé's boyfriend (and the other diner patrons). After everyone else in the diner eats, drinks, and subsequently dies, Gaga, Beyoncé, and a group of background dancers finish the song. With a wink and a nod to the film *Thelma & Louise* (1991), the video ends as Gaga and Beyoncé speed away in the Pussy Wagon, promising never to return.

Several other scholars have commented on TELEPHONE, remarking on Gaga's ability to transcend gender stereotypes and prescribed sexualities. J. Jack Halberstam writes, "In TELEPHONE, Lady Gaga and Beyoncé trip and bounce through a pop anthem about women, desire, and the end of men—the scene is set in a women's prison and does not shy away from 'negative images' of queers: butch prison guards and tranny [*sic*] inmates abound, for example. (This is not a comment on actual prisons so much as on the prison of representation itself and the formulaic sign systems we use to represent otherness)."[16] Discussing the varied forms of gender-non-conformity within the video, Katrin Horn writes that the women in the video are "represented in all shapes and sizes and several constellations of power, antagonism, friendship and desire without being devalued or played off against each other. Rather than using the wardens' nonconforming bodybuilder-physique to divert from Lady Gaga's own rumored sex deviation, the video stresses the connection between these different kinds of women as gender outlaws."[17]

Gender play and role reversal among prisoners is also evident in Ukrainian synthpop band Kazaky's video, CRAZY LAW (2013). The video vacillates wildly between hyper-masculine images and more feminized ones. On the one hand, the video features a number of scenes in which the group's members (all of whom are conventionally attractive, muscular men) are framed as particularly masculine, exercising on examination tables and inside jail cells, licking and masturbating to a pin-up image of Marilyn Monroe, and spitting on the floor. On the other hand, as shown in Figure 6.2, the video includes scenes wherein those same dancers are wearing high-heeled shoes and high fashion and executing dance movements that would generally be gendered female.

A BDSM theme complements the video's prison theme, represented by black leather garments, including a number of leather masks, worn by everyone in the

Figure 6.2 Feminine clothing and choreography in Kazaky's CRAZY LAW (2013). (Screenshot by the author.)

video and the literal bondage that takes place: a man restrained with zip ties at the beginning of the video, and a man trapped in an animal cage later on who is poked and prodded by men wearing masks, chains, and leather aprons.

CRAZY LAW is a direct protest against a bill that was proposed in the Ukrainian parliament in 2012 but defeated, which aimed to outlaw any "pro-homosexual propaganda," including gay pride marches, and films with LGBTQIA+ themes, and any "positive depiction" of gay people.[18] A similar ban was under consideration at that time in nearby Russia, where it was unanimously approved in June 2013. The song opens with the lyrics:

> Why am I feeling this is a crazy law /
> You can have many looks even how you're born /
> Why am I feeling this is a crazy law /
> I'm not trying to show you something wrong

In a subsequent video, PULSE (2014), Kazaky adopts a related theme, dressing as erotic policemen wearing police hats, aviator sunglasses, and black pants; in lieu of shirts, most group members wear fetish-style harnesses or leather gun holsters. Again, gender play is featured in the high-heeled shoes worn by the dancers and many of their feminine-coded dance moves. The plot of PULSE is quite unclear and appears to involve little beyond the group's members dancing in a mirrored dance studio or against a painted brick wall, but the extra focus on costuming and choreography highlights the dichotomy between masculinity and femininity.

Lil Nas X's INDUSTRY BABY (2021), ft. Jack Harlow is yet another homoerotic prison-themed music video that highlights interesting issues concerning the intersectionality of gender and gender roles, race, and sexuality. In a "making of . . . " film about the video produced by Micah Bickham and posted on his own YouTube channel, Lil Nas X says that he selected a prison as the setting for the video because he:

> wanted to go to a place people would least expect me to go to in a music video . . . an overly masculine place and make it gay asf. I also wanted to visualize the theme of breaking free from the shackles society places on you.[19]

The original music video's director, Christian Breslauer, interjects to explain that "this visual is essentially a giant metaphor to represent Nas's unwillingness to conform to the industry standards or be caged in because of his beliefs. No matter the scenario he will be who he is and no prison is strong enough to contain him."[20] These themes are also reflected in the song's lyrics, which Lil Nas X explains "felt like a victory lap . . . but also an underdog anthem, and that's what I wanted the lyrics to reflect."[21]

INDUSTRY BABY opens with a scene from a trailer, released a few days before the actual music video was uploaded to YouTube. In the trailer, Lil Nas X follows in the footsteps of Eddie Murphy and Tyler Perry in playing most of the roles himself: the defendant (himself), the judge, both his own attorney and the prosecutor, and a member of the jury. The Supreme Court trial referenced in the video, "Nike vs. Lil Nas X," is a fake case based on the real legal controversy from 2021 surrounding Lil Nas X's series of Nike Air Max 97 shoes called "Satan Shoes," which Nike claimed infringed on their trademark. These shoes were released in conjunction with the release of his video, MONTERO (CALL ME BY YOUR NAME) (2021), in which Satan can be seen wearing a pair. After the prosecutor asks Lil Nas X "Do your mama know you gay?" he frankly answers, "Yes." As a result, he is sentenced to five years in the fictional Montero State Prison; the actual music video begins with this sentencing.

The music video proper begins three years into Lil Nas X's sentence, during which time he seems to have become well-adjusted to prison life. When we first see him and he begins to rap, he is hanging upside down doing abdominal exercises, polishing his Grammy Award trophies, and straightening a framed certified platinum record from the RIAA. As his cellmates twerk on him, he pats the butt of one and throws one-hundred-dollar bills at the other. Here, Lil Nas X performs a masculinized, dominant role, turning the pockets of his hot pink prison pants inside out; his more feminine-coded cellmates each grab one to be led down the hallway past other cells. When the chorus begins, we see Lil Nas X and eight other black inmates dancing nude in the prison's communal showers (albeit with their genitalia pixelated just out of view). While the choreography in this scene does not read as particularly feminine, it is very reminiscent of what viewers might expect to see women performing in many other hip-hop videos. In the next scene, we see Lil Nas X in the prison's non-contact visitation room, wherein prisoners speak to visitors on the other side of a glass wall via telephone; the group of Black inmates in the background are first seen sitting, then dancing in masculine-coded ways with sharp, forceful moves, and then twerking before finally sitting back down.

Serving as the prison's librarian, the song's featured artist, Jack Harlow, delivers a book, *The Book of Montero*, to Lil Nas X's cell. Interestingly, Harlow is the first white prisoner to appear in the video (at around the 3:55 mark), and he seems to be the only inmate in the entire video to have been afforded a prison job. Opening the book, Lil Nas X finds a pickax hidden inside which he uses to dig a tunnel in the wall behind a poster in his cell. Reaching the end of the tunnel, Lil Nas X drops out of the ceiling, and despite the fact that he is seen on security monitors, he remains unnoticed by the prison's Head of Security, played by gay actor Colton Haynes, who rather than keeping an eye on the monitors, is instead watching Lil Nas X's video MONTERO (CALL ME BY YOUR NAME) on his phone, licking his lips at the sight of Lil Nas X giving Satan a lap dance. His distraction gives Lil Nas X the opportunity to sneak up behind him, spin him around in his chair, and knock him out. With the Head of Security on the floor and unconscious, Lil Nas X presses a big red button (labeled "Do Not Push" in even bigger red letters), setting off alarms throughout the prison.

In the next scene, we see a conspicuously heterosexual Jack Harlow with a prison guard, played by model and social media influencer Vanessa Buchholz, who is mostly undressed and rubbing Harlow's chest and kissing his neck. When the alarms sound, she jumps up and quickly dresses herself, revealing a handprint on her bottom that Harlow had left by spanking her, yet another instance in which the prison/prisoner or punisher/punished roles are subverted in sexualized prison-themed music videos. Buchholz runs out of the cell in which she and Harlow were meeting, blowing Harlow a kiss and offering a cute wave as she leaves. Harlow soon follows, walking through a chaotic cellblock in which it is unclear whether or not the other inmates are fighting, having sex, dancing, or some combination thereof. It is soon revealed that Harlow is on death row as we see him sitting on the electric chair. Although Lil Nas X throws the switch and electrocutes him, Harlow is still able to finish his featured rap verse. After a scene in which Lil Nas X and twenty Black backup dancers perform in the prison yard, Lil Nas X rides out of the gates of Montero State Prison on the roof of the prison's bus as two guard towers burn in the background.

I Guess You Had to Be There: Music Videos from a Prisoner's Point of View

As we have seen throughout this book, identity is often constructed through difference, taking great care to separate "us" from "them," and focusing on "others." As cultural critic Stuart Hall explains:

> Identities can function as points of identification and attachment only because of their capacity to exclude, to leave out, to render "outside," abjected. Every identity has at its "margin," an excess, something more. The unity, the internal homogeneity, which the term identity treats as foundational, is not natural, but a constructed form.[22]

But sometimes, there is some popular cultural cachet in identifying as an outsider, outcast, or outlaw. Even before the advent of music video, prison has played an important role in the history of twentieth-century popular music. Even as early as the 1950s, Elvis's "Jailhouse Rock" and Johnny Cash's concert tour of prisons such as Folsom State Prison and San Quentin State Prison helped to cement a romantic outlaw image for recording artists; "gangsta" rappers and "outlaw country" singers sometimes rely on and build their persona around the notoriety and "street cred" that serving a sentence in prison affords them—even if they haven't actually been to prison. For example, Senegalese rapper Akon (Aliaune Thiam) built his career around a gangster persona and prison record, recounting in interviews and his music how he spent more than four years in prison for his involvement in an extensive luxury car theft ring; however, it turns out that he never spent time in prison. Although he had been arrested six times, he was only charged with one felony for gun possession in 1998, for which he was sentenced to three years' probation. He did spend several months in DeKalb County Jail in Decatur, Georgia for possession of a stolen BMW, but all charges were ultimately dropped.[23] Although Akon did not spend time in prison, care should be taken not to minimize his experience while serving in DeKalb County Jail, a facility notorious for its inhumane living conditions.[24] Nonetheless, Akon's fabricated arrest record has become the subject of a TikTok musical video meme in which creators film themselves using the app's police car filter while Akon's song "Locked Up" (2004) plays in the background. While viewers hear the lyrics "I'm steady tryna find the motive. Why I do what I do? / The freedom ain't getting any closer, no matter how far I go. / The car is stolen, no registration . . . ," creators will superimpose text describing ridiculous reasons why they might be arrested, such as being too sexy, talking baby talk, or eating their own twin in the womb.[25] It is, however, unclear whether or not many of these TikTok creators know about Akon's history of deception or if there is a disconnect between the song and the artist's real or imagined personal history. In his music video LOCKED UP (2004), Akon and Styles P. travel to a prison in a bus and perform from inside a prison. The video's apparent disconnection from reality becomes clearer in that the lyrics do not touch on serious issues that affect the prison population, but instead, only center around the frustration Akon felt in getting caught, being lonely and wanting his friends to come to visit, and running out of money for the commissary.

In contrast, artists who have *actually* been to prison to serve time have created music videos as cautionary tales about "the inside." This type of video, whether created by large record labels, independent artists, or surreptitiously recorded by people currently serving time behind bars, warns against recidivism and raises awareness of the plight and mistreatment of those within the prison-industrial complex. One of the most well-known American rap artists of the last forty years, Calvin Broadus, originally known by the stage name Snoop Doggy Dogg, does have significant personal experience with the criminal justice system and actually living in prison. In 1990, Snoop Dogg was in and out of prison on cocaine possession charges; however, his most famous brush with the law is his 1995–1996 murder trial. Although he was eventually acquitted with the help of celebrity lawyer Johnnie Cochran, Snoop Dogg and his bodyguard were held on charges of first- and second-degree murder and a conspiracy to commit assault in connection with the shooting death of a gang member, Philip Woldemariam, in August 1993. While out of custody on bond, Snoop Dogg produced a short film called *Murder Was the Case* (1994), directed by Dr. Dre and Fab Five Freddy and taking its title from a track from his album, *Doggystyle* (1993), in which the rapper himself is shot and falls into a coma.

The official music video for MURDER WAS THE CASE (1994) is excerpted from this short film. It begins with the sound of helicopters and live, on-location news reports about the fictional shooting of Snoop Doggy Dog, who is rushed to a hospital in an attempt to save his life. As he recovers after surgery and lies in a coma, a crow flies into his hospital room through a window, and after landing on a chair, transforms into the personification of the Devil. The Devil proposes a deal, which Snoop Dogg accepts, restoring him to health. Despite promising to clean up his life, he still falls into a life of drugs and crime, landing him in the California Institute for Men (CIM) in Chino, California. The song's lyrics in the prison section of the video both serve as a dire warning about the dangers of prison and underscore Snoop Dogg's own anxiety about being assassinated while in prison should he be convicted of murdering a rival gang member in his real-life murder trial:

> They send me to a level-three yard, that's where I stay /
> Late night I hear toothbrushes scraping on the floor /

> Niggas getting they shanks, just in case the war, pops off /
> 'Cause you can't tell what's next /
> My little homie Baby Boo took a pencil in his neck /
> And he probably won't make it to see twenty-two.

Several times throughout the song, we hear the whining, high-pitched sawtooth wave of a synthesizer sliding up an octave between two D♭s and then chromatically downward to A♭, musically representing police sirens and, by extension, incarceration.

Snoop Dogg's assassination concerns become a reality—though only within the video—as he ultimately ends up dying at the hands of two other prisoners who stab him with a shank just outside of his cell and a dispassionate prison guard steps over his body as he bleeds to death. In the video's last scene, we see the Devil laughing over Snoop Dogg's open grave; however, because he has eternal life, he wakes up inside his coffin and slowly faces the camera as the video ends with the sound of a flashbulb camera taking a mugshot and a flash of light.

Both his previous experience in prison and his murder trial had a huge impact on Snoop Dogg, the trajectory of his life, and his rap career. In an interview with rapper and radio personality Fatman Scoop, Snoop Dogg explains why his days of rapping to overtly glorify violence and death are behind him, especially after the birth of his first child in 1993:

> When I started writing Tha Doggfather, I lost a lot of fans; I lost a lot of homies because they wanted me to keep it gangsta after beating the murder case... They wanted me to glamorize and glorify, but I was like, somebody's life was lost. My life was changed. This is a real situation.[26]

A notable music video of this warning variety comes from a group of inmates from Rahway State Prison (now East Jersey State Prison) in Avenel, New Jersey called the Lifers Group. This group of inmates and their youth program, the Lifers Group Juvenile Awareness Program, was featured in a 1978 documentary titled *Scared Straight!*, directed by Arnold Shapiro, wherein the group's members would yell in the faces of troubled teens, humiliating them and warning them of the horrors that await them behind bars unless they leave their lives of delinquency.[27]

The Lifers Group's founder, Maxwell Melvins, was able to convince Los Angeles record producer Dave Funken-Klein to travel to Rahway State Prison for three weeks to produce a rap album, titled *#66064*, and a complementary video documentary, *Lifers Group World Tour: Rahway Prison, That's It* (1992) about their lives in prison as another attempt to discourage youth from lives of crime by demystifying life behind bars and to refute all of the romantic notions about prison that were prevalent in rap music of the time. When *Rahway Prison, That's It* (1992) was nominated for a Grammy Award in the "Best Music Video, Long Form" category, *Los Angeles Times* columnist Colum Lynch reported:

> the 30-minute video documentary, directed by Penelope Spheeris ("Wayne's World"), who is also named on the nomination, provides abundant testimony of prison hardships and brutality. Shot in black-and-white 16-millimeter film and color video, it depicts a cramped and dispiriting universe, filled with tiled walls, fences, metal bars and men with huge muscles. The main tracks, "Real Deal" and "Belly of the Beast," are gritty and unsparing. The lyrics, which are written by the inmates, deal in a direct and brutal way with issues like AIDS, murder, betrayal, prison rape, suicide and laundry detail.[28]

Perhaps one of the more positive stereotypes about prison that may actually be true is that the ingenuity and creativity of prisoners know no bounds, extending well beyond the limits placed upon them in their prison cells. Whether fashioning toothbrushes into weapons for protection, old fruit and toothpaste into wine, or a video game controller into a tattoo gun, prisoners are able to accomplish confounding feats of engineering with the everyday materials they find around them. Many inmates are also incredible artists in their own right, expressing themselves through drawing, painting, creative writing and poetry, and music. In 2014, men incarcerated at South Carolina's Kershaw Correctional Institution used a contraband cellphone to record a six-minute cypher-style rap video titled I'M ON (2014).[29] The video was uploaded to YouTube but garnered many more views when it appeared on Worldstar Hip Hop (a content aggregating website aimed at young black audiences), where it now has nearly 1.3 million views.[30] *BET News* reports that as punishment,

> [F]ive of the inmates received 180 days for the video, while the remaining two were given up to 360 days for partaking in social media. Officials at the Kershaw Correctional Facility further punished the group for possessing gang-related materials, contraband and a cell phone . . . the SCDC [South Carolina Department of Corrections] later modified the solitary confinement punishments to a maximum of 60 days for infractions, though social media is measured on the same scale as attacking a guard.[31]

Of course, despite the power that these music videos may have in warning young audiences about the dangers of prison, there is a chance that these messages will go unheard or unheeded. Further, sociologist Tricia Rose notes that the tropes and stereotypes often featured in these videos can also have a deleterious effect on the perception of BIPOC communities, especially Black people:

> By reflecting images of black people as colorful and violent criminals, drug dealers, and sex fiends . . . it crowds out other notions of what it means to be black and reinforces the most powerful racist and sexist images of black people.[32]

Rose also notes that there is pressure to maintain a sense of authenticity in hip-hop music, but since "authentic" urban African American experiences, even prison experiences, are often so distilled through racist stereotypes and tropes it is hard to "keep it real" when few actually know what "real" is:

> The "keeping it real" rhetoric is also a cover for perpetuating gross stereotypes about black people—stereotypes that have deep roots in American culture. Commercialized hip hop's distorted and narrow focus on one aspect of black ghetto street life—under the guise of truth telling—exaggerates and perpetuates negative beliefs about black people and obscures elements of life in poor black neighborhoods that contradict these myths.[33]

As a result, there is a danger of hip-hop becoming a disparaging parody of actual Black American life:

> From listening to too much commercialized, highly visible hip hop, one could get the impression that life in the ghetto is an ongoing party of violence and self destruction with "style," that street culture is an all consuming thing, that poor black folks have created the conditions under which they live.[34]

This same myth that "poor Black folks" have created their own impoverished living conditions is often, by extension, echoed in unsympathetic public opinions about prisoners who "get what they deserve" while incarcerated.

"They Don't Care About Us": Inmates in Music Videos

In 2007, the world was introduced to 1,500 inmates from the Cebu Provincial Detention and Rehabilitation Center in Cebu Province, Philippines, performing dance routines in the prison yard to Michael Jackson's "Thriller" (1982) and the Village People's "Macho Man" (1978) with military precision. Byron Garcia, the security consultant who started the dancing program, claimed that the dance routines added structure to poorly attended exercise sessions and improved inmate behavior.[35] However, critics of the program argue that, in addition to adding an additional layer of surveillance to the lives of the inmates, the dance also discourages critical cultural engagement and effectively extends racial and colonial inequalities.[36]

Although filming a video inside a prison might be a welcome change of pace for the incarcerated, especially when they are included as extras and get to appear in the video, there is certainly a risk that prisoners could be exploited in order to represent commercial or political interests rather than successfully represent themselves. Michael Jackson's THEY DON'T CARE ABOUT US (PRISON VERSION) (1996), directed by acclaimed filmmaker Spike Lee, faced serious criticism at the time of its release, both for its lyrics and visual content, so much so that the "Prison Version" of the video was banned from American airwaves. The song itself includes a number of questionable lyrics, most notably, "Jew me, sue me, everybody do me / Kick me, kike me, don't you black or white me."[37] This controversy likely led to the disclaimer that opens the video which reads: "This film is not degrading to any one race, but pictorializes the injustices to all mankind. May God grant us peace throughout the world." After a prelude scene in which school-aged children sing the song's succinct chorus ("All I wanna say is that they don't really care about us") behind a chain link fence, the video begins with stock footage of the detonation of an atomic bomb; the brutal police beating of Rodney King in Los Angeles and subsequent riots; a Japanese baby crying alone, burned from an atomic blast during World War II; a starving African child covered in flies; the assassination attempt on George Wallace (infamous segregationist governor of Alabama and presidential candidate) in May 1972; and a lone protester facing approaching tanks during the 1989 Tiananmen Square protests and massacre. Jackson himself sings from a stylized prison cell, surrounded by video screens with jagged black frames. Other scenes were shot in an actual prison in Queens, New York City, and feature inmates singing the song's chorus and performing a range of choreographed moves while seated, such as forcefully slamming their fists on the metal dining hall tables, raising their fists in the air, covering their faces, and turning their heads from side to side; meanwhile, police officers patrol the room, slapping their nightsticks in their hand to the beat. Despite these concerns, the fact that actual prisoners were included in the video greatly expanded and strengthened the video's potential message. While the video focused primarily on police brutality and race relations in the United States in the 1990s (and rightly so), the representation of prisoners in the video, most of whom are Black, also draws attention to the racial and ethnic disparity in the incarceration rates of BIPOC Americans.

THEY DON'T CARE ABOUT US (PRISON VERSION) was released in the wake of the 1992 Rodney King Trial and Los Angeles riots, a time when issues such as racial profiling and systematic police brutality were finally gaining national attention in the United States. Further, Jackson had his own humiliating encounter with the LAPD in 1993 as he was arrested (but not charged) on suspicion of child molestation, strip-searched, and photographed nude.

In 2003, hard rock band Metallica filmed their video, ST. ANGER (2003), at the San Quentin State Prison. In exchange for letting them shoot on the prison grounds, Metallica played a ten-song set for the inmates and made a $10,000 donation to support the construction of a field for the prison's resident baseball team, the San Quentin Giants. In addition to scenes from the concert that appeared in the video, many other scenes reveal elements of daily life within the prison, including exercise, visitation, time spent in a cell block, praying in the prison's chapel, and so on. Discussing the making of the video, co-director Brendan Malloy explains his intentions on ensuring that the video was not exploitative, remarking, "We tried to strip it down and make the video about them, really give it an organic feel . . . At first a lot of the prisoners were stand-offish to the crew almost as if we were there to exploit them, but when they heard it was a Metallica video they were all lining up to be in it."[38]

Other instances of filming music videos in prison are not handled with as much care and concern. For example, in 2004, rapper T.I. was permitted to leave jail on work release while serving his sentence for a probation violation charge in Cobb County, Georgia to shoot part of a promotional music video in the neighboring Fulton County Jail in Atlanta. The situation resulted in accusations of gross mismanagement by city officials, due in part to them having given permission for T.I. to use the facility for a music video. The resulting investigation brought several other human rights violations to light. Further, another prisoner, dressed in scrubs and acting as an extra in the video, escaped during the taping, sparking additional criticism of the jail's inadequate security and regard for the safety of its inmates.[39]

Copaganda in Music Videos

One of the most visible elements of the carceral state in and outside of prison is the police force. Popular music and criticism of the police seemingly go hand in hand, and there is a long legacy of distrust and disparagement of the police in the music and music videos of many artists in a wide range of genres. However, in addition to artists who avidly support the police and write songs about this support, police officers and police departments are creating music videos in an effort to improve public relations.

In July 2018, police officers in Norfolk, Virginia created a music video in which they dance and lip-sync to Mark Ronson and Bruno Mars' "Uptown Funk" (2014) in a bald-faced attempt to shine a more positive light on the department.[40] Corporal William Pickering, a public information officer with the department, commented, "It is allowing the country to see us in another way . . . We aren't all robots."[41] Although the video received more than 70 million views in its first month on social media, it probably comes as no surprise that many viewed the video as being tone-deaf, especially considering the fact that BIPOC people were still being victimized by police in Virginia, including Marcus-David Peters, an unarmed Black man who was shot by police in Richmond in May 2018 while experiencing a mental health crisis.

These music videos, described by some as "copaganda," a *portmanteau* of the words "cop" and "propaganda," describe a disturbing viral trend to create videos as a way to distract public attention away from instances of police brutality and other injustices at the hands of police officers by framing cops as down-to-earth, friendly good guys and public servants. As Black popular culture scholar Mark Anthony Neal explains:

> Simply put, copaganda actively counters attempts to hold police malfeasance accountable by reinforcing the ideas that the police are generally fair and hard-working and that Black criminals deserve the brutal treatment they receive.[42]

Copaganda comes in a variety of forms, including television series and franchises, such as *COPS*, *Law & Order*, and *NCIS*; police films; and even children's cartoons, such as *Paw Patrol*. And it can also take the form of music videos.

In July 2023, country singer Jason Aldean released the particularly controversial music video TRY THAT IN A SMALL TOWN (2023) as an ode to vigilante justice at the hands of small-town citizens and as a not-so-veiled threat to outsiders who might come to a small town to protest social injustices. The video stokes unfounded fears and accusations that go back to 2020 regarding rumors spread online claiming that busloads of Black Lives Matter or Antifa protesters would come to small towns to sow chaos and destroy property.[43] Standing in front of the courthouse in Columbia, Tennessee, a particularly infamous lynching sight during the Jim Crow era, Aldean sings about sensationalized (and proportionally rare when population rates are taken into account), instances of crime and violence committed in big cities before moving to more political territory:

> Cuss out a cop, spit in his face /
> Stomp on the flag and light it up /
> Yeah, ya think you're tough /
> Well, try that in a small town /
> See how far you make it down the road /
> Around here, we take care of our own.

During the song, stock footage of property destruction during Black Lives Matter protests, a woman flipping off riot police, and a police officer being yelled at by an angry protester, are either projected onto the side of the courthouse (seemingly insinuating that the property destruction in the videos defaces civic buildings and institutions everywhere) or interjected as cutaway scenes, clearly but furtively expressing unwavering and uncritical support for police in the way. The song's title and lyrics hearken back to "Sundown Towns," all-white towns and cities scattered across the Jim Crow South in which BIPOC people were not allowed after dark, and where law enforcement and citizens alike would enforce this segregation through violence. Of course, the type of vigilante justice for which Aldean advocates in the music video is obviously antithetical to actual support for law enforcement, since taking the law into one's own hands would imply a distrust that the small town's police force or sheriffs would be able to keep its citizens safe. Since its release, Aldean has had to edit the video, including removing the footage of BLM marches, not due to issues related to the content but because the video clips were used without permission of the copyright owners—although Aldean blames "cancel culture."[44]

Afterword

"You'll Never Look at Music *Videos* the Same Way Again"

Other Others, Music Videos, and Allyship

As scholars, creators, and consumers of music videos, it is our collective responsibility to ensure that "others" are represented in these videos with dignity and respect. It is also our responsibility to work together to ensure that everyone is represented in music videos. I do not mean to make excuses for myself here, but it is obviously an impossible task to comprehensively cover the representations in music videos of the marginalized communities discussed in this book, and a large struggle I continually faced in the writing process was coming to terms with this fact. That is to say nothing of the even deeper anxiety I feel when considering the groups that—due to time, word count, unfamiliarity, and a host of other issues—I have left out altogether. For example, interesting work from scholars working at the intersections of ethnomusicology and disability studies on hip-hop music and music videos created by Deaf artists (known as Dip Hop) would certainly warrant more investigation, especially considering the primacy of visual elements, that is, hand signs, in that genre of music.[1] Also, British rapper M.I.A.'s video BORDERS (2016) and others like it that focus on the plight of refugees, unfortunately, become ever more relevant as the global refugee crisis grows deeper and the representation of refugees in contemporary media becomes increasingly tainted by politics and the commercial priorities of cable news. In fact, there are hosts of ethnicities, religions, and people groups that are both underrepresented in or altogether missing from the scholarly literature about music videos and popular music, and misrepresented or underrepresented in Western music videos.

Similarly, I hope that as you have read this book, you have also found yourself asking, "What about . . . " as you think of marginalized communities and *other* others whose representation within music videos deserves further attention and discussion. Not only are we as individual viewers responsible for our interpretation and construction of meaning in the media we make, study, or consume, but we are also collectively constructing meanings for this media. Writing about the ways in which music videos resist "structural listening," Andrew Dell'Antonio argues that, as with the experiences of other performances as an audience, the

Audiovisual Alterity. Michael L. Austin, Oxford University Press. © Oxford University Press 2024.
DOI: 10.1093/oso/9780190277789.003.0008

evaluation and interpretation of a music video is not an individualized activity, but rather a collective one. He writes:

> A performance is a quintessentially social activity, since the members of the group witnessing a performance are connected by their shared processing of the codes/signs generated by the performance . . . much more self-consciously than solitary readers of the same text can ever be. In other words, the specific message of a performance/video (and I would contend with Frith, a music video) is not as crucial as the way the performance/video reinforces understandings about what is collectively meaningful—whether politically, socially, or aesthetically—and how the collective arrives at such meanings . . . I would thus suggest that the critical model that music videos establish is one of collective negotiation; thus the Ideal Appraiser they construct is a collective, not an individual.[2]

Dell'Antonio goes on to describe how MTV facilitates a communal assessment of music videos, particularly in the late 1990s and early 2000s, in the form of shows such as *12 Angry Viewers*, *Total Request Live* (TRL), and to a lesser extent, the animated *Bevis and Butthead*. With the advent of social media such as Facebook and Twitter, and especially video-driven apps such as TikTok, YouTube, and the future platforms that will follow and/or replace them, the collective construction of a music video's meaning is much less scripted and controlled by the video's producers, and instead, created and re-created by the audience.

As an audience of music videos, especially those of us who view from a position of privilege, we have a collective responsibility to listen to the communities represented in music videos, making sure not to overstep and speak *for* marginalized groups, while using our privilege to speak truth to power whenever possible. Realistically speaking, few of us have access to major record label executives, and even if we did, the chance they would listen to us would be quite small. But as a reader of an academic monograph—one who made it all the way to the afterword no less—you likely find yourself in higher education teaching, working with, or studying to become the next generation of leaders in the music industry. If nothing else, I hope this book has been a useful contribution to a much larger conversation about the ways in which we create and maintain accountability for ourselves and those in positions of power with respect to how others are represented, about doing the hard but important work to rebuild trust and repair damaged relationships that misrepresentations have caused, and about finding ways to relinquish control and power so that marginalized others truly have a say in how they are represented.

Notes

Introduction

1. Coincidentally, Florida Georgia Line's CRUISE also features a colored chalk fight that has been culturally misappropriated from Hindu celebrations of a religious holiday called Holi.
2. It should be noted, however, that The Specials' RAT RACE was the fifty-eighth video to play on MTV's first broadcast day and included both Black and white performers.
3. Margena A. Christian, "Why It Took MTV So Long to Play Black Music Videos," *Jet Magazine*, October 9, 2006, 17.
4. Deborah French, "The Return of the Michael Jackson Video Vanguard Award," *Stereoboard.com*, September 2, 2011, https://www.stereoboard.com/content/view/167512/9#:~:text=%22A%20lot%20of%20Black%20asses,are%20missing%20exposure%20and%20sales.%22.
5. Rob Tannenbaum and Craig Marks, *I Want My MTV: The Uncensored Story of the Music Video Revolution* (New York: Dutton Plume, 2011), 138.
6. Although it was broadcast from New York City, MTV was only available to some cable subscribers in suburban New Jersey at the time of its launch, and it was not available in Manhattan until its second year of existence. See Sall Bedell, "All-Rock Cable-TV Service Is A Hit," *New York Times*, August 2, 1982, https://www.nytimes.com/1982/08/02/arts/all-rock-cable-tv-service-is-a-hit.html.
7. Christian, "Why It Took MTV So Long,"18.
8. Tamara Palmer, "How the 'Billie Jean' Video Changed MTV," *The Root*, March 10, 2013, https://www.theroot.com/how-the-billie-jean-video-changed-mtv-1790895543.
9. Mark Anthony Neal, "Sold Out on Soul: The Corporate Annexation of Black Popular Music," *Popular Music & Society* 21, no. 3 (1997), 129. For an in-depth look at this phenomenon, see Bakari Kitwana, *Why White Kids Love Hip-Hop: Wankstas, Wiggers, Wannabes, and the New Reality of Race in America* (Cambridge, MA: Civitas Books, 2005).
10. Bill Ashcroft, Gareth Griffiths, and Helen Tiffin, "Hegemony," in *Post-colonial Studies: The Key Concepts*, 2nd ed. (New York: Routledge, 2007), 106.
11. Jack Banks, *Monopoly Television: MTV's Quest to Control the Music* (New York: Routledge, 2018), 196.
12. Richard A. Rogers, "From Cultural Exchange to Transculturation: A Review and Reconceptualization of Cultural Appropriation," *Communication Theory* 16 (2006): 477.
13. Helene A. Shugart, "Counterhegemonic Acts: Appropriation as a Feminist Rhetorical Strategy," *Quarterly Journal of Speech* 83 (1997): 210. Emphasis in original.
14. For an in-depth discussion of the many fascinating uses of this tune, see Robert J Branham and Stephen J. Hartnett, *Sweet Freedom's Song: 'My Country 'Tis of Thee' and Democracy in America* (New York: Oxford University Press, 2002).
15. Harry Brant, "The Look: Annie Lennox," *Interview Magazine*, September 23, 2014, https://www.interviewmagazine.com/fashion/the-look-annie-lennox.
16. For example, see Keri Koh Eason, "Reppin' and Rice: How Asian and Pacific Islander American Hip Hop Fans Negotiate Their Racial Identities and Make Meaning of Their Experiences in the US Hip Hop Community," *Sociological Inquiry* 92, no. 4 (2021): 1255–1280.
17. Minh-Ha T. Pham, "Racial Plagiarism and Fashion," *QED: A Journal in GLBTQ Worldmaking* 4, no. 3 (Fall 2017): 69.
18. The term "cultural plagiarism" exists in scholarly literature, but it is used to describe the differences in values and attitudes of students from various minority cultures about plagiarism within the context of academic writing.
19. For one of many examples of this argument, see John McWhorter, "You Can't 'Steal' a Culture: In Defense of Cultural Appropriation," *The Daily Beast*, April 14, 2017, https://www.thedailybeast.com/you-cant-steal-a-culture-in-defense-of-cultural-appropriation.

20. See Will Witt, "Are Native Americans Offended by Cultural Appropriation," *PragerU.com*, January 8, 2019, https://www.prageru.com/video/are-native-americans-offended-by-cultural-appropriation.
21. Edward Said, *Orientalism* (New York: Random House, 1978), 332.
22. Cherokee intellectual, feminist, and anti-violence activist Andrea Smith argues that Orientalism (and its manifestation as war), is one of the three pillars of white supremacy (along with Slavery/Capitalism and Genocide/Colonialism). See Andrea Smith, A. "Heteropatriarchy and the three pillars of white supremacy: Rethinking women of color organizing," in *Are All the Women Still White?: Rethinking Race, Expanding Feminisms*, ed. Janell Hobson (Albany: State University of New York Press, 2016), 61–71.
23. Said, *Orientalism*, 283.
24. bell hooks, *Black Looks: Race and Representation* (Boston, MA: South End Press, 1992), 21.
25. Antonio Gramsci, *Prison Notebooks* (London: Lawrence & Wishart, 1971), Notebook 3, §14.
26. Antonio Gramsci, *Quaderni del carcere*, ed. Valentino Gerratana (Turin: Einaudi Editore, 1975), 3:2279–2294, as cited in Marcus Green, "Gramsci Cannot Speak: Presentations and Interpretations of Gramsci's Concept of the Subaltern," *Rethinking Marxism* 14, no. 3 (2020): 2.
27. Ranajit Guha, "Preface," in *Selected Subaltern Studies* (New York: Oxford University Press, 1988), 35.
28. Gayatri Chakravorty Spivak, *The Post-colonial Critic: Interviews, Strategies, Dialogues*, ed. Sarah Harasym (New York: Routledge, 1990), 141.
29. Leon de Kock, "Interview with Gayatri Chakravorty Spivak: New National Writers Conference in South Africa," *ARIEL: A Review of International English Literature* 23, no. 3 (July 1992): 45–46.
30. Robert J.C. Young, *Postcolonialism: A Historical Introduction* (Oxford: Blackwell, 2003), 32.
31. "Epistemic violence" is a phrase Michel Foucault used to describe the structural cost of colonialism, further developed and extended by Spivak and others to include the damage done by the politics of privilege.
32. See Gayatri Chakravorty Spivak, "Can the Subaltern Speak?," in *Marxism and the Interpretation of Culture*, ed. Cary Nelson and Lawrence Grossberg (Urbana: University of Chicago Press, 1988), 275.
33. Said, *Orientalism*, 81.
34. Reni Eddo-Lodge, *Why I'm No Longer Talking to White People About Race* (New York: Bloomsbury, 2017), xii.
35. BIPOC is an acronym for Black, Indigenous, and people of color.
36. Loretta Ross, "I'm a Black Feminist. I Think Call-Out Culture Is Toxic," *New York Times*, August 17, 2019, https://www.nytimes.com/2019/08/17/opinion/sunday/cancel-culture-call-out.html.
37. Ross, "I'm a Black Feminist."
38. I should note that I understand that many artists, especially when they first start out in the business, rarely have control over the content of their music videos, and the imbalance of power between them and their label is enormous; this is especially true in the case of artists from marginalized communities or identities.
39. Eddo-Lodge, *Why I'm No Longer Talking*, 215.
40. bell hooks, "Marginality as a Site of Resistance," in *Out There: Marginalization and Contemporary Cultures* (Cambridge, MA: MIT Press, 1990), 341–343.
41. hooks, "Marginality as a Site of Resistance," 342.
42. Marc Colvincenzo, "Can the Postcolonial Critic Speak—and if So, Who is Listening?," in *Bodies and Voices: The Force-Field of Representation and Discourse in Colonial and Postcolonial Studies*, ed. Merete Falck Borch, Eva Rask Knudsen, Martin Leer, and Bruce Clunies Ross (New York: Rodopi, 2008), 408.
43. bell hooks, "Madonna: Plantation Mistress or Soul Sister," in *Black on White*, ed. David R. Roediger (New York: Random House, 1998), 307–308.
44. Diane Railton and Paul Watson, *Music Video and the Politics of Representation* (Edinburgh: Edinburgh University Press, 2011), 12–13.
45. Karine Nahon and Jeff Hemsley, *Going Viral* (Cambridge: Polity, 2013), 16.

Chapter 1

1. *Zoonosis* is a term used to describe the transmission of diseases from animals to humans or *vice versa*. As of September 2023, the prevailing theory regarding the origin of the COVID-19

pandemic is traced to zoonosis occurring in a wet market in China in which the virus was passed from infected animals to humans.

2. Aisha Harris, "The Troubling Viral Trend of the 'Hilarious' Black Neighbor," *Brow Beat: Slate's Culture Blog*, May 7, 2013, http://www.slate.com/blogs/browbeat/2013/05/07/charles_ramsey_amanda_berry_rescuer_becomes_internet_meme_video.html.
3. John Kosich, "Interview with Charles Ramsey." *Special Coverage*, WEWS NewsNet5 Cleveland, May 6, 2013, https://youtu.be/uPoA2f11UPk?si=PSjDjAcpy1J_gPkB, beginning 1:09 of posted video.
4. The Gregory Brothers, "Dead Giveaway!" schmoyoho, YouTube video , May 7, 2013, http://youtu.be/nZcRU0Op5P4, accessed March 13, 2014.
5. For an excellent critique of the Gregory Brothers' practice of inserting themselves into their videos, and the stark juxtaposition of their appearance and the appearance of the video's subjects, see Corella Di Fede, "How the World is Being Remade: The Case of Antoine Dodson and the Limits of Samplings as a Transcultural and Cross-Class Expression," in *Sampling Media*, ed. David Laderman and Laurel Westrup, eds. (New York: Oxford University Press, 2014), 212–227.
6. The most astounding example of this type of work that I have ever seen is a series of videos created for "The Tonight Show Starring Jimmy Fallon" wherein the creators pored over years' worth of news footage of Brian Williams, anchor and managing editor of NBC Nightly News, to edit together, word-by-word, video clips that made Williams appear to "rap" hip-hop classics such as The Sugar Hill Gang's "Rapper's Delight" (1979), Sir Mix-A-Lot's "Baby Got Back" (1992), and Snoop Doggy Dogg's "Gin and Juice" (1993).
7. Studies have even been conducted to test whether traits such as sexual orientation, sex appeal, and physical height are also discernible through a person's voice; for example, see Maddalena Daniele, "Gay Voice: Stable Marker of Sexual Orientation or Flexible Communication Device?," *Archives of Sexual Behavior* 49 (2020): 2585–2600.
8. Adriana Cavarero, *For More Than One Voice: Toward a Philosophy of Vocal Expression*, trans. Paul A. Kottman (Stanford, CA: Stanford University Press, 2005), 5.
9. Wim Mertens, *American Minimal Music*, trans. J Hautekiet (New York: Broude, 1983), 88.
10. Sampling is the practice of taking material from a pre-existing recording and using it another work. Although sampling was developed as an experimental practice in the 1960s, it has been an important part of popular music composition since the late 1970s, especially in hip-hop music.
11. Steve Reich, "Notes," liner notes, *Early Works: Come Out/Piano Phase/Clapping Music/It's Gonna Rain*, Electra/Nonesuch 9 79169-2, 1987, compact disc.
12. Lloyd Whitesell, "White Noise: Race and Erasure in the Cultural Avant-Garde." *American Music* 19, no. 2 (Summer 2001): 176–177.
13. Whitesell, "White Noise," 177.
14. Mitchell Morris, "Musical Virtues," in *Beyond Structural Listening? Postmodern Modes of Hearing*, ed. Andrew Dell'Antonio (Berkeley and Los Angeles: University of California Press, 2014), 63.
15. Richard Dawkins, *The Selfish Gene* (Oxford: Oxford University Press, 1976), 192.
16. Limor Shifman, *Memes in Digital Culture* (Cambridge, MA: MIT Press, 2014) 56.
17. Shifman, *Memes in Digital Culture*, 63.
18. Fidel Martinez, "Are 'Hilarious Black Neighbor' Videos a Modern Minstrel Show?" *The Daily Dot*, May 9, 2013, http://www.dailydot.com/opinion/hilarious-black-neighbor-modern-minstrel.
19. J. Stanley Lemons, "Black Stereotypes as Reflected in Popular Culture, 1880–1920," *American Quarterly* 29, no. 1 (Spring, 1977), 102.
20. Alexandria Agloro "Contemporary Coon Songs and Neo-Minstrels: Auto-Tune the News, Antoine Dodson, and the 'Bed Intruder Song,'" *Gnovis Journal* 11, no. 2 (Spring 2011), http://gnovisjournal.org/2011/04/04/contemporary-coon-songs-and-neo-minstrels-Auto-Tune-the-news-antoine-dodson-and-the-bed-intruder-song/.
21. In the original interview, Ramsey goes on to say, "Something is wrong here. Dead giveaway;" the Gregory Brothers took this phrase to be the title of their song and it is repeated many times throughout the chorus.
22. "OKC apartment complex catches fire, 5 units damaged; Sweet Brown explains," narrated by Joleen Chaney, online video, April 8, 2012, http://kfor.com/2012/04/08/okc-apartment-complex-catches-fire-5-units-damaged.

23. "Make Sure The Kiddies Are Sleeping Before .....," freshalina, YouTube video, August 4, 2010, http://youtu.be/3PpYasA94sU, transcribed by the author.
24. "Blaxploitation," in *Dictionary of Media Studies* (London: A&C Black), 2006, accessed May 17, 2014, from Credo Reference.
25. Stephanie Yarbough, "Blaxploitation Films," in *Encyclopedia of Black Studies*, ed. Molefi Kete Asante and Ama Mazama (Thousand Oaks, CA: Sage Publications, 2004), accessed May 17, 2014, from Credo Reference.
26. Nelson George, *Hip-Hop America*, rev. ed. (New York: Penguin Books, 2005),104.
27. Junius Griffin, "Black Movie Boom—Good or Bad?," *New York Times*, December 17, 1972.
28. M.A. Reid, "The Black Action Film: The End of the Patiently Enduring Black Hero," *Film History* 2 (1988): 23–36.
29. Ed Guerrero, *Framing Blackness: The African American Image in Film* (Philadelphia, PA: Temple University Press, 1993), 69.
30. Cedric J. Robinson, "Blaxploitation and the Misrepresentation of Liberation," *Race and Class* 40, no. 1 (July–September 1998): 1.
31. Many times, Dodson's interview will be transcribed in non-standard English to emphasize his alterity or "ghetto-ness" for humorous affect: "Welll, obvioouuuslly we have a RAPIST in Lincoln Park. He's climbing in yo' windows, he's snatching yo' people up, tryin' to rape 'em. So y'all need to hide yo' kids, hide yo' wife, and hide yo' husband 'cause they're rapin' 'er'body out here."
32. See Chris Watson and Molly Horan, "Antoine Dodson/Bed Intruder," *Know Your Meme*, 2012, http://knowyourmeme.com/memes/antoine-dodson-bed-intruder, and Eliot Van Buskirk, "Gregory Brothers of 'Bed Intruder' Fame Discuss TV Pilot, Antoine Dodson," *Wired Magazine*, August 2010, https://www.wired.com/2010/08/gregory-brothers-bed-intruder-antoine-dodson-autotune/, accessed May 13, 2014.
33. Pontente Susurro, "On Feminism, Liberals, Black Folks and Antione [*sic*] Dodson," *Like a Whisper Blog*, September 4, 2010, http://likeawhisper.wordpress.com/2010/09/04/on-feminism-liberals-black-folks-and-antione-dodson/. Many blogs, both academic and more casual and personal, provide astute and through-provoking critiques of these videos; a more thorough examination of this literature as a critical body of work in social theory is certainly warranted.
34. Susurro, "On Feminism, Liberals, Black Folks."
35. Dave Itzkoff, "The Gregory Brothers Auto-Tune the Internet," *New York Times*, August 11, 2011, http://www.nytimes.com/2011/08/14/magazine/the-gregory-brothers-Auto-Tune-the-internet.html?pagewanted=all&_r=0.
36. Andy Carvin, "'Bed Intruder' Meme: A Perfect Storm of Race, Music, Comedy and Celebrity," *NPR's All Tech Considered*, August 5, 2010, http://www.npr.org/blogs/alltechconsidered/2010/08/05/129005122/youtube-bed-intruder-meme.
37. Carvin, "'Bed Intruder' Meme."
38. "Sweet Brown Commercial | 1-800-2-SellHomes," 18002sellhomes, YouTube video, May 12, 2012, http://youtu.be/2WEMHmyF5BI, transcribed by the author, accessed August 30, 2014.
39. See Jamilah King and Jorge Rivas, "Antoine Dodson Not Happy About 'Bed Intruder' Costume," *Colorlines: News for Action*, September 27, 2010, http://colorlines.com/archives/2010/09/antoine_dodson_not_happy_about_bed_intruder_halloween_costume.html, accessed May 17, 2014.
40. Again, for more in-depth discussion on this topic, see Corella Di Fede, "How the World is Being Remade: The Case of Antoine Dodson and the Limits of Samplings as a Transcultural and Cross-Class Expression," in *Sampling Media*, ed. David Laderman and Laurel Westrup (New York: Oxford University Press, 2014), 212–227.
41. Rush Limbaugh, "The 47% Speaks: She's Voting for Obama Because He Gave Her a Free Phone." Transcript from "The Rush Limbaugh Show," September 27, 2012, http://www.rushlimbaugh.com/daily/2012/09/27/the_47_speaks_she_s_voting_for_obama_because_he_gave_her_a_free_phone, accessed May 24, 2014.
42. Di Fede, "How the World is Being Remade," 218.
43. Melissa Harris-Parry, *Sister Citizen: Shame, Stereotypes, and Black Women in America* (New Haven, CT: Yale University Press, 2011), 102–103.
44. Harris-Parry, *Sister Citizen*, 116–117.

Chapter 2

1. When the song was released, many people presumed that the phrase "I'm turning Japanese" and the accompanying gesture was a reference to the face that someone might make when reaching sexual climax, although Fenton gave no such indication. See "How I wrote 'Turning Japanese' by The Vapors' David Fenton." *Songwriting Magazine*, Spring (2017): 9. I should note that this gesture was also considered offensive at the time the video was released.
2. Bep Schrieke, *Alien Americans: A Study of Race Relations* (New York: The Viking Press, 1936), 10.
3. Schneke, *Alien Americans*, 11.
4. Jean Pfaelzer, *Driven Out: The Forgotten War Against Chinese Americans*, (Berkeley and Los Angeles: University of California Press, 2007), 79–80.
5. Edward W. Said, *Orientalism* (New York: Vintage Books, 1978), 3.
6. Gina Marchetti, *Romance and the "Yellow Peril": Race, Sex, and Discursive Strategies in Hollywood Fiction* (Berkeley and Los Angeles: University of California Press, 1993), 2.
7. Pfaelzer, *Driven Out*, 21.
8. Samuel Gompers, "Imperialism—Its Dangers and Wrongs: A Speech by Samuel Gompers," in *Save the Republic*, Anti-Imperialist Leaflet No. 11 (Anti-Imperialist League: Washington, DC, 1898–1899), para 3. Available at https://www.loc.gov/item/rbpe.2390200h.
9. George Sutherland and Supreme Court of the United States, 1922. *U.S. Reports: Ozawa v. United States*, 260 U.S. 178. 1922. Available at https://www.loc.gov/item/usrep260178. As I have stressed implicitly and explicitly throughout this book, terminology is important, especially when discussing the lived experience and treatment of minority communities and issues surrounding their representation. This is also true of the way that we white, European-Americans describe ourselves. Although the term is still widely used today in the United States to describe European Americans, the racial signifier "Caucasian" (as opposed to the demonym for people who live in the Caucasus region) has roots in eugenics and scientific racism. The founder of physical anthropology, Johann Friedrich Blumenbach (1752–1840), undertook an empirical study titled *Degeneris humani varietate nativa* ([1795] 1865), in which he sought to classify various human races based on skull shape. Because of the symmetry and other pleasing aesthetic qualities of the skull of a young Georgian girl in his collection, he concluded that the "Caucasian" race was the "highest type and also the original race from which other were subsequently derived by a process called 'degeneration.'" Gustav Jahoda, "Towards Scientific Racism," in *Race and Racialization: Essential Readings*, ed. Tania Das Gupta, Carl E. James, Chris Andersen, Grace-Edward Galabuzi, and Roger C.A. Maaka (Toronto: Canadian Scholars' Press, Inc., 2007), 24.
10. George Sutherland and Supreme Court of the United States, *U.S. Reports*, 1922.
11. Using terms such as "internment camps" or "war camps" as euphemisms to describe the concentration camps in which Japanese immigrants and Japanese Americans with US citizenship were detained, treated like cattle, and experienced violations of their constitutional—and human—rights is a form of epistemic violence that delegitimizes the experience of those who suffered in them. For a deeper look at the importance of calling Japanese "internment camps" what they really were, that is, concentration camps, see Roger Daniels, "Words Do Matter: A Note on Inappropriate Terminology and the Incarceration of the Japanese Americans," in *Nikkei in the Pacific Northwest: Japanese Americans and Japanese Canadians in the Twentieth Century*, ed. Louis Fiset and Gail Nomura (Seattle: University of Washington Press, 2005), 183–207. Answering critics who believe that the term should only be reserved for those camps used by the Nazis in Europe during World War II, Daniels suggests that "death camp" or "extermination camp" would serve as more aptly descriptive terms.
12. Eugene Franklin Wong, *On Visual Media Racism: Asians in the American Motion Pictures* (New York: Arno Press, 1978), 156.
13. Wong, *On Visual Media Racism*, 150.
14. The myth that MSG is carcinogenic began in the 1960s based on early studies linking MSG to "Chinese Restaurant Syndrome." According to the FDA, MSG is generally safe, especially when reasonable amounts are consumed. See US Food and Drug Administration, "Questions and Answers on Monosodium glutamate (MSG)," January 4, 2018, https://www.fda.gov/food/food-additives-petitions/questions-and-answers-monosodium-glutamate-msg.
15. Robert Lawson, *At That Time* (New York: William Heinemann, 1948), 43–45.

16. David Desser, "The Kung Fu Craze: Hong Kong Cinema's First American Reception," in *The Cinema of Hong Kong: History, Arts, Identity*, ed. Poshek Fu and David Desser (Cambridge: Cambridge University Press, 2000), 38.
17. Sucheng Chan, "The Exclusion of Chinese Women, 1870–1943," in *Entry Denied: Exclusion and the Chinese in America, 1882–1943*, ed. Sucheng Chan (Philadelphia, PA: Temple University Press, 1991), 94.
18. Chan, "The Exclusion of Chinese Women," 132.
19. Chan, "The Exclusion of Chinese Women," 138.
20. See Brendan Lantz and Marin R. Wenger, "Anti-Asian Xenophobia, Hate Crime Victimization, and Fear of Victimization During the COVID-19 Pandemic," *Journal of Interpersonal Violence* 38, nos. 1–2 (2023): NP1088–NP1116, https://pubmed.ncbi.nlm.nih.gov/35544766.
21. For a discussion of musical orientalism, see Derek B. Scott, "Orientalism and Musical Style," *The Musical Quarterly* 82, no. 2 (1998): 309–335. For a thorough discussion of the use of the "oriental lick" in particular, see Martin Nilsson, "The Musical Cliché Figure Signifying The Far East: Whence, Wherefore, Whither?" (2007). Archived version available at https://web.archive.org/web/20120618021011/http://chinoiserie.atspace.com/index.html.
22. See Leonard Bernstein and the New York Philharmonic, Young People's Concert: "Folk Music in the Concert Hall" (CBS Television Network, original broadcast date: April 9. 1961) and "Omnibus: Introduction to Modern Music" (CBS Television Network, original broadcast date: January 13, 1957).
23. Siouxsie and the Banshees' HONG KONG GARDEN (1978) is a performance video that features a version of the "oriental riff" played on a marimba that is not seen in the video. Unlike Douglas in KUNG FU FIGHTING or Aneka in JAPANESE BOY, the band does not adopt any stereotypically East Asian dress.
24. For a detailed history of Afong Moy and her influence on American culture in the nineteenth century, see Nancy E. Davis, *The Chinese Lady: Afong Moy in Early America* (New York: Oxford University Press, 2019).
25. Kurt Loder, "David Bowie: Straight Time," *Rolling Stone*, May 12, 1983, https://web.archive.org/web/20160116030557/http://www.rollingstone.com/music/features/straight-time-19830512?page=4 (emphasis in original).
26. Despite its proposed meaning, scholars such as music theorist Ellie M. Hisama argue that CHINA GIRL still misrepresents Asian women by not allowing Ching to speak for herself within the video, instead leaving her to serve as a nameless, racialized sex object. See Ellie M. Hisama, "Postcolonialism on the Make: The Music of John Mellencamp, David Bowie and John Zorn," *Popular Music* 12, no. 2 (1993): 91–104. Others, such as journalist Ruth Tam, read Bowie's original intent in the video, that is, a parody of racism and stereotyping. See Ruth Tam, "How David Bowie's 'China Girl' Used Racism to Fight Racism," *Washington Post*, January 20, 2016, https://www.washingtonpost.com/news/morning-mix/wp/2016/01/20/how-david-bowies-china-girl-used-racism-to-fight-racism.
27. At this point, a square border composed of mint green square spirals also appears around the edge of the screen. I was unable to ascertain this symbol's connection to Chinese symbolism (if one exists).
28. The "Tiger Mom," or strict, controlling Asian mothers who micromanage their children's lives in order to guarantee academic and social success, is a popular contemporary version of the "Dragon Lady" trope.
29. Jesa Marie Calaor, "Gwen Stefani: "I Said, 'My God, I'm Japanese,'" *Allure Magazine*, January 10, 2023, https://www.allure.com/story/gwen-stefani-japanese-harajuku-lovers-interview.
30. Calaor, "Gwen Stefani."
31. Margaret Cho, "Harajuku Girls," *MargaretCho.com*, October 31 2005, https://margaretcho.com/2005/10/31/harajuku-girls..
32. MiHi Ahn, "Gwenihana," *Slate*, October 12, 2007, https://web.archive.org/web/20071013051650/http://dir.salon.com/story/ent/feature/2005/04/09/geisha/#share.
33. Nolan Feeney, "Gwen Stefani: I Don't Regret the Harajuku Girls At All," *Time Magazine*, December 8, 2014, https://time.com/3622594/gwen-stefani-harajuku-girls-spark-the-fire.
34. For a more thorough examination of Gwen Stefani's performance of Japaneseness in her appropriation of the Harajuku street style, see Chris Tonelli, "From Delocalization to Performances of Japaneseness: Shifting Identities in Transnational Popular Music in and after Japan's Period of 'Gross National Cool,'" *Journal of World Popular Music*, 1, no. 2 (2014): 284–306.

35. For more on the objectified femininity and sexual fetishization of the school girl uniform, especially within the context of Japanese street fashion, see Laura Miller, "Cute Masquerade and the Pimping of Japan," *International Journal of Japanese Sociology* 20 (2011): 18–29.
36. Leila Madge, "Capitalizing on 'cuteness': The Aesthetics of Social Relations in a New Postwar Japanese Order," *The Journal of the German Institute for Japanese Studies* 9 (1997): 158.
37. Michael Rothman, "Avril Lavigne Says Her 'Hello Kitty' Video Is Not Racist," *ABC News*, April 24, 2014, https://abcnews.go.com/Entertainment/avril-lavigne-kitty-video-racist/story?id=23453019.
38. Avril Lavigne (@AvrilLavigne), "RACIST??? LOLOLOL!!! I love Japanese culture and I spend half of my time in Japan. I flew to Tokyo to shoot this video . . . " Twitter post, April 24, 2014, https://twitter.com/AvrilLavigne/status/459151232628580353?s=20.
39. For a discussion of "ethnic type," see "Stereo Types," *Print Magazine*, June 17, 2009, https://www.printmag.com/design-resources/stereo_types.
40. Phil Yu, "Okay, So This Is Pretty Much the Worst Thing Ever Made," *Angry Asian Man Blog*, July 30, 2013, http://blog.angryasianman.com/2013/07/okay-so-this-is-pretty-much-worst-thing.html.
41. Valerie Reich and Aaron Couch, "Band Apologizes After 'Racist' 'Asian Girlz' Video Causes Uproar," *The Hollywood Reporter*, August 2, 2013, https://www.hollywoodreporter.com/news/music-news/band-apologizes-racist-asian-girlz-598859.
42. Derrick Clifton, "Q&A: 'Asian Girlz' Singer Joe Anselm of Day Above Ground," *Huffington Post*, August 5, 2013, https://www.huffpost.com/entry/asian-girlz-day-above-ground_b_3705655.
43. Reich and Couch, "Band Apologizes After 'Racist' 'Asian Girlz' Video."
44. Reich and Couch, "Band Apologizes After 'Racist' 'Asian Girlz' Video."
45. Jose Antonio Vargas, "'Slanted Screen' Rues the Absence of Asians," *The Washington Post*, May 25, 2007, https://www.washingtonpost.com/wp-dyn/content/article/2007/05/24/AR2007052402573.html.
46. Grace Kao, Kelly Stamper Balistreri, and Kara Joyner, "Asian American Men in Romantic Dating Markets," *Contexts* 17, no. 4 (2018), 48–53, https://journals.sagepub.com/doi/10.1177/1536504218812869
47. Clara L. Wilkins, Joy F. Chan, and Cheryl R. Kaiser, "Racial Stereotypes and Interracial Attraction: Phenotypic Prototypicality and Perceived Attractiveness of Asians." *Cultural Diversity and Ethnic Minority Psychology*, 17, no. 4 (2011): 427–431, https://psycnet.apa.org/doiLanding?doi=10.1037%2Fa0024733.
48. C. Winter Han, *Geisha of a Different Kind: Race and Sexuality in Gaysian America* (New York: New York University Press, 2015), 18.
49. William Petersen, "Success Story, Japanese-American Style," *New York Times*, January 9, 1966, 186.
50. See "Success Story of One Minority Group in the U.S.," *U.S. News & World Report*, December 26, 1966, and "Success Story: Out-whiting the Whites," *Newsweek*, June 21, 1971, 24–25.
51. Gustavo López, Neil G. Ruiz, and Eileen Patten, "Key Facts about Asian Americans, a Diverse and Growing Population," *Pew Research Center*, September 8, 2017, http://www.pewresearch.org/fact-tank/2017/09/08/key-facts-about-asian-americans.
52. Rakesh Kochhar and Anthony Cilluffo, "Key Findings on the Rise in Income Inequality within America's Racial and Ethnic Groups," *Pew Research Center*, July 12, 2018, http://www.pewresearch.org/fact-tank/2018/07/12/key-findings-on-the-rise-in-income-inequality-within-americas-racial-and-ethnic-groups.
53. Kochar and Cillufoo, "Key Finds on the Rise in Income Inequality."
54. For more on the "bamboo ceiling," see Jane Hyun, *Breaking the Bamboo Ceiling: Career Strategies for Asians* (New York: Harper Business, 2005).
55. Eleonora Pilastor, "BTS and Their 23 Records Enter the Guinness World Records 2022 Hall of Fame," *Guinness World Records*, September 2, 2021, https://www.guinnessworldrecords.com/news/2021/9/bts-and-their-23-records-enter-the-guinness-world-records-2022-hall-of-fame.
56. "BTS," *Billboard.com*, https://www.billboard.com/artist/bts, accessed August 24, 2023.
57. Isha Aran, "America Is in Love with Asian Music, but Asian American Artists Still Can't Catch a Break," *Splinter News*, March 1, 2018, https://splinternews.com/america-is-in-love-with-asian-music-but-asian-american-1823038498.
58. Lauren Nostro, "Rich Chigga Breaks Down 'Dat $tick' On Genius' Video Series 'Verified,'" *Genius.com*, May 26, 2017, https://genius.com/a/rich-chigga-breaks-down-dat-tick-on-genius-video-series-verified.

59. See Zach Gelfand, "Rapper Rich Chigga on Power of Social Media, His Idol Donald Glover," *RollingStone Magazine*, July 18, 2017, https://www.rollingstone.com/music/music-features/rapper-rich-chigga-on-power-of-social-media-his-idol-donald-glover-206055.
60. Eric Diep, "Rich Brian Returns with 'Yellow' and Talks New Album 'The Sailor,'" *Complex Magazine*, June 26, 2019, https://www.complex.com/music/a/eric-diep/rich-brian-interview-yellow-the-sailor.
61. Diep, "Rich Brian Returns."
62. Rich Brian, 2019, "Rich Brian - Yellow ft. Bekon," 88rising, YouTube video, June 26, 2019, https://www.youtube.com/watch?v=yeW1cCw3-Hc.

Chapter 3

1. David Stirrup, "Introduction," in *Tribal Fantasies: Native Americans in the European Imaginary, 1900–2010*, ed. James Mackay and David Stirrup (Basingstoke: Palgrave Macmillan, 2013), 7.
2. Daniel Francis, *The Imaginary Indian: The Image of the Indian in Canadian Culture* (Vancouver: Arsenal Pulp Press, 1992), 4–5.
3. The vast majority of this monograph was written in various parts of what is now known as the United States of America on the traditional lands of the Nacotchtank (Anacostan), Caddo, Choctaw, Osage, and Quapaw communities.
4. Shari M. Huhndorf, *Going Native: Indians in the American Cultural Imagination* (Ithaca, NY: Cornell University Press, 2001), 2.
5. Gregory D. Smithers, "Why Do So Many Americans Think They Have Cherokee Blood?" *Slate Magazine*, October 1, 2015, https://slate.com/news-and-politics/2015/10/cherokee-blood-why-do-so-many-americans-believe-they-have-cherokee-ancestry.html.
6. 1491s. I'M AN INDIAN, TOO. Directed and edited by Sterlin Harjo, YouTube video, September 21, 2012, https://www.youtube.com/watch?v=9BHvpWP2V9Y.
7. RedCorn is also a comedian and staff writer for Hulu's hit series, "Reservation Dogs," a critically acclaimed show that focuses on the lives of four Indigenous teenagers in rural Oklahoma, winning numerous awards for its healthy representation of Indigenous communities. I'M AN INDIAN, TOO also features Bobby Wilson (Sesseton-Wahpeton Dakota), another member of the 1491s, who appears dancing in several scenes, but he is not the central focus of the video.
8. Lisa Nakamura, *Cybertypes: Race, Ethnicity, and Identity on the Internet* (New York: Routledge, 2002), 40–42. For a similar discussion of this issue as it relates to white appropriation of Black identities in hip-hop-themed video games, see Michael Austin, "Playas' and Players: Racial and Spatial Trespassing in Hip Hop Culture Through Video Games," in *The Oxford Handbook of Hip Hop Music*, ed. Justin D. Burton and Jason Lee Oaks (New York: Oxford University Press, 2018), https://doi.org/10.1093/oxfordhb/9780190281090.013.55.
9. Katie J.M. Baker, "A Much-Needed Primer on Cultural Appropriation," *Jezebel*, November 13, 2012. http://jezebel.com/5959698/a-much-needed-primer-on-cultural-appropriation.
10. Susan Cheever, "In a Broken Land," *People Magazine*, May 17, 1993, https://people.com/archive/in-a-broken-land-vol-39-no-19.
11. Dean Ferguson, "'Half-Breed': Cher and the Problem of Cultural Appropriation," *CherFanClub.com*, March 25, 2023, https://www.cherfanclub.com/post/half-breed-cher-and-the-problem-of-cultural-appropriation?commentId=2d0ace6c-07f3-490c-81cd-5c1e78953c38.
12. Larry Flick, "Single Reviews," *Billboard Magazine*, February 5, 1994, 71.
13. Steve Hochman, "Country Hit 'Indian Outlaw' Hits a Nerve: Pop Music: Some Native American Groups Say the Fast-rising Single from Tim McGraw's 'Not a Moment Too Soon' is Stereotypical and Ask Stations to Ban It," *Los Angeles Times*, March 24, 1994, https://www.latimes.com/archives/la-xpm-1994-03-24-ca-38103-story.html.
14. For an in-depth discussion of many of these musical tropes, see Michael V. Pisani, *Imagining Native America in Music* (New Haven, CT: Yale University Press, 2005).
15. See William J. Schafer and Johannes Ridel, "Indian Intermezzi ('Play It One More Time, Chief!')," *The Journal of American Folklore* 86, no. 342 (Oct–Dec 1973): 382–387. The University of Illinois discontinued the use of this music in 2017; it is still used by Florida State University as of 2023.
16. Richard Lei, "Catchy Tune Catches Controversy," *The Washington Post*, April 8, 1994, https://www.washingtonpost.com/archive/lifestyle/1994/04/08/catchy-tune-catches-controversy/2ca0a30e-bd4b-4f6f-8122-5fbb57db7698.

17. For example, see Noel Davis, "O.C. POP MUSIC REVIEW: Pam Tillis: Highbrow but Down to Earth," *Los Angeles Times*, May 19, 1993, https://www.latimes.com/archives/la-xpm-1993-05-19-ca-36961-story.html.
18. Gil-Soo Han, "K-pop Nationalism: Celebrities and Acting Blackface in the Korean Media," *Continuum: Journal of Media & Cultural Studies* 29, no. 1 (2015): 2–16.
19. Roald Maliangkay, "Catering to the Female Gaze: The Semiotics of Masculinity in Korean Advertising," *Situations* 7, no. 1 (2013): 48.
20. Jon Caramancia, "Korean Pop Machine, Running on Innocence and Hair Gel," *New York Times*, October 25, 2011, http://www.nytimes.com/2011/10/25/arts/music/shinee-and-south-korean-K-pop-groups-at-madison-square-garden-review.html?_r=0.
21. Karen Kramer, Jay Calderín, and Madelein M. Kropa, *Native Fashion Now: North American Indian Style* (Salem, MA: Peabody Essex Museum, 2015), 19.
22. "Urban Outfitters Wins Latest Round in Navajo Nation Case," *The Fashion Law*, July 12, 2016, https://www.thefashionlaw.com/home/urban-outfitters-wins-latest-round-in-navajo-nation-case.
23. Tim Blanks, "Runway: Dsquared2 Fall 2015 Ready-to-Wear," *Vogue Runway*, March 2, 2015, https://www.vogue.com/fashion-shows/fall-2015-ready-to-wear/dsquared.
24. Blanks, "Runway."
25. Boran Choi, "이트라이브, 티아라 신곡 '야야야' 가사 직접 해설" ["E-Tribe directly explains the lyrics of T-ara's new song 'Yayaya'"], *Star News*, December 3, 2010, https://www.starnewskorea.com/stview.php?no=2010120311174020392&type=1&outlink=1 (emphasis mine).
26. Michael Fuhr, *Globalization and Popular Music in South Korea: Sounding Out K-Pop* (New York: Routledge, 2016), 115.
27. Fuhr, *Globalization and Popular Music in South Korea*, 119.
28. See Catherine Walthall, "The Story Behind the One-Hit Wonder 'Hooked on a Feeling' by Blue Swede," *American Songwriter*, May 5, 2022, https://americansongwriter.com/the-story-behind-the-one-hit-wonder-hooked-on-a-feeling-by-blue-swede.
29. I should note that unlike other videos in this chapter (and many other misappropriations of Plains-style war bonnets), the war bonnet worn by MC Mong in INDIAN BOY is similar to, although smaller than, Geronimo's iconic headdress.
30. Henry Jenkins, *Fans, Bloggers, and Gamers: Exploring Participatory Cultures* (New York: New York University Press, 2006), 156.
31. Paige Skinner, "K-pop Fans Flood Dallas PD's App to Help Protect BLM Protesters," *Dallas Observer*, June 1, 2020, https://www.dallasobserver.com/arts/K-pop-fans-troll-dallas-police-trying-to-arrest-protesters-11916023.
32. Kristin April Kim, "Stifled, Invisible, and Threatened: Cultural Appropriation in K-pop Through the Lens of Identity-negotiating Fans of Color," *Communication, Culture and Critique* 17, no. 1 (2023): 17–23.
33. "How K-pop Is Responding to Its Longstanding Appropriation Problem," *Dazed Digital*, August 12, 2020, https://www.dazeddigital.com/music/article/50045/1/how-k-pop-is-responding-to-cultural-appropriation.
34. Ella Shohat, "The Struggle over Representation: Casting, Coalitions, and the Politics of Identification," in *Late Imperial Culture*, ed. Roman de la Campa, E. Ann Kaplan, and Michael Sprinkler (New York: Verso, 1995), 173.
35. Stuart Hall, "The Whites of Their Eyes: Racist Ideologies and the Media (revised)," in *The Media Reader*, ed. Manuel Alvarado and John O. Thompson (London: BFI, 1990), 11.
36. Hall, "The Whites of Their Eyes," 14.
37. Helene A. Shugart, "Counterhegemonic Acts: Appropriation as a Feminist Rhetorical Strategy," *Quarterly Journal of Speech* 83 (1997): 210.
38. Nicholas Bourriaud, *Postproduction* (New York: Lukas and Sternberg, 2002), 17–18.
39. Danny Hoch, "Toward a Hip-Hop Aesthetic: A Manifesto," in *Total Chaos: The Art and Aesthetics of Hip-Hop*, ed. Jeff Chang (New York: Basic, 2006), 349.
40. William Uricchio, "Cultural Citizenship in the Age of P2P Networks," in *European Culture and the Media*, ed. I.B. Bondebjerg and Peter Golding (Bristol: Intellect Books, 2004), 148.
41. Jean Burgess and Joshua Green, *YouTube: Online Video and Participatory Culture* (Hoboken, NJ: John Wiley & Sons, 2018), 81.
42. Tony Mitchell, "Doin' Damage in My Native Language: The Use of 'Resistance Vernaculars' in Hip Hop in France, Italy, and Aoetaroa/New Zealand," *Popular Music and Society* 24, no. 3 (2000): 52.

43. Jordan Farrar, "Hip Hop Gains Popularity among Native American Youth," *People's World*, June 28, 2011, https://www.peoplesworld.org/article/hip-hop-gains-popularity-among-native-american-youth.
44. Taki Telonidis, "Supaman: Rapping on the Reservation," *All Things Considered*, National Public Radio, October 11, 2011. Transcript available at: http://www.npr.org/2011/10/11/141238763/supaman-rapping-on-the-reservation.
45. Telonidis, "Supaman."
46. As of September 1, 2023.
47. Dawn Turner Trice, "Native American Rapper Looks to Break Stereotypes," *Chicago Tribune*, April 22, 2014, https://www.chicagotribune.com/news/ct-xpm-2014-04-22-ct-native-american-hiphop-trice-met-0421-20140422-story.html.
48. Taté Walker, "Music as Medicine: Life and Lyrics of Frank Waln," *Native Peoples Magazine* (October 2014), http://www.nativepeoples.com/Native-Peoples/September-October-2014/Music-asMedicineLifeandLyricsofFrankWaln.
49. Walker, "Music as Medicine."
50. Dodai Stewart, "Frank Waln's New Music Video for 'Wokiksuye' Honors Indigenous Peoples Day," *Teen Vogue*, October 8, 2018, https://www.teenvogue.com/story/frank-waln-music-video-wokiksuye-Indigenous-peoples-day.
51. Stewart, "Frank Waln's New Music Video."
52. Stefan Benz, "'Still we all gon rise': Indigenous Hip Hop, Racial Capitalism, and the Quest for Indigenous Sovereignty in the Work of Snotty Nose Rez Kids," *The Journal of the German Association for American Studies* 68, no. 2 (2003): 257.
53. Tamara Ikenberg, "Boujee Natives: Snotty Nose Rez Kids Infuse Hip-Hop with Indigenous Identity and a Wicked Sense of Humor," *Native News Online*, November 10, 2020, https://nativenewsonline.net/arts-entertainment/boujee-natives-snotty-nose-rez-kids-infuse-hip-hop-with-Indigenous-identity-and-a-wicked-sense-of-humor.
54. Nick Krewen, "Snotty Nose Rez Kids Give Listeners Some Pandemic Relief with 'I'm Good, HBU?'," *The Toronto Star*, December 2, 2022, https://www.thestar.com/entertainment/music/snotty-nose-rez-kids-give-listeners-some-pandemic-relief-with-i-m-good-hbu/article_1264eda3-40d2-53c1-a057-72c2767e7e7c.html.
55. Although bannock bread originally comes from the British Isles, some Indigenous communities / First Nations, especially in British Columbia, have applied the name to native unleavened bread-like foods.
56. "Fugazi" is a slang term that refers to a person or object that is fake.
57. Texas Parks & Wildlife Department, *Palo Duro Canyon State Park*, https://tpwd.texas.gov/state-parks/palo-duro-canyon/park_history.
58. Reed Jackson, "Drezus Walks: Meet the Native American Rapper merging Old Sounds and New," *Vice.com*, October 29, 2014, https://www.vice.com/en/article/rqgadr/drezus-native-american-rapper-warpath-indian-summer-red-winter-interview-profile.
59. Jackson, "Drezus Walks."
60. "Drezus Big Winner at Indigenous Music Awards in Winnipeg," *CBC News*, September 11, 2015, https://www.cbc.ca/news/Indigenous/Indigenous-music-awards-1.3224505.
61. Burgess and Green, *YouTube*, 82.

Chapter 4

1. Michael Bane, "Hillbilly Band," *Country Music* (March 1977): 51.
2. Justin McCarthy, "U.S. Same-Sex Marriage Support Holds at 71% High," *Gallup*, June 5, 2023, https://news.gallup.com/poll/506636/sex-marriage-support-holds-high.aspx.
3. Nadine Hubbs, *Rednecks, Queers, and Country Music* (Berkeley and Los Angeles: University of California Press, 2014), 23–24.
4. Jim Wilke, "Frontier Comrades: Homosexuality in the American West," in *Out in All Directions: A Treasury of Gay and Lesbian America*, ed. Lynn Witt, Sherry Thomas, and Eric Marcus (New York: Warner Books, 1995), 635.
5. Wilke, "Frontier Comrades," 635.
6. Graeme Thomson, "Country Music's Gay Stars: 'We're Still Kicking Down the Closet Door'," *The Guardian*, April 9, 2014, http://www.theguardian.com/music/2014/apr/10/country-music-gay-stars-kicking-closet- door-lavender-country.

7. Thomson, "Country Music's Gay Stars."
8. To highlight his effeminacy, this man riddles his clothing stories with interjections that could be at once offbeat, *dernier cri*, and queer, such as "Isn't that scooby-dooy?" and "It's me again—the world's 10 best-dressed men all rolled up into one gorgeous little ball!"
9. See R. Kirk Mauldin, R. Kirk. "The Role of Humor in the Social Construction of Gendered and Ethnic Stereotypes," *Race, Gender & Class* 9, no. 3 (2022): 76–95.
10. Chris Gibson, "The Global Cowboy: Rural Masculinities and Sexualities," in *Sexuality, Rurality, and Geography*, ed. Andrew Gorman-Murray, Barbara Pini, and Lia Bryant (Plymouth, UK: Lexington Books, 2013), 199–218.
11. Russell Smith, "'Feed Jake' Video Clip Gives Rise to Questions," *Dallas Morning News*, July 4, 1991, https://news.google.com/newspapers?id=P2FWAAAAIBAJ&sjid=w_ADAAAAIBAJ&dq=feed-jake&pg=5254%2C1477194.
12. Smith, "'Feed Jake' Video Clip."
13. Lawrence Kramer, "Tropes and Windows: An Outline of Musical Hermeneutics," in *Music as Cultural Practice, 1800–1900* (Berkeley and Los Angeles: University of California Press, 1990), 9–10.
14. Kramer, "*Tropes and Windows*," 10.
15. Kramer, "*Tropes and Windows*," 9.
16. Alexander Doty, *Making Things Perfectly Queer: Interpreting Mass Culture* (Minneapolis: University of Minnesota Press, 1993), 8.
17. Kramer, "*Tropes and Windows*," 1.
18. Kyle Anderson, "Taylor Swift Battles Bullies, Critics, and Silent Movie Villains in New 'Mean' Video: Watch it here," *Entertainment Weekly*, May 9, 2011, http://music-mix.ew.com/2011/05/09/taylor-swift-mean-video.
19. Mark Booth, *Camp* (London: Quartet Books, 1983), 67.
20. Booth, *Camp*, 69.
21. Dmitry Patukhov, "Music Market Focus: Sizing Up the US Music Industry," *Soundcharts Blog*, March 16, 2022, https://soundcharts.com/blog/us-music-market-overview.
22. Grady Smith, "Every country song has these lyrics. Right?," YouTube video, September 18, 2020, https://www.youtube.com/watch?v=48ZxNFGJTo8. Gibbon's lyric analysis is also available online: https://danagibbon.github.io/country-music-lyrics-grady/gibbon_report.html#summary.
23. See Laura McClellan, "Six Country Hits Become One Epic Song in Awesome Mashup," *Taste of Country*, January 8, 2015, https://tasteofcountry.com/six-country-song-mashup-sir-mashalot. The songs used by Sir Mashalot are "Sure Be Cool If You Did" (Blake Shelton, 2013), "Drunk on You" (Luke Bryan, 2012), "Chillin' It" (Cole Swindell, 2013), "Close Your Eyes" (Parmalee, 2013), "This Is How We Roll" (Florida Georgia Line, 2014), and "Ready, Set, Roll" (Chase Rice, 2013).
24. Eric Weisbard, "Brad Paisley's 'Accidental Racist' And The History of White Southern Musical Identity," *The Record: Music News from NPR*, National Public Radio, April 9, 2013, http://www.npr.org/blogs/therecord/2013/04/09/176675002/brad-paisleys-accidental- racist-and-the-history-of-white-southern-musical-identi.
25. Hubbs, *Rednecks, Queers, and Country Music*, 150.
26. Andrew Ross, "Uses of Camp," in *Camp Grounds: Style and Homosexuality*, ed. David Bergman (Amherst: University of Massachusetts Press, 1993), 58.
27. Andrew Ross, *No Respect: Intellectuals and Popular Culture* (London: Routledge, 1989), 136.
28. Cynthia Morrill, "Revamping the Gay Sensibility: Queer Camp and *dyke noir*," in *The Politics and Poetics of Camp*, ed. Moe Meyer (London: Routledge, 1994), 99.
29. Andrew Britton, "For Interpretation: Notes Against Camp" (1979), in *Camp—Queer Aesthetics and the Performing Subject: A Reader*, ed. Fabio Cleto (Ann Arbor: University of Michigan Press, 2022), 142.
30. Chris Gibson. "The Global Cowboy: Rural Masculinities and Sexualities," in *Sexuality, Rurality, and Geography*, ed. Andrew Gorman-Murray, Barbara Pini, and Lia Bryant (Lanham, MD: Lexington Books, 2013), 214.
31. Country-themed gay bars are discussed in more detail later in this chapter.
32. I should note that despite the claim made by many media outlets hailing Grand as the first openly gay male country music star, Canadian artist Drake Jensen came out in February 2012 and released the video for his overtly queer song "Scars," which addresses the trauma of bullying experienced by many LGBTQIA+ youth, nearly a month before ALL-AMERICAN BOY was released.

Unfortunately, neither Jensen nor the video enjoyed the same popular appeal and attention as Grand's video.

33. Before launching his singing career, Steve Grand was a successful underwear model, so some critics attribute part of the success of his music videos, especially among the gay community, more to Grand's physique than his musical talent. Others question whether a former underwear model is a suitable role model for LGBTQIA+ youth.
34. Raj Rudolph, "Watch 'Stay' by Steve Grand," *EQ Music Blog*, September 9, 2013, https://eqmusicblog.com/watch-stay-by-steve-grand.
35. See Dan Renzi, "Steve Grand Is Not A Country Singer (But You Can Say He Is)," *Huffington Post*, August 9, 2017, https://www.huffpost.com/entry/steve-grand-is-not-a-country-singer-but-you-can-say_b_5983d0a7e4b00833d1de26f6.
36. Shana Goldin-Perschbacher, *Queer Country* (Urbana: University of Illinois Press, 2022), 2.
37. Rylie Jones, "Reclaiming Country: LGBTQ+ Artists Forging a New Tradition," *KVRX 91.7 Blog*, May 18, 2021, https://kvrx.org/app/blog/features/reclaiming-country-lgbtq-artists-forging-a-new-traditi.
38. Stephen L. Betts, "Why Chely Wright Had to Wait 10 Years to Play the Opry After Coming Out," *Rolling Stone Magazine*, August 20, 2019, https://www.rollingstone.com/music/music-country/chely-wright-coming-out-opry-873928.
39. See Carena Liptak, "Story Behind the Song: Katie Pruitt, 'Loving Her,'" *The Boot*, March 11, 2020, https://theboot.com/katie-pruitt-loving-her-lyrics-information.
40. Elias Leight, "Lil Nas X's 'Old Town Road' Was a Country Hit. Then Country Changed Its Mind," *Rolling Stone Magazine*, March 26, 2019, https://www.rollingstone.com/music/music-features/lil-nas-x-old-town-road-810844.
41. In an interview with *Time Magazine* about the *Billboard* chart on which "Old Town Road" belongs (Billboard Hot Country Songs or Hot R&B/Hip-Hop Songs), Lil Nas X argues, "The song is country trap. It's not one, it's not the other. It's both. It should be on both." See Andrew R. Chow, " Lil Nas X Talks 'Old Town Road' and the Billboard Controversy, *Time Magazine*, March 30, 2019, https://time.com/5561466/lil-nas-x-old-town-road-billboard.
42. "Five Burning Questions: Billboard Staffers Discuss Lil Nas X's Top 40 Breakout Hit 'Old Town Road,'" *Billboard Pro*, March 26, 2019, https://www.billboard.com/pro/lil-nas-x-old-town-road-five-burning-questions.
43. Kyle Coroneos, "Billboard Must Remove Lil Nas X's 'Old Town Road" From Country Chart," *Save Country Music.com Blog*, March 23, 2019, https://www.savingcountrymusic.com/billboard-must-remove-lil-nas-xs-old-town-road-from-country-chart.
44. Coroneos, "Billboard Must Remove Lil Nas X's 'Old Town Road.'"
45. Lil Nas X (@pussy), "old town road is literally about horses," Twitter post, July 1, 2019, https://twitter.com/LilNasX/status/1145724580834623488?s=20.
46. Francesca T. Royster, *Black Country Music: Listening for Revolutions* (Austin: University of Texas Press, 2022), 6.
47. I would be remiss if I did not point out the symbolism of a white homeowner shooting at a Black teenager, especially considering the fact that the video was released in 2019, several years after the beginning of the national Black Lives Matter movement in 2013 (in response to the 2012 killing of Trayvon Martin, an innocent, unarmed Black teenager), but just before the George Floyd protests during the summer of 2020.
48. Esther Newton, *Mother Camp: Female Impersonators in America* (Chicago, IL: University of Chicago Press, 1972).
49. Dan Weiss, "Q&A: Miranda Lambert on Her New 'Platinum,' Country Radio, and the Damn Tabloids," *Spin Magazine*, March 13, 2014, http://www.spin.com/articles/miranda-lambert-interview-platinum-tabloids. Although fans seem to welcome Lambert's acceptance in the lyrics of "All Kinds of Kinds" and in subsequent interviews, many saw the music video as a missed opportunity to support the LGBTQIA+ community by representing them visually alongside other "kinds" of people, such as the "farmer kind," the "helping kind," and the "father figure kind."
50. Considering intersectional identities as discussed earlier in this chapter, it is worth noting that Firkus was raised in rural Wisconsin and is mixed-race (white and Ojibwe), although it is unclear how much involvement he had or currently maintains with this community.
51. "Interview: Trixie Mattel," *Merry-Go-Round Magazine*, April 29, 2017, https://merrygoroundmagazine.com/interview-trixie-mattel-2/.

52. Christoph Büscher, "Q&A: Trixie Mattel On Her Debut Album 'Two Birds,'" *Medium*, May 11, 2017, https://medium.com/artmagazine/q-a-trixie-mattel-on-her-debut-album-two-birds-c1ae15b1f84c.
53. Goldin-Perschbacher, *Queer Country*, 177–178.
54. Goldin-Perschbacher, *Queer Country*, 178.
55. David Floyd, "Eureka O'Hara Excited to Represent Johnson City on 'RuPaul's Drag Race,'" *Johnson City Press*, March 18, 2017, https://www.johnsoncitypress.com/living/arts-entertainment/eureka-ohara-excited-to-represent-johnson-city-on-rupauls-drag-race/article_d8090764-4666-5ed6-9c04-1788d7cc2f66.html.
56. The print is called "Wranglers" and is designed by Alexander Henry Fabrics. Available at http://www.ahfabrics.com/collections/category/347-wranglers. Tom of Finland (1920–1991) is a well-known Finnish artist who specialized in homoerotic illustrations featuring men with exaggerated genital sizes and tight clothing.
57. Daniel Valdez, "How the Round-Up Became a Dallas Favorite of Celebrities," *Central Track*, November 8, 2019, https://www.centraltrack.com/how-the-round-up-became-a-dallas-favorite-of-celebrities/.
58. Lars Rains, "The Bear Essentials of Country Music," in *The Bear Book: Readings in the History and Evolution of a Gay Male Subculture*, ed. Les K. Wright (Binghamton, NY: Haworth Press, 1997), 194.
59. Rains, "The Bear Essentials of Country Music," 196.
60. "The Round-Up Saloon Music Philosophy," *The Round-Up Saloon*, February 27, 2022, https://roundupsaloon.com/our-music.
61. Darryl W Bullock, *David Bowie Made Me Gay: 100 Years of LGBT Music* (New York: Overlook Duckworth, 2017), 193.
62. Kristin M. Hall, "Country Artists Condemn LGBT Laws, but Labels Silent," *Associated Press*, April 13, 2016, https://apnews.com/article/b534afb2b24e44fcbd4d4921fd2d4d1b.
63. Matthew Leimkuehler, "Music Industry Leaders Ask Tennessee Lawmakers to Stop 'Disastrous' Anti-LGBTQ Legislation," *The Tennessean*, April 16, 2021, https://eu.tennessean.com/story/entertainment/2021/04/16/tennessee-lgbtq-legislation-nashville-music-industry-gov-bill-lee/7261159002.
64. Matthew Leimkuehler, "Miley Cyrus' 'Stand By You': 4 Moments from Her Pride Month Special at the Ryman," *The Tennessean*, June 25, 2021, https://eu.tennessean.com/story/entertainment/2021/06/25/miley-cyrus-stand-by-you-best-moments-pride-month-show/7583124002.
65. See Kristin M. Hall, "Musicians Flight Threat of Tennessee Anti-LGBTQ, Drag Bills," *Associated Press*, March 22, 2023, https://apnews.com/article/music-drag-lgbtq-laws-nashville-3bc931615f13ab5762ae97436e811d41.
66. Hall, "Musicians Fight Threat of Tennessee Anti-LGBTQ, Drag Bills."
67. Nardine Saad, "Kelsea Ballerini Catches Heat for 'Woke' CMT Awards Performance with Drag Queens," *Los Angeles Times*, April 3, 2023, https://www.latimes.com/entertainment-arts/music/story/2023-04-03/kelsea-ballerini-drag-queens-2023-cmt-awards-drag-race-stars.
68. Jon Freeman, "Why Country Music Was (Finally) Ready to Come Out," *Rolling Stone Magazine*, August 18, 2021, https://www.rollingstone.com/music/music-country/gay-country-music-1212415.

Chapter 5

1. Made popular by the Beatles in the late 1960s, the process of hiding audible messages in "plain sight" (or hearing as the case may be) by recording them, reversing them, and planting them within a standard, forward-playing audio recording is called "backmasking." In order to properly hear the "secret" message, listeners would need to play the recording in reverse, and intentional mishearings and pareidolia (i.e., the psychological tendency to recognize patterns within data, even those that may not actually be present) led to many accusations of nefarious, satanic activity and subliminal brainwashing.
2. On August 16, 2018, Russell M. Nelson, seventeenth president and prophet of the Church of Jesus Christ of Latter-day Saints, released a press statement suggesting that God had impressed upon him that members of the Church should no longer be referred to as "Mormons" (except in proper titles, such as *The Book of Mormon*) and that the abbreviation "LDS" should no longer be used. Instead, the Church's style guide indicates that "Church of Jesus Christ" or simply

"the Church" is the preferred shortened reference to the church, and "Latter-day Saints" is the preferred title for its members. In this chapter, in acknowledgement of the Church's wishes regarding its own representation, the term "Mormon" is used only to indicate historical references to the Church or its members by its own members and in quoted references, or when referring to former members of the Church who call themselves "ex-Mormons." See Sarah Jane Weaver, "'Mormon' is Out: Church Releases Statement on How to Refer to the Organization." *Church News*, August 16, 2018, https://www.churchofjesuschrist.org/church/news/mormon-is-out-church-releases-statement-on-how-to-refer-to-the-organization?lang=eng.

3. Some scholars even credit these groups as the creators of mass media in the United States; see Paul David Nord, *Faith in Reading: Religious Publishing and the Birth of Mass Media in America* (New York: Oxford University Press, 2004).
4. Dennis N. Voskuil, "Reaching Out: Mainline Protestantism and the Media," in *Between the Times: The Travail of the Protestant Establishment in America, 1900–1960*, ed. William R. Hutchison (New York: Cambridge University Press, 1989), 81–82.
5. Ben Armstrong, *The Electric Church* (New York: Thomas Nelson Publishers, 1979), 38.
6. In this context, the term "corporate" is used to refer to worship as a group, usually in a church service.
7. Randall J. Stephens, *The Devil's Music: How Christians Inspired, Condemned, and Embraced Rock 'n' Roll* (Cambridge, MA: Harvard University Press, 2018), 174–175.
8. Lisa McGirr, *Suburban Warriors; The Origins of the New American Right, Politics and Society in Twentieth-Century America* (Princeton, NJ: Princeton University Press, 2001), 243.
9. Chris R. Armstrong, "Sound, Style, Substance: New Directions in Evangelical Spirituality," in *The Future of Evangelicalism in America*, ed. Candy Gunther Brown and Mark Silk (New York: Columbia University Press, 2016), 58.
10. For an in-depth overview of Oral Roberts' television ministry, see Jim Ernest Hunter, "Where My Voice is Heard Small: The Development of Oral Roberts' Television Ministry," *Spiritus* 3, no. 2 (2018): 239–257. Although there does not seem to be a reason to question the article's objectiveness, it should be noted that *Spiritus* is a publication of Oral Roberts University.
11. Ed Harrison, "Shedding Light Along the Way," *Billboard Magazine*, October 2, 1982.
12. See Janice Dorothea Terrell, "The Growth of Contemporary Christian Music in the Last Ten years (1973–1983)" (Master's thesis, The American University, 1984).
13. "Lamb and Lion Act to be Seen and Heard on MTV," *Billboard Magazine*, November 20, 1982.
14. Chuck Davis, "Thank God for Rock Bands Like DeGarmo & Key, Petra," *The Oklahoman*, November 9, 1986, https://www.oklahoman.com/story/news/1986/11/09/thank-god-for-rock-bands-like-degarmo-key-petra/62709606007.
15. Mark Powell, "Deliverance," in *Encyclopedia of Contemporary Christian Music*, ed. Don Cusic (Peabody, MA: Hendrickson Publishers, Inc., 2002), 252.
16. Z Music Television, "Great Things Start with A Great Service," advertisement, *Broadcasting & Cable Magazine*, June 24, 1996.
17. David Tobenkin, "Cable: More than Just MTV. Viacom Service Remains Leader, but New Networks Look to Make Music of Their Own," *Broadcasting & Cable*, September 2, 1996.
18. Ed Christian, "Music for Contemporary Christians: What, Where, and When?" *Journal of the Adventist Theological Society* 13, no. 1 (Spring 2002): 194.
19. Christian, "Music for Contemporary Christians," 194.
20. "General Instruction of the Roman Missal," Chapter II, Section II: 40. Published in *The Roman Missal*, 3rd edition (Washington, DC: United States Conference of Catholic Bishops, 2010), https://www.usccb.org/prayer-and-worship/the-mass/general-instruction-of-the-roman-missal.
21. Eric Gormly, "Evangelizing Through Appropriation: Toward a Cultural Theory on the Growth of Contemporary Christian Music," *Journal of Media and Religion* 2, no. 4 (2003): 261.
22. "Who Killed the Contemporary Christian Music Industry? *The Week*, June 21, 2017, https://theweek.com/articles/555603/who-killed-contemporary-christian-music-industry.
23. 2021 MRC Data Year-End Report, presented in collaboration with *Billboard Magazine*, January 6, 2022, https://web.archive.org/web/20220124064822/https://mrcdatareports.com/mrc-data-2021-u-s-year-end-report.
24. "MRI-Simmons USA 2021 Fall Database Survey," Radio Advertising Bureau (February 2022), http://www.rab.com/whyradio/reportresults.cfm.
25. John Medearis, "Sparrow Finds Markets Beyond Gospel," *Los Angeles Times*, November 14, 1989.

26. Elmer L. Towns and Vernon M. Whaley, *Worship through the Ages: How the Great Awakenings Shape Evangelical Worship* (Nashville, TN: B&H Publishing Group, 2012), 517.
27. William D. Romanowski, "Evangelicals and Popular Music: The Contemporary Christian Music Industry," in *Religion and Popular Culture in America, Revised Edition*, ed. Bruce David Forbes and Jeffrey H. Mahan (Berkeley and Los Angeles: University of California Press, 2000), 108.
28. Fredric Jameson, *Postmodernism, Or, The Cultural Logic of Late Capitalism* (Durham, NC: Duke University Press, 1991), 17.
29. Joshua Busman, "(Re)Sounding Passion: Listening to American Evangelical Worship Music, 1997–2015" (PhD diss., University of North Carolina at Chapel Hill, 2015).
30. Towns and Whaley, *Worship Through the Ages*, 519.
31. Wallace Stegner, *Mormon Country* (Lincoln: University of Nebraska Press, 2003), 347.
32. There are two classes of priesthood in the LDS church. The first is the Aaronic priesthood (named for Moses' son, Aaron), which is bestowed upon male church members at the age of twelve or upon conversion. The second is the Melchizedek priesthood (named for the king of Salem mentioned in Genesis 14, a title ascribed to Jesus in Hebrews 7 as the "priest of the Most High God"), which is usually conferred upon a man around age eighteen (and often in time for him to leave on his mission) or a year after becoming an Aaronic priest for new converts. Men must prove a certain level of moral worthiness to receive the laying on of hands and ordination into each level of priesthood, which excluded Black men until 1978 because of their race, and still excludes male children who live in households led by same-sex couples. All of this is important to keep in mind when discussing the Church's parody music videos, since priesthood is sometimes mentioned, and all male missionaries presumably usually hold both of these priesthood levels considering the work they are required to do while on their mission at the notable exclusion of women missionaries.
33. Joseph Smith, History 1:8, 10. This citation is from *The Pearl of Great Price* (originally published in 1851 and hailed as "A Selection from the Revelations, Translations, and Narrations of Joseph Smith First Prophet, Seer, and Revelator to The Church of Jesus Christ of Latter-day Saints" as it was a collection of Smith's published teachings. It is one of the four books of scripture canonized by the LDS Church and other offshoot denominations. In addition to an authorized, "Inspired" Mormon version of the *Holy Bible* used by the rest of Christendom, the LDS Church includes the aforementioned *Pearl of Great Price* (the name of which comes from Jesus' Parable of the Pearl found in Matthew 13 of the *Holy Bible*), the Book of Mormon (published in 1830 as "another testament of Jesus Christ" and is described in more detail in this chapter), and *Doctrine and Covenants* (which is the open scriptural canon of the Church that includes previous lectures and established church doctrines and allows for newer updates, or "covenants," which are said to be revealed to contemporary church presidents by God).
34. *Doctrine and Covenants* (often abbreviated D&C) 1:30.
35. For more on the Church's history and doctrine, see Church of Jesus Christ of Latter-Day Saints, *The Doctrine and Covenants of the Church of Jesus Christ of Latter-Day Saints. The Pearl of Great Price* (Salt Lake City, UT: Church of Jesus Christ of Latter-Day Saints, 1989); and Missionary Department of the LDS Church, *Preach My Gospel* (Salt Lake City, UT: LDS Church, Inc., 2004).
36. From "Facts and Statistics: Worldwide Church," *The Church of Jesus Christ of Latter-Day Saints Newsroom*, https://newsroom.churchofjesuschrist.org/facts-and-statistics, accessed September 15, 2023.
37. Peggy Fletcher Stack, "Mission Metamorphosis." *The Salt Lake City Tribune*, June 30, 2007, http://archive.sltrib.com/article.php?id=6262037&itype=NGPSID. BYU, or Brigham Young University, is the Church's flagship university and located in Provo, UT.
38. A stake president is a high priest in the LDS church who oversees a stake, which is a cluster of congregations within a particular geographic area, similar to a diocese in Catholic and Episcopal church polity.
39. The Church of Jesus Christ of Latter-day Saints, *Missionary Handbook* (Salt Lake City, Utah: Intellectual Reserve, Inc., 2006), 8–9.
40. The Church of Jesus Christ of Latter-day Saints, *Missionary Handbook*, 12.
41. The Church of Jesus Christ of Latter-day Saints, "Dress and Appearance," February 25, 2022, https://www.churchofjesuschrist.org/callings/missionary/dress-and-appearance?lang=eng.
42. The Church of Jesus Christ of Latter-Day Saints, *Young Church-Service Missionary Guiding Principles Handbook* (Salt Lake City, UT: Intellectual Reserve, Inc., 2014),18.
43. The Church of Jesus Christ of Latter-day Saints, *Young Church-Service Missionary Guiding Principles Handbook*, 19.

44. Jason Swensen, "Church Plans to Decrease Missions, Utilize Tech Savviness to Locate Religious-Minded People," *The Church of Jesus Christ of Latter-day Saints Church News*, October 21, 2017, https://www.lds.org/church/news/church-plans-to-decrease-missions-utilize-tech-savviness-to-locate-religious-minded-people?lang=eng.
45. The Church of Jesus Christ of Latter-day Saints, *Missionary Handbook*, 25–26.
46. The Church of Jesus Christ of Latter-day Saints, *Missionary Handbook*, 25 (emphasis mine).
47. The Church of Jesus Christ of Latter-day Saints, *Young Church-Service Missionary Guiding Principles Handbook*, 19.
48. Michael Hicks, *Mormonism and Music: A History*, 2nd ed. (Urbana: University of Illinois Press, 2003), 197.
49. Fred L.W. Bennett, "Why Not Abolish Jazz?" *Improvement Era*, January 1926, 272–273.
50. Edward P. Kimball, "A Reprehensible Practice," *Improvement Era*, June 1932, 490.
51. Ezra Taft Benson, "A Plea to Strengthen Our Families." General Conference Address, October 1970.
52. See "Music to a Missionary's Ears," *Mormon Tabernacle Choir Blog*, August 21, 2014, https://www.mormontabernaclechoir.org/articles/music-for-missionaries.html.
53. Hicks. *Mormonism and Music*, 204.
54. For more on youth, popular music, and identity formation, see Simon Frith, *Sound Effects: Youth, Leisure, and the Politics of Rock* (London: Constable, 1983); Andrew Ross and Tricia Rose, *Microphone Fiends: Youth Music and Youth Culture*, London: Routledge, 1994); and Andy Bennett, *Popular Music and Youth Culture: Music, Identity, and Place*. London: Macmillan, 2000).
55. Hicks, *Mormonism and Music*, 229.
56. Robert Hariman, "Political Parody and Public Culture," *Quarterly Journal of Speech* 94, no. 3 (August 2008): 249.
57. Linda Hutcheon, *A Theory of Parody: The Teachings of Twentieth-century Art Forms* (New York: Methuen, 1985), 34.
58. Hutcheon, *A Theory of Parody*, 57.
59. Hutcheon, *A Theory of Parody*, 225.
60. Elisha McIntyre, "Knock Knocking on Heaven's Door: Humour and Religion in Mormon Comedy," in *Handbook of New Religions and Cultural Production*, ed. Carole Cusack and Alex Norman (Leiden and Boston: Brill, 2012), 71.
61. Joseph & Smith (@josephsmith7830), "Adele - Hello (Missionary Parody)," YouTube video, April 5, 2016, https://www.youtube.com/watch?v=ckLqfX62u_I.
62. Erica Tempesta, "'Hello from the Other Side . . . We Must Have Knocked a Thousand Times!' Mormon Missionaries' Brilliant Parody of Adele's Hit Hello Earns 500,000 Views in TWO DAYS," *The Daily Mail*, April 7, 2016, https://www.dailymail.co.uk/femail/article-3528942/Hello-knocked-thousand-times-Mormon-missionaries-brilliant-parody-Adele-s-hit-Hello-earns-500-000-views-TWO-days.html.
63. Kellie Jeppson (@kellcakes21), "Virtue Makes You Beautiful," YouTube video, September 24, 2013, https://www.youtube.com/watch?v=oartIE7rKuM. A discussion of one such video can be found in Sarah Petersen, "Mormon Teenage Boys Tell Girls They're Beautiful Through One Direction Music Video Covers," *Deseret News*, November 13, 2012, https://www.deseretnews.com/article/865566595/Young-men-in-Mesa-Ariz-tell-girls-theyre-beautiful-through-music-video.html?pg=all. For a version of this parody from the perspective of young LDS women, see Henk Prinsloo Productions (@woodenpalette), "Virtue Makes You Beautiful (Girls Version)," YouTube video, December 3, 2014, https://www.youtube.com/watch?v=WZDwLOhSytA.
64. The Church of Jesus Christ of Latter-day Saints, *Handbook 2: Administering the Church* (Salt Lake City, Utah: Intellectual Reserve, Inc., 2010), https://www.lds.org/handbook/handbook-2-administering-the-church/young-women/10.8?lang=eng&_r=1#10.8.5. Although there are many other publications that admonish young men to remain sexually pure, it is notable that I was unable to find mention of similar standards events for young men in this handbook. See also: The Church of Jesus Christ of Latter-day Saints, *For the Strength of the Youth* (Salt Lake City, Utah: Intellectual Reserve, Inc., 2001).
65. Sarah Peterson, "Why LDS Artist Alex Boye Took Part in a Viral Mormon Version of 'That's What Makes You Beautiful,'" *Deseret News*, October 3, 2013, https://www.deseretnews.com/article/865587589/Why-LDS-artist-Alex-Boye-takes-part-in-viral-Mormon-version-of-Thats-What-Makes-You-Beautiful.html.

66. Andy Emit, "Tyler Glenn's New Album Is a Goodbye Letter to the Mormon Church," *Vice*, 24 October 24, 2016, https://www.vice.com/en/article/7bm4m4/tyler-glenns-new-album-is-a-goodbye-letter-to-the-mormon-church-neon-trees.
67. Audacity, "Tyler Glenn Explains Symbolism in 'Trash' Video," *Radio.com Interviews*, YouTube video, October 14, 2016. https://www.youtube.com/watch?v=_c-S4s7Ebt0.
68. Zelph On the Shelf (@ZelphOntheShelf), "Joseph Smith Rap – Ain't No Man Know My History," YouTube video, November 11, 2016, https://www.youtube.com/watch?v=1TqEVSotMqI.
69. Zelph On the Shelf (@ZelphOntheShelf), "Brigham Young Rap," YouTube video, September 4, 2018, https://www.youtube.com/watch?v=0lN6jGTcVzU.
70. See Peggy Fletcher Stack, "Church Posts Pictures, Video Explaining Mormon 'Garments,'" *The Salt Lake Tribune*, March 3, 2015, https://www.sltrib.com/religion/2015/03/03/church-posts-pictures-video-explaining-mormon-garments.
71. See Michael De Groote, "What Was the Real Date of Jesus' Birth?," *Deseret News*, December 24, 2010, https://www.deseret.com/2010/12/24/20162745/what-was-the-real-date-of-jesus-birth.
72. The Church of Scientology, "What is Scientology?" https://www.scientology.org/what-is-scientology, accessed March 11, 2023.
73. Scientology Media Productions, "Trail of Discovery," *L. Rob Hubbard: In His Own Voice*, video series, Season 1, Episode 1. Originally aired March 18, 2018. https://www.scientology.tv/series/l-ron-hubbard-in-his-own-voice/trail-of-discovery.html. For a more objective, balanced biography, see Hugh B. Urban, *The Church of Scientology: A History of a New Religion* (Princeton, NJ: Princeton University Press, 2011).
74. "What is Auditing?" Scientology Newsroom Frequently Asked Questions," *Scientology Newsroom*. https://www.scientologynews.org/faq/what-is-auditing.html, accessed April 4, 2023.
75. Likely due to court cases arising from FDA complaints in the 1960s in which the government argued that the Church misrepresented the medical applications of the device, resulting in a raid on January 4, 1963, in which US marshals raided the Washington, DC branch of the Church and confiscated three tons of property. The Church of Scientology overtly states at seemingly every opportunity that the E-meter is not intended or effective for the diagnosis, treatment, or prevention of any disease and is, in fact, only a religious artifact used to aid auditors in pastoral care and counseling.
76. "Medicine: Of Two Minds," *Time Magazine*, July 24, 2050, https://content.time.com/time/subscriber/article/0,33009,812852,00.html.
77. For a more thorough and nuanced discussion of the theology and mythology of Scientology, see Urban, *The Church of Scientology*. Although there are many valid reasons to criticize the Church of Scientology, its leaders, and perhaps even some of its followers, as I will discuss further in this chapter, this particular mythology is no more or less probable or demonstrably true than the creation myths found in many other major world religions.
78. The L. Ron Hubbard Library, *L. Ron Hubbard: A Profile* (Glostrup, Denmark: New Era Publications International, 2012), 149.
79. The Church of Scientology, *Music Maker, Composer & Performer: The L. Rob Hubbard Series, The Complete Biographical Encyclopedia, Book 12* (Los Angeles: Bridge Publications, Inc., 2012), 37. Here, his biographer incorrectly notes that Hubbard's observations are "altogether inarguable" in light of later punk and rap trends.
80. Hubbard, *Music Maker*, 49.
81. See Mark Evans, "L. Ron Hubbard's Foray into the World of Music," in *Scientology in Popular Culture: Influences and Struggles for Legitimacy*, ed. Stephen A. Kent and Susan Raine (Santa Barbara, CA: Praeger, 2017), 333–354.
82. Church of Scientology. "Third Set of Responses to the IRS in support of Scientology's application for 501(c)(3) tax exemption." 1992. Available online: https://www.scribd.com/document/267513033/Church-of-Scientology-Nov-23-1992-Third-Set-of-Responses-to-the-IRS, accessed April 11, 2023.
83. Evans, "L Ron Hubbard's Foray into the World of Music," 339.
84. The Church of Scientology, *Music Maker*, 62.
85. L. Ron Hubbard, "HCO Policy Letter of 23 May 1976 R; Revised 10 January 1991: Celebrities." *Scientology Celebrities & Human Rights*. Church of Scientology International, 1976. Available at: https://archive.ph/2013.07.14-223516/http://scientologycelebrity.wordpress.com/2013/05/01/scientology-definition-of-celebrity, accessed 4 April 2023.
86. L. Ron Hubbard, "HCO Policy Letter of 23 May 1976 R."

87. The Church of Scientology, *Music Maker*, 38–39.
88. Scientology Singers, "We Stand Tall," video, archive.org, September 9, 2018. https://archive.org/details/WeStandTall.
89. See Hugh B. Urban "Appendix: A Timeline of Major Events in Scientology's Complex Journey to Becoming a 'Religion,'" in *The Church of Scientology: A History of A New Religion* (Princeton, NJ: Princeton University Press, 2011), 217–220.
90. Tony Ortega, "Saturday Night Live's Genius Spoof of Scientology: Lyrics and Images," *The Underground Bunker*, April 5, 2015, https://tonyortega.org/2015/04/05/saturday-night-lives-genius-spoof-of-scientology-last-night-lyrics-and-images/#comment-1947530397.
91. Although viewers see a man walk across each night scene at the beginning of the video wearing a light shirt or jacket, it becomes clear that the man discussed here has not yet appeared in the video; in fact, it appears as though each of the previous scenes features an altogether different person.
92. The Church of Scientology claims that the points of the cross indicate various "dynamics" of life in which an individual is striving to survive, and make special mention of the fact that the symbol of the cross predates Christianity. The first use of the eight-pointed cross was in 1954, presumably to coincide with the establishment of the first Church of Scientology. The symbol became even more prominent in the late 1960s, even to the point of becoming a symbol worn by auditors, along with the black suits and white collars commonly worn by mainline Christian ministers, to help legitimize the Church as a real religion in the face of persecution and hostile press coverage.
93. Angry Gay Pope (@angrygaypope), "Scientologists sing 'We Stand Tall" 2010 at Shrine Auditorium," YouTube video, June 17, 2018, https://www.youtube.com/watch?v=YZyWal1mYho.
94. Saturday Night Live (@SaturdayNightLive), "Neurotology Music Video—SNL," YouTube video, April 5, 2015, https://www.youtube.com/watch?v=fOpapeX6Vzs. See also "All Hail Gretchen," a brief parody of this video featuring a choir singing dressed in matching polo shirts and khaki pants singing praises to their cult leader, from Season 4, Episode 9 of the Netflix show *Unbreakable Kimmy Schmidt* (2019).
95. Kids on Stage for a Better World Official Website, http://www.betterworldkids.com, accessed April 14, 2023.
96. CCKids, (@CCKids), "Starts With Me 1993," YouTube video, November 25, 2008. https://www.youtube.com/watch?v=ylC6Wh-3u_E.

Chapter 6

1. For a discussion of representation of the subaltern voice in prison work songs, see Mary-Ann Constantine and Gerald Porter, "Beating Time: Resistance and the Subaltern Voice in Prison Work Songs," in *Fragments and Meaning in Traditional Song: From the Blues to the Baltic* (New York: Oxford University Press, 2003), 142–154.
2. Michel Foucault, *Discipline and Punish: The Birth of the Prison* (New York: Random House, 2012), 9.
3. Lawrence Law, "Images and Everyday Life," *Spectacular Times* 1–2 (2007): 2–3, https://archive.org/details/SpectacularTimesImagespdf/page/n3/mode/2up.
4. Barbara Ellen, "Up Front," *Observer Magazine* (March 4, 2007): 5.
5. Ian Marsh, "The Media Representation of Prisons: Boot Camps or Holiday Camps," *SOLON Law, Crim and History* 3, no. 2 (2013): 167.
6. See Shannon Sullivan and Nancy Tuana, eds., *Race and Epistemologies of Ignorance* (Albany: State University of New York Press, 2007).
7. Franklin B. Krohn and Frances L. Sauzo, "Contemporary Urban Music; Controversial Messages in Hip-Hop and Rap Lyrics," *ETC: A Review of General Semantics* 52, no. 2 (Summer 2005): 149.
8. Anna Clark and Omar Lee, "Jail Bait: Rethinking Images of Incarcerated Women," *Bitch Magazine* no. 27 (Winter 2005), https://www.bitchmedia.org/article/jail-bait.
9. See Kristine Levan, Katherine Polzer, and Steven Downing, "Media and Prison Sexual Assault: How We Got to the 'Don't Drop the Soap' Culture," *International Journal of Criminology and Sociological Theory* 4, no. 2 (December 2011): 674–682.
10. Christopher Doll, "Rockin' Out: Expressive Modulation in Verse-Chorus Form," *Music Theory Online* 17, no. 3 (October 2011), http://www.mtosmt.org/issues/mto.11.17.3/mto.11.17.3.doll.html.

11. Corey Moss, "Jail Cells, Whips, Sexual Energy—Yup, It's a Blink-182 Video," *MTV News*, October 6, 2003, https://web.archive.org/web/20181208172840/http://www.mtv.com/news/1479587/jail-cells-whips-sexual-energy-yup-its-a-blink-182-video.
12. The Harajuku Girls in Gwen Stefani's music videos are discussed in detail in Chapter 2.
13. lankalion, "Best of Women in Prison Movies," *Internet Movie Database*, http://www.imdb.com/list/ls000024224, accessed September 9, 2016.
14. See Chandra Bozelko, "Why We Let Prison Rape Go On," *New York Times*, April 17, 2015, https://www.nytimes.com/2015/04/18/opinion/why-we-let-prison-rape-go-on.html.
15. Neil McCormick, "We're Going to Blow People Away," *The Telegraph*, January 6, 2005, https://www.telegraph.co.uk/culture/music/3634438/Were-going-to-blow-people-away.html.
16. J. Jack Halberstam, *Gaga Feminism: Sex, Gender, and the End of Normal* (Boston, MA: Beacon Press, 2012), 62.
17. Katrin Horn, "Follow the Glitter Way: Lady Gaga and Camp," in *The Performance Identities of Lady Gaga: Critical Essays*, ed. Richard J. Gray, II (Jefferson, NC: McFarland & Company, Inc., 2012), 97.
18. See David Stern, "Ukraine Takes Aim against 'Gay Propaganda,'" *BBC News*, October 11, 2012, https://www.bbc.co.uk/news/magazine-19881905.
19. Micah Bickham, "Lil Nas X - The Making of 'Industry Baby' (Vevo Footnotes) ft. Jack Harlow," YouTube video, October 14, 2021, https://www.youtube.com/watch?v=0dkJUweVWKk&t=2s.
20. Bickham, "Lil Nas X - The Making of 'Industry Baby.'"
21. Bickham, "Lil Nas X - The Making of 'Industry Baby.'"
22. Stuart Hall, "Who Needs Identity?" in *Questions of Cultural Identity*, ed. Stuart Hall and Paul du Gay (London: Sage, 1997), 5.
23. See Rosie Swash, "FBI Casts Doubts on Akon's Criminal Past," *The Guardian*, April 17, 2008, https://www.theguardian.com/music/2008/apr/17/news.akon.
24. See Gloria Tatum, "Activists Accuse DeKalb County Jail of Inhumane Conditions," *Atlanta Progressive News*, August 10, 2019, https://atlantaprogressivenews.com/2019/08/10/activists-accuse-dekalb-county-jail-of-inhumane-conditions.
25. See Kelly Corbett, "Akon's 'Locked Up' Song Started a Hilarious TikTok Trend, and We're Guilty of Loving It," *Distractify*, August 24, 2022, https://www.distractify.com/p/locked-up-tiktok-trend.
26. Victoria Moorwood, "Snoop Dogg Reveals Why He Stopped Rapping about Death after 1993 Murder Case," *Revolt*, January 26, 2021, https://www.revolt.tv/article/2021-01-26/61210/snoop-dogg-reveals-why-he-stopped-rapping-about-death-after-1993-murder-case.
27. It should be noted that in the nearly forty years since the "Scared Straight" program was introduced, many critics have argued that these types of juvenile delinquency programs are ineffective, are not backed by empirical evidence, and may in fact be potentially harmful to the teenagers involved in the programs. See Lauri O. Robinson and Jeff Slowikowski, "Scary—and Ineffective," *Baltimore Sun*, January 31, 2011, http://articles.baltimoresun.com/2011-01-31/news/bs-ed-scared-straight-20110131_1_straight-type-programs-straight-program-youths.
28. Colum Lynch, "Inmates Take Rap—to the Grammys: Pop music: Lifers Group Can't Attend Ceremonies, but the Band is Nominated for Its Stark Long-form Video," *Los Angeles Times*, February 25, 1992, http://articles.latimes.com/1992-02-25/entertainment/ca-2648_1_lifers-group.
29. A cypher is an informal hip hop "jam session" that includes MCs/rappers, beatboxers, and breakdancers.
30. World Star Hip Hop, "South Carolina Inmates Film 1st Ever Music Video In Prison!" *World Star Hip Hop*, March 17, 2014, http://www.worldstarhiphop.com/videos/video.php?v=wshh9d14sLHAcSMVlotr, accessed September 15, 2023.
31. Latifah Muhammad, "South Carolina Inmates Get Years in Solitary Confinement for Rap Video," *BET News*, October 22, 2015, http://www.bet.com/news/music/2015/10/22/south-carolina-inmates-years-in-solitary-confinement-for-rap-video.html.
32. Tricia Rose, *The Hip Hop Wars: What We Talk About When We Talk About Hip Hop — and Why It Matters* (New York: Basic Books, 2008), 138–139.
33. Rose, *The Hip Hop Wars*, 141.
34. Rose, *The Hip Hop Wars*, 141
35. Ian MacKinnon, "Jailhouse Rocks: Philippine Inmates' Thriller Routine an Internet Hit," *The Guardian*, July 27, 2007, https://www.theguardian.com/world/2007/jul/27/ianmackinnon.

36. J. Lorenzo Perillo, "'If I Was Not in Prison, I Would Not Be Famous': Discipline, Choreography, and Mimicry in the Philippines," *Theatre Journal* 63, no. 4 (December 2011): 607.
37. Bernard Weinraub, "In New Lyrics, Jackson Uses Slurs," *New York Times*, June 15, 1995, https://www.nytimes.com/1995/06/15/arts/in-new-lyrics-jackson-uses-slurs.html.
38. Blabbermouth.net, "Director Brendan Malloy Discusses the Metallica 'St. Anger' Music Video," *Blabbermouth.net*, July 31, 2003, https://blabbermouth.net/news/director-brendan-malloy-discusses-the-metallica-st-anger-music-video.
39. Kristen Wyatt, "Rapper Makes Video While Jailed," *CBS News*, June 18, 2004, https://www.cbsnews.com/news/rapper-makes-video-while-jailed.
40. See WTKR 3 (@WTKR3), "Norfolk Police Department Lip Sync Battle," YouTube video, July 10, 2018, https://www.youtube.com/watch?v=NZO7ADSwXAc.
41. Laura M. Holson, "Police Officers Lip-Sync as Part of Public Relations Dance," *New York Times*, July 23, 2018, https://www.nytimes.com/2018/07/23/us/police-lip-sync-challenge.html?smtyp=cur&smid=tw-nytimes.
42. Mark Anthony Neal, "Pop Culture Helped Turn Police Officers Into Rock Stars—And Black Folks Into Criminals," *Medium*, October 6, 2020, https://level.medium.com/pop-culture-helped-turn-police-officers-into-rock-stars-and-black-folks-into-criminals-1ac9e3faffa1.
43. For example, see Kate Payne, "Social Media Misinformation About 'Buses of Rioters' Fuels Real Fears in Iowa And Across the Country," *Iowa Public Radio*, June 11, 2020, https://www.iowapublicradio.org/news/2020-06-11/social-media-misinformation-about-buses-of-rioters-fuels-real-fears-in-iowa-and-across-the-country.
44. Adrian Horton, "Jason Aldean's Controversial Video Reportedly Edited to Remove BLM References," *The Guardian*, July 26, 2023, https://www.theguardian.com/music/2023/jul/26/jason-aldean-try-that-in-a-small-town-video-edited-blm.

Afterword

1. For example, see Katelyn E. Best, "Expanding Musical Inclusivity: Representing and Representing Musicking in Deaf Culture through Hip Hop," in *Music and Democracy*, ed. Marko Kölbl and Fritz Trümpi (Vienna: mdwPress, 2021), 235–266.
2. Andrew Dell'Antonio, "Collective Listening: Postmodern Critical Processes and MTV," in *Beyond Structural Listening? Postmodern Modes of Hearing*, ed. Andrew Dell'Antonio (Berkeley and Los Angeles: University of California Press, 2004), 212–213.

Index

For the benefit of digital users, indexed terms that span two pages (e.g., 52–53) may, on occasion, appear on only one of those pages.

Figures are indicated by an italic *f* following the page number.